LEARNING ABOUT ISLAM

Student Textbook

Yahiya Emerick

IB TS

First printing: July 1998

Published and distributed by:
International Books & Tapes Supply
PO Box 5153
Long Island City, NY 11105, USA
Tel: (718) 721 4246
Fax: (718) 728 6108

Cover design: Richard Henry

e-mail: itsibts@aol.com
WWW.ITSIBTS.COM

Manufactured in the United States of America

ISBN: 1-889720-19-4

Dedicated to my second mother,
Mrs. Suraiya Baig,
for all her strength and inspiration

Other Books by

Yahiya Emerick

The Holy Qur'an For Students: Juz 30 in American English
Layla Deen and the Case of the Ramadan Rogue
Ahmad Deen and the Curse of the Aztec Warrior
The Seafaring Beggar and Other Tales
Ahmad Deen and the Jinn at Shaolin
How to Tell Others About Islam
In the Path of the Holy Prophet
What Islam is All About
The Story of Yusuf
Full Circle
Isabella

Bismillahir Rahmanir Raheem

In the Name of Allah,
The Compassionate Source of all Mercy.

Learning About Islam

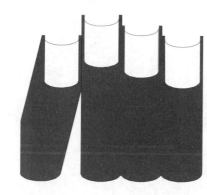

Reading for Comprehension.
Textbooks for Today and Tomorrow.

The Islamic Arts Series
Grade Level: 4-6

Reshma Baig	Literature Consultant/ Design Consultant/ Editor
M. Shamsheer Ali Baig	Program Reviewer
Ibrahim Negm	Consultant
Samina Najar	Consultant
Qasim Najar	Reviewer
Yahiya Emerick	Author

Reading for Comprehension: Textbooks for Today and Tomorrow, is a new effort to present information on Muslims and Islam in a manner which is in keeping with current educational research. This is the second textbook in a series which will encompass all grade levels from KG to High School. Test Masters and enrichment literature complete the usefulness of this program and teachers are recommended to acquire the other components of this system as they become available.

Contents

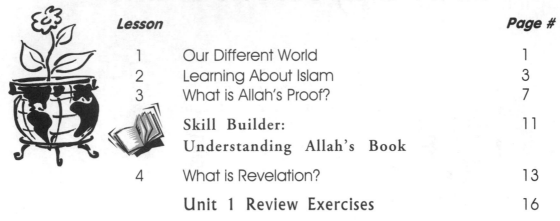
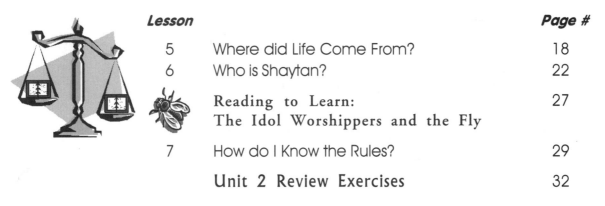

Unit 4: Meet New Muslim Friends

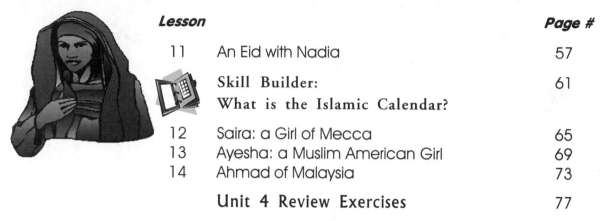

Unit 5: Prophets of the Past

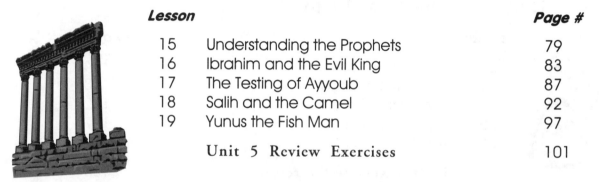

Unit 6: Three Prophets, One Way

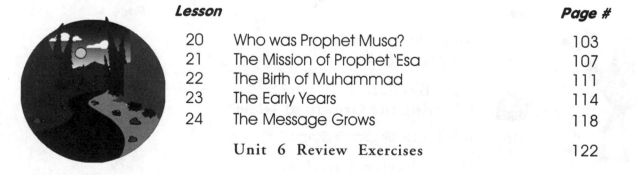

Unit 7:   The Great Tests

Unit 8:   The Final Victory

Unit 9:   The Golden Age of Islam

Unit 10:   Islamic Arts

Reference Section

Foreword

All praise is due to the One Who created humans with a will to survive and a mind to understand. We are the creatures who agreed to accept the burden of consciousness and self-awareness. We have chosen to be the ones to be granted the ability to reason and choose the course of our actions. Allah, the Exalted, did not force us to be self-aware. Indeed, He offered this blessing and burden to the rest of creation first. There were no takers. This is a mighty responsibility which rests upon our shoulders.

Our task in this life is clear: surrender our wills to the perfect will of Allah, and then do what is morally right to our fellow living beings. In order to facilitate our understanding of and selection of such a way of life, Allah has revealed His guidance to humans, from time to time, and sometimes even put it in the hearts of people to write these messages down. The only one of these messages that has been preserved in its original form has been the Holy Qur'an.

"Islam" is the last installment humanity will receive of Allah's codified guidance. There will be no new prophets or faiths born. The Blessed Prophet Muhammad assured us of that. Consequently, any group that has arisen in the world since the time of the Blessed Prophet Muhammad, claiming to have a different "truth", is, in fact, deceived and deceivers. Allah has said, *"This day I have perfected your way of life for you and completed My favor upon you. I have chosen Islam (surrender to My will) as your way of life."* (Qur'an 5:3) This is the way we must follow ourselves and teach to our children.

After having worked in Islamic schools for several years, this author has noticed a need for a new approach to Islamic studies and the teaching of the Qur'an. Our American born and raised children do not take any interest in "traditional" methods of teaching such as those found in many non-Western societies.

Modern society teaches our children to question everything and to demand relevance. They also want to be able to learn in a language style they can understand and enjoy. Such is the nature of our modern, fast-paced global way of life. There is nothing inherently wrong in this approach. Indeed, it was exactly this way of thinking which caused Islam to attract millions of converts throughout the past centuries to begin with! For most of the last five centuries, however, this spirit of inquiry in the Muslim world has given way to dogmatism and close-mindedness. The time to reawaken ourselves has come!

Unless the message of Islam is imbibed by the students, they will be aimless and adrift like most people are in the world today. Even our Muslim communities are adrift! They forgot how to study and ponder upon the Book, and they are the lowest of the low in world affairs. Our children do not want to be the lowest of the low and are given alternatives in Western nations to be something else.

If they associate Islam with ignorance and backwardness, then you will have failed to keep your descendants Muslim after you. (Can you imagine seeing all your children and their children on down being thrown in the fire on Judgment Day, all because you were negligent?)

On the other hand, if they know and understand the message of Islam, then they will be filled with an enthusiastic zeal to live and promote the Deen. Then they will utilize whatever technological advantages the modern world offers to make the Deen of Allah prominent in the world, Insha'llah. The key is instilling in their hearts the truth of the Qur'an, the message of Islam and the sincerity of Iman and true Taqwa.

In the interests of furthering Qur'anic and Islamic literacy, I have assembled this textbook which will enhance any student's knowledge and understanding. As you will see quickly, this textbook is not set up in the usual style. Each lesson is structured with a reading selection followed by review questions. This enables the teacher to explore each topic in detail without having many small topics crammed together on the same page. In addition, the writing style is closer to modern English than most other textbooks to better enable our children to understand more of what they read. To complete the review questions, a student must learn to ponder upon the meanings of Qur'anic ayat, ahadith and Islamic teachings and how they relate to the lesson they read. Of course, that is the way Islamic education should be!

We hope and pray for the mercy and reward of our Lord. May He grant us the best in this short life of ours, and may He grant us the best in Paradise. Not according to what we deserve, which is a trifling, but according to His mercy and compassion. May He protect us from the punishment of the grave and the trials of the Day of Judgment. If we do not pass on the spirit of Islam to our next generation, who will? Think long and ponder over why you are alive and how soon you will die. Insha'llah, we will all have lives that are useful in the Cause of Allah. *Amin.*

Yahiya Emerick
1998/1419

How to Use This Book

This book contains lessons on Islam for use by students to increase their knowledge of Islam. It is part of a three-tiered program which consists of a <u>textbook</u>, (which you hold in your hands,) <u>enrichment literature</u> and <u>test masters</u> (which can be obtained separately). These materials can be implemented in any size class in one of two ways. The first method is preferable. (New teachers are recommended to read, "<u>Teaching Tips and Effective Strategies...</u>" by Mohammad Ismail.)

Method One

1. The teacher will introduce the topic with a story, lesson, question or example. Such an item is already provided on the first page of every lesson. The students will write their one or two sentences answers in their notebooks. Next, the students will take turns reading the lesson aloud. The teacher will pause periodically to write notes on the board which the students <u>must</u> copy, add supplementary information or ask and answer students' questions and concerns. This procedure should take about half an hour for each lesson. Then, for the last fifteen minutes of class, the students can work independently on the review questions at the end of each lesson. This is considered to be one of the most effective teaching methods.

Method Two

*2. The teacher can introduce the topic of the day with a story or example. Then he or she can develop the whole content of the lesson, adding whatever information they like. Notes are the heart of this approach and will be copied by the students. The teacher must be careful not to bore the students with a lecture, however. Rather the students should do most of the speaking during the class period. The teacher acts as a guide and moderator. The book can be referenced as needed. Then the lesson in the textbook can be assigned as class work or homework. The students will read the lesson on their own and do the questions. This method is for the more prepared and knowledgeable teacher. It must be remembered, however, that in our day and age, most students **will not read anything** you tell them to whether it's at home or to themselves in class.*

Whichever method is followed, after the completion of a **Unit** (a unit is a group of lessons), the students should spend one class period working on the **Unit Review Exercises** which are found at the end of each of the units. This acts as a test review for them and it enables the teacher to check up on the progress of students and help them. The following class is when the teacher should give the test. It is recommended that the teacher look over each lesson before beginning it in class so as to be better able to answer whatever questions the students may have.

There is no answer key provided for the teacher. This is done for two reasons. 1) The teacher should know the material already and should have no problem correcting the assignments. This acts as a constant refresher for the teacher. 2) If I did write an answer key, in some sort of a teacher's edition, because of the nature of our community, every child in the world would get his or her hands on the answer key, thus negating the value of homework. Can you imagine walking into a convention bazaar and watching some of <u>your students</u> buying an answer book off some person's book table! Think about it and understand why no answer key is provided.

Each of the book's units cover different themes. Activities are preceded by a heading at the top of each page. The title contained therein gives a pretty good explanation of what skill or issue the lesson will explore. Under the heading there will be a reading selection or explanation of the topic, followed by review exercises.

The teacher will need to have Qur'ans in the class for demonstration, access and supplementary material for the students. This is in keeping with our goal of getting the students used to seeing the Qur'an and using it. The most useful translations for use in the classroom by very young students are ranked in order as follows:

1. The Holy Qur'an for Students (When available)................Yahiya Emerick *(Most helpful)*
2. The Noble Qur'an...Al Hilali & Khan *(Helpful)*
3. Al Qur'an..Mohammad Malik. *(Good)*
4. The Meaning of the Holy Qur'an.........Abdullah Yusuf Ali *(Difficult to understand, but resource-rich)*

If use the translation by Pickthal, Daryabadi, Shakir, Asad, Malik or Nooruddin, then it may be necessary to provide some sort of classroom guidance in how to understand the difficult English. Our own translation should be available by the year 2000 and will be designed in such a way that it will be very accessible and useful for our students.

Teachers: Do not be too quick to give the answers to the students. Let them figure out the answers for themselves. Students should do assignments from this book as your lessons require. When the students are finished with the assignment, collect all the homework for grading. ***It is recommended not to return graded homework to the students until <u>after</u> you have collected all the students' papers.*** This is because cheating and homework-copying are <u>***epidemic***</u> among students today and <u>***many, many***</u> Muslim children are also swayed by this easy way out of doing assignments. *(I've taught Muslim children of all ethnic backgrounds in two different states and can attest to this fact.)*

<u>Suggested Enrichment Literature consists of the following books:</u>

Unit 1	Layla Deen and the Case of the Ramadan Rogue. By Yahiya Emerick. (IBTS)
Unit 2	Finders Keepers and Other Stories. By Samina Najar & Qasim Najar. (IBTS)
Unit 3	Burhaan Khan. By Qasim Najar. (IBTS)
Unit 4	Adventures in Nile Valley. By Susan Omar. (Ta Ha Publishers)
Unit 5	Stories of the Prophets. A. Nadwi. (IBTS)
Unit 6	The Long Search. By Khurram Murad. (Islamic Foundation)
Unit 7	Marvelous Stories From the Life of Muhammad. Iman Tarantino. (IBTS)
Unit 8	The Broken Idol and the Jewish Rabbi. Khurram Murad. (Islamic Foundation)
Unit 9	Stories From the Muslim World. By Huda Khattab. (Ta Ha Publishers)
Unit 10	Islamic Designs for Artists and Craftspeople. By Eva Wilson. (Sound Vision)

We are planning to add more textbooks in this series which will be a continuation of the themes stressed in the other ones. Future textbooks will contain an overview of Islamic history and culture, Muslim achievements, Muslims today, geography and the Muslim experience in the West. May Allah give us time to complete them! May your efforts be successful and may your teaching bear fruit. Insha'llah, *Allahumma Amin.*

(Note: Due to the large number of times the name of the Blessed Prophet Muhammad and other Blessed people are mentioned, we have chosen to omit any salutations. The earliest scholars of Islam also followed this practice of not writing "peace be upon him" every time a holy name or a pronoun referencing one was written. We request that the readers should say silently to themselves, "Peace be upon him/her" upon seeing a noble name, because the Prophet encouraged us to say it when we **hear** his name. Reading it on a page is a way of hearing it. Writing it is a way of **saying** it- to which others are to respond to when they **hear** it.)

An Explanation of the Methodology

After having taught in full-time Islamic schools, Sunday schools, summer schools and youth camps for several years, I often became frustrated by the lack of good materials for use by the students. Of course there are hundreds of books in print to choose from, but none of them seem to have been designed with any understanding of the needs of students and teachers. There is a reason that textbooks used in public schools are designed the way they are.

Textbook companies spend millions of dollars testing formats, styles, designs, educational methodologies and even artwork! This because they are only interested in one thing: getting school districts to select their products for use by students. Therefore, they are in the business of making information as digestible to students as possible. Muslims must take note and benefit from the fruit of their research.

All too often, I've seen Muslim students subjected to boring lectures on Islam from teachers who didn't have proper materials from which to teach. If the teachers had a textbook available which outlined the lessons for them, they could spend less time coming up with haphazard lectures and more time thinking up enrichment activities. Likewise, the students often dislike Islam, Qur'an and Arabic classes intensely because they don't see them as relevant subjects. They either receive photo-copies to learn or study from at worst, or books that are not properly suited to educational uses at best.

After having seen the lack of modern-style textbooks in the study of the most important subject- Islam- I have decided to do what I can to rectify the situation. The methodology used in this textbook is simple. I merely studied the format, style and presentation of several current public school social studies textbooks and designed the "look" and "feel" of this book in the same way. The style of questions and enrichment activities are similar to the style of questions which modern educators have found most effective.

All of the information contained in the text was written using well-known sources of Islamic information. I have tried as much as possible to present the material in a fresh and relevant way. At every stage of writing I have relied upon authentic Islamic literature which is recognized and accepted by the community. The following main sources for reference were used in this book:

Main General Islamic Sources

The Holy Qur'an. (In Arabic)
The Holy Qur'an. Abdullah Yusuf Ali.
The Message of the Qur'an. Muhammad Asad.
The Holy Qur'an for School Children: Juz 30. Yahiya Emerick.
Sahih Al Bukhari.
Riyadh us Saliheen.
The Cultural Atlas of Islam. I. & L. Faruqi.
Selections From the Hadith. Abdul Hamid Siddiqui.
Guidance From the Messenger. Mazhar Kazi.
An Nawawi's Two Hadith Collections.
Arabic-English Dictionary. Hans-Wehr.
A Glossary of Islamic Terminology. B. Abughosh & W. Shaqra.
The 'Alim Database.
Bent Rib. Huda al Khattab.
What Islam is all About. Yahiya Emerick.
Jesus: A Prophet of Islam. M. A. Rahim.
Imam Bukhari's Book of Morals and Manners. Imam Bukhari.
Woman in Islam. A'isha Lemu.

Islamic Beliefs

Islam: A Comprehensive Guidebook. Altaf Kherie.
What Islam is All About. Yahiya Emerick.
Thinking About God. Ruqaiyyah W. Maqsood.
I am a Muslim. (2 Vols.) Sheikh Abubaker Najaar.

History of the Blessed Prophet

The Life of Muhammad. M.H. Haykal.
Muhammad The Last Prophet. Vehbi Ismail.
The Life of Muhammad. Tahia Ismail.

The Lives of Famous Muslims

The Beauty of the Righteous and the Ranks of the Elite. M. Al Akili.
God-Oriented Life. Wahiduddin Khan.
Muslim Heroes of the World. M. Atiqul Haque.
Companions of the Prophet. Abdul Wahid Hamid

Fiqh, Shari'ah, Islam in Society

The Lawful and Prohibited in Islam. Yusuf al Qaradawi.
Fiqh us Sunnah. Sayyid Sabiq.
Everyday Fiqh. Yusuf Islahi.
The Islamic ruling on Music and Singing. Mustafa al Kanadi.
Manners and Morals in Islam. Ibrahim Kaysi.

Islamic History

Concise History of the Muslim World. Vols. 1-3. Rafai A. Fidai.
The Illustrated History of Islam. M. Abdul Rauf
Studies In Islamic History. Dr. Ali.
The Encyclopedia of Islam. Cyril Glase.
The Atlas of Islamic History Since 1500. Francis Robinson.
The History of Al Khilafah Al Rashidah. IQRA.

Other Misc. Materials

Anecdotes of Sadi Shirazi. Sadi Shirazi.
The Incomparable Nasruddin. Idris Shah.
Mythology and Folklore of the Hui. Luckert and Li.
Jewels of Remembrance. Camille Helminski.
Islamic Art and Spirituality. Syed H. Nasr.

I have tried to be as accurate and thorough as possible. In the end, only Allah is Mighty and Supreme. If you have any suggestions, comments or corrections, please convey them to the publisher at the address on the copyright page. We look forward to bringing out future, improved editions, Insha'llah and we all must participate in the struggle for our way of life. May Allah reward us by what He wills, not with what little we may or may not deserve. Amin.

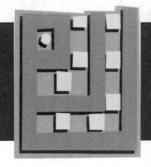

Unit 1

Looking for the Truth

Think About It

What is a belief and why is it important?

Vocabulary Words

Belief   Spiritual   Religion

What to Learn

Islam is not a religion but a way of living your life.

A. People are Different.

There are all kinds of people in our big, blue world. There are tall people, short people, skinny people and strong people. But those differences are only about how we look. Are there other things that make one person different from another? Let's see if we can answer that question.

In addition to all the physical differences there are also differences in how people behave and in what people believe is right and wrong. If one person steals and another person is honest, would you say they are the same? Of course not! If one person drinks alcohol and another says it's wrong, are they different too. Indeed they are!

What about other differences? Is it possible for one person to be different from another in their beliefs and way of living? Does a person's religion make them different from others? As you will see, people can be very different in what they believe and in how they live their lives.

B. Different Beliefs.

A **Belief** is an idea that a person feels is true. Any belief can be true or false. If a person believes in a false idea and doesn't know it's false, then it may still be real for them. Just because we believe in something doesn't always make it right. The value of our beliefs must be tested for truth.

Many people have different beliefs about why they are alive in this world. Some people believe we are here to have fun and take whatever we want. Other people believe we're here to be good and to do nice things to every living creature. (17:18-19)

Sometimes a person's beliefs may include spiritual concepts or ideas. **Spiritual** means anything having to do with the hidden world of our soul or an after-life. The word soul means the hidden spirit inside your body. When people talk about spiritual things in our country, they usually say they are talking about religion.

C. Islam is not a Religion.

In English, the word **Religion** means a group of beliefs that a person follows in the hopes of getting a reward from their god. Usually the rewards are thought to be either good luck in this life or going to Heaven in the next life for free. People in America, Canada and England follow many different religions and belief systems.

Islam is not a religion, however, because it teaches people more than just to believe in something. We do have beliefs to follow, but it doesn't just stop with praying or going to a church once in a week or year. To get to Heaven, and live a good life, a Muslim must not only believe in God, but they must also follow His teachings as best as they can. Islam is a part of our lives every day. (45:15)

As a Muslim, or follower of Islam, we learn that our whole life is for God, who we call Allah. Allah is the Creator of the Universe. We pray to Allah and believe in Him, and when we're not praying, we remember our Creator in other ways by living by His rules.

So Islam is not a religion but a way to live your life everyday. Our beliefs become our life and our life becomes our beliefs. This is what makes a Muslim different from all the other people of the world.

D. How Do I Live With Different People?

Even though there are so many different kinds of beliefs among the people of the world, Islam teaches us that we must respect others. Allah

Islam calls for world peace

created everyone in the world and He wants people to accept His way of life, called Islam.

But a Muslim is never allowed to force someone else to become a Muslim. This is not the Islamic way. Everyone must choose to accept Islam or reject it. (2:256)

It is important for us to remember that a person's beliefs are real to them. It's what gives a person their feelings of value inside. A person's heart is like a fortress, or strong castle. (45:14)

If people are going to change their beliefs to something else, then the way the new beliefs are introduced must be very careful and planned. Otherwise the fortress of their heart will keep them from understanding. (16:125)

In a world of different kinds of people and different beliefs it is important that we respect the rights of others to believe in whatever they want to. This is what Islam tells us to do: respect others first and then you can tell them about your beliefs.

Questions to Answer

1. What are some things that make people different from each other?
2. What is a religion?
3. Why do we say that Islam is not a religion?
4. Who is the One Who made the Universe?
5. How should Muslims deal with people who have different beliefs from us?

2 Learning About Islam

Think About It

Why did Allah give us the ability to love?

Vocabulary Words

Arabic   Islam   Muslim   Rasul

What to Learn

Islam means to surrender to Allah and find peace.

A. A Special Way of Life.

When we mention the name, Islam, what do we mean when we say it? When I say I'm a Muslim, what am I trying to tell people? If we don't know what those things mean then we might as well say nothing at all!

The word Islam comes from a language called Arabic. **Arabic** is the language that people speak in Arabia. Find Arabia on the map on the next page.

Islam means two important things: first, it means to surrender or give up to someone. Who are we surrendering to? You guessed it, Allah. In Islam we surrender to Allah. What does that mean? It means that we try to do what Allah told us to do and we try to stay away from what He told us to stay away from. We don't go against His rules, we surrender to them.

The second meaning of the word Islam is to find peace. If we always disobey our father and make him mad at us, can we say that our day will be easy? No, it will be hard because there will be nothing but arguing and yelling. Maybe we will be punished also and that makes us afraid.

In the same way, if we disobey Allah and don't care about Him, then our life will be filled with fear, anger and trouble. We will feel lost inside and might behave badly with others. When we listen to our parents we know we will be safe. When we listen to Allah, we will be safe in another way also. This is the peace that Islam brings to our hearts. We don't worry or fear things as much anymore. (16:97)

B. Who is a Muslim?

What is the same between the two words, "Islam" and "Muslim?" Look real hard at those two words and compare them. Do you see how they both use some of the same letters? Which letters are the same in both the words?

If you looked very hard, you will see that both the words have the letters "S", "L" and "M." In Arabic, every word is based on what they call "Root Letters." Root letters are the basic meaning of something from which you can make other, similar words.

Islam means Surrender to Allah and Peace

3

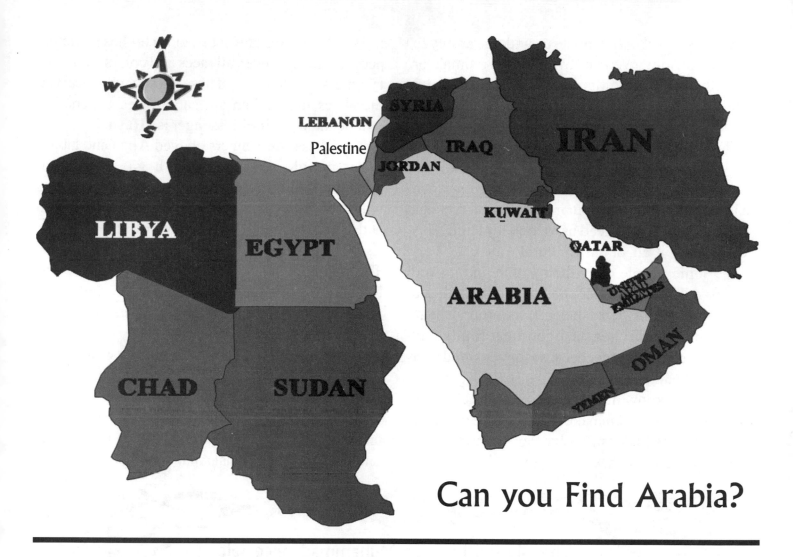

Can you Find Arabia?

For example, pronounce the root word, "SLM." This word means both surrender and peace. To make it mean surrender more, we add a few vowels and we get, "Islam." To make it mean peace more, we add different vowels and we get "Salam." Salam means peace without surrender being thought of.

That's why Arabic is so wonderful. If you can learn the root letters of any word you can make lots of other words out of it. Your Arabic teacher can show you more about this. So what about the closeness of the two words, "Islam" and "Muslim?" How are they related?

In Arabic, you can often-times make any action or describing word into a person or thing by adding a "Mu" in front of it. If we have the word "Islam" meaning to surrender and find peace, what would a person be called who is doing this? You guessed it! If we add a "Mu" in front and change the vowels a little bit, "Islam" becomes "Muslim." Cool, isn't it!

So a **Muslim** is a person who surrenders to Allah and is finding peace. The more you surrender to Allah, the more you follow His ways, the more peace and good feelings you will get. (17:19)

C. How Do We Find Out How Allah Wants Us To Live?

Allah made us so that we could obey Him. He's not going to make you love Him, however, because He wants you to come to Him by yourself. Just like we can't force other people to believe as we do, Allah will not force us to believe in Him.

We have learned before that the best way of living our life is to follow Allah. This is called Islam. But now that we know it, how do we find out what Allah wants us to do? How can we learn to love Allah and obey Him? Allah didn't leave us alone with no help. Let's see what He gave us to help us learn to love Him.

First of all, Allah made us with the ability to feel love inside. We can love people, animals or even other things like games, jobs or ideas. But there's one other thing our love does. It makes us realize that we need something else in this world besides ourselves.

The people who listen to their hearts the most eventually see that the greatest love of all is when we love Allah. So Allah put in us the good feelings that would eventually lead us to look for Him. This is called our Fitrah, or basic natural way.

Some people obey their Fitrah and go and look for Allah while other people ignore Allah and keep on loving only what they can see around them. Oftentimes their hearts become clouded in ignorance, pain and anger because they covered over what their heart wants most.

So we know our love can bring us closer to Allah. We know it can make us want to be nearer to Allah, but that still doesn't solve the question: "How can I know what Allah wants me to do?"

Allah took care of that too. He chose different people long ago, from all races and colors, and gave His messages to them. These people who received messages from Allah are called Messengers. In Arabic the word for Messenger is "**Rasul**."

These Messengers obeyed Allah and taught other people whatever Allah gave to them. Sometimes Allah even gave some of the Messengers whole books so people far and wide could read them and learn how to follow Allah's ways. (18:54-59)

The last book Allah gave is called the Qur'an. The name of the Messenger who brought it was Muhammad, peace be upon him. Because the Qur'an is the last message from Allah, it covers everything important for us.

When we read the Qur'an and do what it says, then we can say we are following what Allah wants. This is how we come closer to Allah.

If you don't have a Qur'an- with the Arabic text and a translation- in your house, you should get one right away! It's what Allah wants you to have.

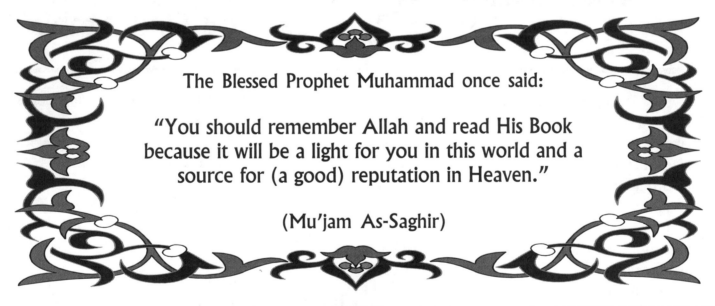

The Blessed Prophet Muhammad once said:

"You should remember Allah and read His Book because it will be a light for you in this world and a source for (a good) reputation in Heaven."

(Mu'jam As-Saghir)

Questions to Answer

1. What does the word Islam mean?
2. What are root words?
3. What does the word Muslim mean?
4. What makes us want to come closer to Allah?
5. How do we know what Allah wants us to do?
6. What is a Rasul?
7. What is the name of the last message Allah sent to us?

What Does Allah Say?

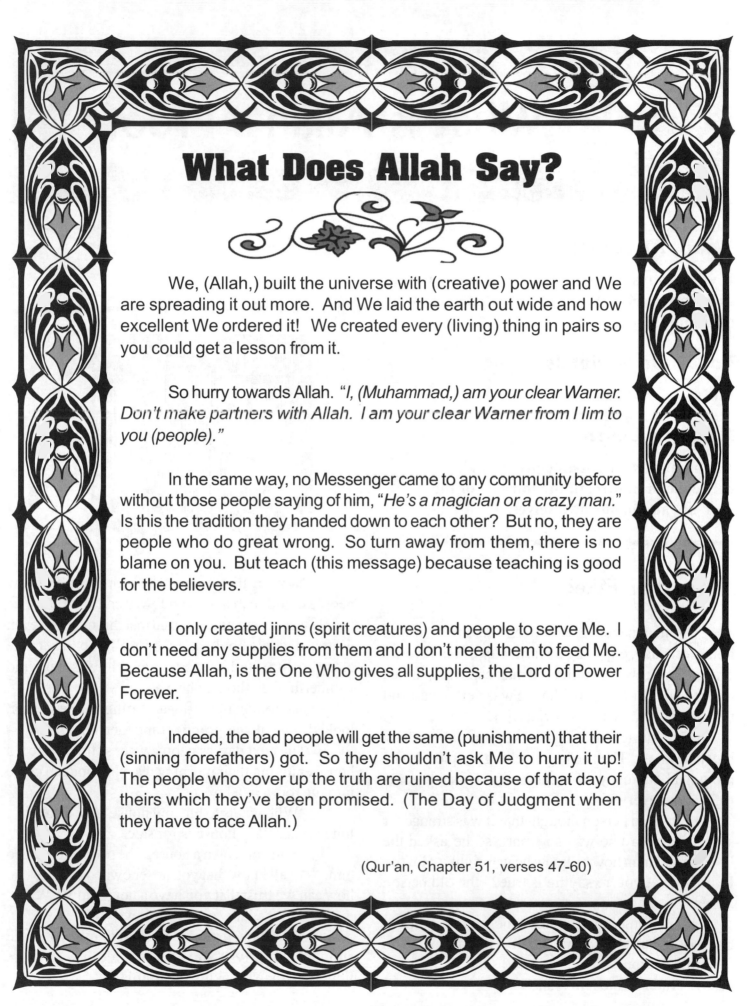

We, (Allah,) built the universe with (creative) power and We are spreading it out more. And We laid the earth out wide and how excellent We ordered it! We created every (living) thing in pairs so you could get a lesson from it.

So hurry towards Allah. *"I, (Muhammad,) am your clear Warner. Don't make partners with Allah. I am your clear Warner from I lim to you (people)."*

In the same way, no Messenger came to any community before without those people saying of him, *"He's a magician or a crazy man."* Is this the tradition they handed down to each other? But no, they are people who do great wrong. So turn away from them, there is no blame on you. But teach (this message) because teaching is good for the believers.

I only created jinns (spirit creatures) and people to serve Me. I don't need any supplies from them and I don't need them to feed Me. Because Allah, is the One Who gives all supplies, the Lord of Power Forever.

Indeed, the bad people will get the same (punishment) that their (sinning forefathers) got. So they shouldn't ask Me to hurry it up! The people who cover up the truth are ruined because of that day of theirs which they've been promised. (The Day of Judgment when they have to face Allah.)

(Qur'an, Chapter 51, verses 47-60)

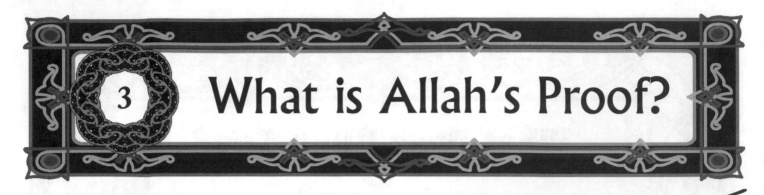

3 What is Allah's Proof?

Think About It

If you always thought something was true, but then you found out it was false, what should you do about it?

Vocabulary Words

Idols   Allah

What to Learn

Allah gave us all possible proof of His existence in nature, in the miracle of the Qur'an, and in our own selves.

A. Real or Fake?

A man named Nasroodeen was sitting in a tea house one day, enjoying a warm cup of his favorite drink. Suddenly, a long-haired man came into the tea house and told everyone that he was very smart and that he could answer every question.

He started to brag to everyone about how much he knew. Then he began telling people what he thought about many different things. He said he was right about everything.

One old person thought that it was strange for someone to say he was so smart, so he asked the long-haired man how he knew he was right. "How do I know what you're saying is true?" the old person asked.

The long-haired man stood up and pulled a book from out of his coat pocket. He slammed it on the table in front of everyone and said, "This is my proof! And I wrote it myself!"

Now in that part of the world, only a few people could read and even fewer could write. The people were even more amazed that this man had even written a whole book- all by himself! So they came close to him and started saying how smart and wonderful they thought he was.

Nasroodeen, who was sitting in the corner, looked at what was going on and then left silently.

The next day, as people were sitting in the tea house enjoying their morning tea, Nasroodeen came into the room in a hurry.

"Who wants to buy my house?" he asked in a loud voice. "My house is for sale."

"You don't own a house," the people reminded him. "We all know that you never owned a house. So how can we trust that you have a house now? Where is your proof? How can we believe you?"

Nasroodeen moved in front of everyone and shouted happily, "Showing something is more important than speaking the truth!"

The brick flew across the table!

Then he took a brick from his coat pocket and threw it on the table in front of everyone.

"Here is my proof!" he shouted. "Look at the brick and see how well it's made. And I built the whole house myself!"

B. We Must Know Truth.

Nasroodeen didn't have a house, of course. He was only trying to show the people how dumb they were. When the people asked the long-haired man for proof about what he was saying, what did he do?

He showed the people a book that he wrote himself. But just because someone writes their words in a book doesn't mean that they're automatically true. The long-haired man just put whatever he had to say on paper. What kind of proof is that?

The dumb people thought that the man's own book was enough proof that whatever he said was right. Nasroodeen put a brick on the table to *prove* he had a house. But anyone can bring in a brick and say that, even if they don't really have a house, like Nasroodeen.

The people should have known that proof for something has to come from a different person or thing. Otherwise, it may be just one person fooling you over and over. This is good advice: always look for proof and don't just take someone else's words by themselves. That is the best way. (See the Qur'an, 49:6)

C. What is Love?

Some people are short, others are tall. Some people laugh a lot, others are quiet. But no matter what the differences are, we all want to be loved and happy. When we are scared we want someone to help us. When we are lonely, we want someone to be our friend. When we look at something beautiful, like a mountain or a lake or a flower, we feel good inside.

This is because people like good things such as beauty, friendship and happiness. Where do all these feelings come from? They come from love. Love is our ability to have feelings that are good. How did we get all of these things? How did we get this ability to love?

The reason is because we were made that way! Allah put those feelings in us so deeply that everyone shares them, no matter where or when they are born. In this way, all people are basically born the same.

D. What Can the World Teach Me About Allah?

Allah is not a person or a thing like us and He is not something we can see right now. Allah is the invisible force that created everything. So what is the proof that He exists? We wouldn't want to be fooled like the people in the Tea House were. How do we know Allah is real? That's an easy question to answer because the proof is all around us. (67:22-24)

Allah gave us the Qur'an. In that book, Allah tells us to look at the world around us and to see how perfect the plants, animals and stars are.

Allah said, *"Our Signs are all around them and in themselves."* (See Qur'an, 45:3-4)

Everything in nature is just too perfect! If you threw a pile of sticks on the ground would they suddenly become a house? Of course not! But if you took your time and worked very hard, could you make the sticks into some kind of house? Yes!

In the same way, for all the world to be so perfect, it would also take someone to plan and work for it. Allah did that for us. We look at ourselves and see all the wonderful feelings we can have and then we look at nature and see His power there too.

Allah is giving us all the proof in the world because the whole world is the proof! (21:30-35)

The Qur'an tells us a lot more about Allah. In the Qur'an we learn that Allah is not only very powerful, but also that He loves us a lot. Why do you think you have love in you too?

E. What Else Can I Know About Allah?

What is Allah like? There are some people in the world who say that Allah is a man. The Jews say this. The Christians say Allah is a white man who has children. The Buddhists think that Allah is some strange power but not really much more than that. People called Hindus say that there are many different gods and then they make statues called **idols** and pray to them. For them rats are gods, monkeys are gods and grasshoppers are gods. Sounds foolish doesn't it? What does Allah tell us about Himself in His book, the Qur'an?

Allah says He is only One, all alone. He doesn't need any helpers to do what He wants done because He can do anything and everything. (21:22-29) Allah also says He is not a man or a woman and He certainly is no bug or animal. (23:91-92) We only use the word "He" when we mention His name because it doesn't sound nice to call Allah an "it." That doesn't sound very nice does it?

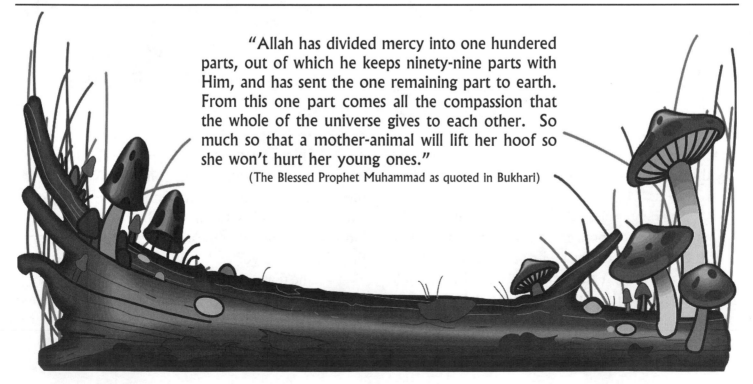

"Allah has divided mercy into one hundered parts, out of which he keeps ninety-nine parts with Him, and has sent the one remaining part to earth. From this one part comes all the compassion that the whole of the universe gives to each other. So much so that a mother-animal will lift her hoof so she won't hurt her young ones."
(The Blessed Prophet Muhammad as quoted in Bukhari)

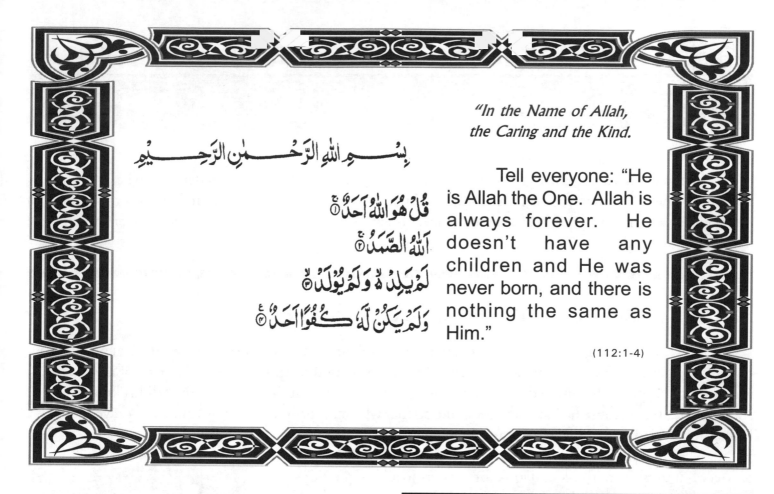

بِسْمِ اللهِ الرَّحْمٰنِ الرَّحِيمِ

قُلْ هُوَ اللهُ أَحَدٌ ۞
اللهُ الصَّمَدُ ۞
لَمْ يَلِدْ وَلَمْ يُولَدْ ۞
وَلَمْ يَكُنْ لَّهُ كُفُوًا أَحَدٌ ۞

"In the Name of Allah, the Caring and the Kind.

Tell everyone: "He is Allah the One. Allah is always forever. He doesn't have any children and He was never born, and there is nothing the same as Him."

(112:1-4)

Because Allah is not a boy or a girl this means that He also doesn't have any children or a wife or a husband. Those things are for us, the people He made.

Can you imagine the One Who made all the stars, clouds, bumble bees and fish having children? Of course not! Whoever has children is like us and none of us could ever make anything so wonderful.

What does Allah tells us about Himself? The small section of verses from chapter 112 in the Qur'an that you see on this page sums up Islamic teachings nicely. Read it and smile. But before we read the Qur'an we always ask Allah to protect us from the bad Shaytan (Devil).

Can you Read the Arabic Text Above?

We say, "Owthzu billahi mina Shaytan ir Rajeem." "I want Allah to protect me from the bad Shaytan." (16:98)

The next time you look at the stars at night or see a beautiful bird or tree, remember that it is so beautiful because Allah made it. Allah made it for you because He loves you to have good things. So shouldn't we love Allah in return? Of course!

Questions to Answer

1. Why did the people start loving the long-haired man?
2. How did Nasroodeen prove that the people were foolish for believing everything they were told?
3. What are some proofs of Allah's power?
4. List three false ideas people have about Allah.
5. Memorize the short chapter from the Qur'an on this page in Arabic and English.

When we talk about the Qur'an, there are a few things we must learn so we understand what it is and how to use it to help us. Below you will find some vocabulary words and exercises that can help you come closer to the Book of Allah. Try your best and remember to always write your answers on your paper in complete sentences. Good luck!

Part A. Where did the Qur'an Come From?

The Qur'an was given by Allah to a man named Muhammad. The book wasn't given all at once. Allah revealed, or gave, the book to him a little at a time over the period of 23 years. The first part of the Qur'an was given to Prophet Muhammad when he was forty years old. At that time, Muhammad didn't know much about Allah. But because he hated the idols and statues which his people bowed down to and prayed to, Muhammad tried to find his true Creator in his own way.

Muhammad used to go to a mountain outside of his home town of Mecca, in Arabia, to think and look for answers to all his questions. Everyone in town thought Muhammad was nice, honest and friendly, but Muhammad wanted more than just to be a nice guy. He wanted to know what was true and what was false. Soon his wish was going to be answered because Allah was going to choose him to be His last Messenger to the people of the earth.

On that lonely mountain, in a small cave in the side, Muhammad was resting after a lot of heavy thinking. Suddenly a bright angel appeared in front of him and said the word, "READ."

Muhammad was born in a place where there were no schools so he never learned to read or write. He was so scared of the bright creature that all he could say was, "I..I can't read."

The angel took hold of him and squeezed him tightly and repeated the word he said before, "Read."

Muhammad cried, "I can't read!"

The angel grabbed him again and squeezed the breath out of his chest and repeated, "Read."

To save himself from any further pain, Muhammad answered quickly, "What should I read?"

Then the angel gave the new Prophet his first message from Allah. He said, "Read in the Name of your Lord Who created humans from a clinging (embryo). Read for your Generous Lord. He is the One Who taught people with the pen what they didn't know before."

Muhammad ran home to his wife who comforted him from his strange vision. But from then on, the angel, whose name was Jibra'il, came back to him often and taught him more and more of the Qur'an and about Islam. The last Messenger from Allah began his mission and the Qur'an wouldn't be completed until 23 years later. When it was finally done, the world would be changed forever.

Part B. Vocabulary of the Qur'an.

The Qur'an has vocabulary words that are special for it alone. When we talk about the Qur'an or parts of it, we use these words because they have special meanings. Look at the list below and learn the vocabulary words and when to use them.

Ayah: This means one verse, or line from the Qur'an.

Ayat: More than one ayah.

Hafiz: Someone who memorized the whole Qur'an by heart.

Juz: One section of the Qur'an out of thirty equal parts.

Kitab: This word means "Book."

Qari: A good recitor of the Qur'an.

Mus-haf: This means the written Arabic text of the Qur'an.

Surah: This means one chapter of the Qur'an.

Translation: When you take something from one language and say or write its meaning in another language.

Part A Exercises.

Answer the following questions in complete answers. Use a separate piece of paper.

1. Why did Muhammad go to the mountain outside of town a lot?
2. What did people think about Muhammad?
3. What was the name of Muhammad's home town?
4. Describe what happened to Muhammad in the cave.
5. How many years did it take for the whole Qur'an to be finished?
6. What did Muhammad do after he received his first revelation and why do you think he did it?

Part B Exercises.

Look at the vocabulary chart under section B and write each word in a sentence of your own on a separate piece of paper. Make sure to construct a sentence that makes sense with the meaning of the word.

4 What is Revelation?

Think About It

Why do people forget things after a long time?

Vocabulary Words

Revelation   **Nabi**   **Qur'an**

What to Learn

Allah sent Prophets and Messengers to all people.

A. There Were Many Teachers From Allah.

People have been on the earth for a long time. Allah said so in the Qur'an. People who study the ancient, or old days, say that people have been here for hundreds of thousands of years.

In addition, people live all over the world. Some people live in jungles in South America. Other people live in deserts in Africa while others live on plains or mountains. People are everywhere! How did Allah get His messages to all those people, especially in ancient times?

We have already learned that Allah chose people to give his messages to. Those special people were called Rasuls, or Messengers. They were the ones who got rules, teachings and good words from Allah.

A few of them left books of Allah's words for their communties. Any words or messages given by Allah to a person are called **Revelation**.

Prophet's Named in the Qur'an

Adam	Idris	Nuh	Hud
Salih	Ibrahim	Isma'il	'Esa
Is-haq	Ya'qub	Yusuf	Lut
Shu'aib	Yunus	Ilyas	
Ayyub	Musa	Harun	
Dhu'l Kifl	Dawud	Suleiman	
Al Yasa'	Zakariyya	Yahya	

and

Muhammad!

Peace be upon them all

Revelation comes from the word "Reveal" which means to make something known to your heart and mind suddenly.

Besides Messengers, there is also another group of people who got revelation from Allah. They didn't get books, but they did get some good and wise teachings so they could share them with other people. This kind of person is called a Prophet, or **Nabi**. Some very special people were both Messengers and Prophets at the same time! But only a few, like Muhammad, had this great honor.

B. The Prophets and Messengers of Old.

Allah tells us in the Qur'an that He sent a Prophet or Messenger to every group of people that lived in the old times. (See Qur'an, 35:24.) This means that no matter where the people lived, whether in the jungles, deserts, mountains or plains, someone was there who told them about Allah.

Some people would listen to their Prophet or Messenger while others would make fun of him and say he was stupid. But in the end, every teacher from Allah told the people what they had to. No one in the old days will be able to say they didn't know about Allah.

Whenever a Prophet was sent to a community and taught people about Allah, many times the people would either forget or change the teachings the Prophet had brought. Sometimes they did this on purpose, other times they were just being forgetful. But in the end, the pure and true message from Allah would always be lost.

Think about it: If I tell you something and you tell your friend and they tell their friends, after a while, the secret might have changed to something totally different. You can try it for yourself. If you are in a classroom with a lot of other children, try to whisper a secret from one person to another. What the last person says out loud may be a lot different from what the first person said!

When you learn about people in far away places you may find that they have beliefs that are against Islam. Maybe their communities had Prophets from Allah a long time ago but the message was lost or changed completely.

Many different religions have their roots in the real teachings of an ancient Prophet from Allah. The message was just changed over the years until today it seems most religions teach things that are not true about Allah and His way of life. (22:34)

C. The Only Unchanged Book.

If a Messenger brought a book from Allah to his people, they might change that as well over many years. There were five books from Allah that we know the names of. All of them except for one have been lost, damaged or changed by people. (3:3-4)

The four that were lost or changed are called: 1) The Suhuf (Scrolls) of Prophet Ibrahim. 2) The Taurah of Prophet Musa. 3) The Zaboor of Prophet Dawud. And 4) The Injeel of Prophet 'Esa.

The last book from Allah to the world, the one brought by Prophet Muhammad, the Holy Qur'an, was never lost or changed. The name "**Qur'an**" means something you read. Indeed, from the very first day of the mission of Prophet Muhammad, the Qur'an has been read over and over.

In our own times, many people have the entire Qur'an memorized and we even have old copies of

the Qur'an that go all the way back to near the Prophet Muhammad's time that say exactly the same thing as today. This is important because while other Prophets and Messengers in the past have been sent mostly to their own local communities, the Prophet Muhammad was sent as a Messenger for the whole world. The Qur'an is for all people every where.

Allah said, "*We, (Allah,) have sent you, Muhammad, as a bringer of good news and a warner for all people.*" (Qur'an, 34:28)

Allah promised that He would never let His last message, the Qur'an, be lost. He has kept His promise to us.

D. What is the Qur'an?

The Qur'an is the last book sent by Allah to the world. It has stories, rules, advice, teachings and examples. Everything in the Qur'an is true because it is from Allah. We already saw the proof that Allah is there, now we can accept His book and live by it. He made us so He knows what the best teachings are for us. (3:7)

The Qur'an is written in the Arabic language. That is because the Prophet Muhammad lived in Arabia and spoke that language. Arabic is an easy language to learn and Muslims all over the world learn at least enough Arabic to say their prayers or to read the Qur'an. (12:2, 16:103, 19:97)

There are many translations of the Qur'an into English, Chinese, Spanish and other languages. People who don't know Arabic read the meanings of the Qur'an in their own language so they can learn about Islam also.

Allah says that the Qur'an is easy to remember. If you have ever memorized portions of

it, you will agree because it ryhmes and sounds nice to hear, even if you don't understand all the words yet. (44:58)

The Qur'an is over 1,500 years old and will last until the end of the world! We should read the Qur'an and learn from it because it's the best way to learn what Allah has to say to us. It can't be lost or changed like the other books were and it is enough to teach everyone in the world about Allah.

Qur'an!

Urdu
Turkish
Bangla
Thai
Spanish
Malay
French
Swahili
Farsi
Chinese
English
Swedish

Questions to Answer

1. What is a Nabi?
2. Where did Allah send His teachers to?
3. What happened to Allah's teachings after a long time?
4. What are the five books of Allah that we know the names of?
5. Which of those five books is the last one with no changes?
6. Describe how the Arabic language and the Qur'an are related.
7. What is a Rasul?

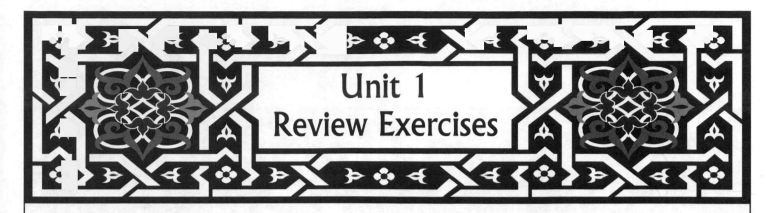

Unit 1
Review Exercises

Vocabulary Review

On a separate piece of paper, write the meaning of each word below. Remember to write in complete sentences.

1. Qur'an
2. Ayah
3. Belief
4. Spiritual
5. Idols
6. Islam

7. Root Letters
8. Nabi
9. Muslim
10. Arabic
11. Rasul
12. Spiritual

Remembering What You Read

On a separate piece of paper, answer the questions below. Remember to answer as best as you can and write in complete sentences.

1. What is the Qur'an for?
2. What is the proof Allah gives us that He is there?
3. How did people in the old days find out about Allah?
4. Who was Nasroodeen and what did he do?
5. How are the words Islam and Muslim related?
6. What is the definition of the word Islam?
7. Where were Prophets and Messengers sent to?
8. How does a Muslim deal with people who have different beliefs?
9. Explain why you think a Muslim is not allowed to force someone to believe in Allah.

Thinking to Learn

Read the following statement and explain whether it is true or false. Write in complete sentences on a separate piece of paper.

Islam is a religion just like other religions.

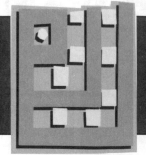

Unit 2

Who Am I?

5 Where Did Life Come From?

Think About It

If you found out something was going to happen that you didn't understand, what would you do?

Vocabulary Words

Universe	Meteor	Dinosaur
Angels	Jinn	

What to Learn

We are not alone in this universe.

A. Where Did Life Come From?

Allah made the universe a long time ago. The **Universe** is what we call the stars, planets, moons and galaxies all together. It took billions of years for it to be finished. After the universe was ready, Allah decided to make living things to live in it.

Why did He want to make things that were alive? If you ever held a rock in your hand, and saw how cold and plain it was, or got tired of looking at a flame, then you'll understand why a whole universe full of just dead rocks (planets) and big fireballs (stars) could get pretty boring after a while. Living creatures are much more interesting because they actually do things and can show feelings.

Allah doesn't need anyone or anything, of course, He just made life because He wanted to. The Holy Qur'an tells us that He made life in many places around the universe, but we are concerned right now only with life here on our own planet, earth. Let's explore how Allah made life:

First, He made tiny creatures that you have to use a microscope to see. Then He made the plants, fish, amphibians, lizards and much later He made the dinosaurs.

The **dinosaurs** are giant reptiles that lived millions of years ago. Have you ever seen a dinosaur skeleton in a museum or a movie with dinosaurs in it? Those big creatures aren't around anymore. They died a long time ago when a meteor from space crashed into the world millions of years ago.

A **meteor** is a big chunk of rock that falls from space to the earth. How did that make all the dinosaurs die? The huge meteor made a lot of dust go up in the air because it hit the earth so hard. (Scientists say the meteor hit in the south of the present-day country of Mexico.)

With all that dust in the air, sunlight couldn't get through to feed the plants so a lot of jungles just disappeared. Many kinds of dinosaurs ate plants to live, but since the plants were gone, they starved and died.

A Meteor Crashed to Earth!

The big dinosaurs, like the T-Rexes and Velociraptors, which ate the plant-eating dinos, lost their food supply also so they died too. Other animals that could survive the difficult days then took over the earth. Those are the animals that live in our world right now.

Today the only evidence we have that the dinosaurs were ever here is in fossil bones that we find sometimes. Have you ever found a fossil? What was it like? If you have one at home you can bring it in and show your class!

A Fossil!

B. What Other Kinds of Creatures are Out There?

Allah made other kinds of living things also. Creatures that are not like the people and animals we see around us. They are more like us than the animals, but they're still a little different.

One of these kinds of living creatures are called Jinn. The **Jinn** are made out of fire-energy. We cannot see them but they can see us. They are born, they live and then they die. Although we can't see them, we can feel what they do.

The word Jinn means "hidden" and that is a good name for them. There are good Jinn and bad Jinn. The good Jinn leave us alone while the bad Jinn bother us. How do they bother us? They whisper bad thoughts into your mind and try to get you to be bad also.

Have you ever felt a bad thought come in your mind and you didn't know where it came from? Chances are a Jinn was whispering to you. Allah told people to avoid the Jinn and to ignore them.

Some people try to contact the Jinn with Astrology, Ouija Boards or fortune-telling. These are all bad things to use. People who try to contact the Jinn become the slaves of the Jinn and are helpless in their power. (7:200-201)

The people who become slaves of the Jinn lead bad lives filled with bad deeds and sins. They forget Allah and feel terrible inside all the time. They often drink alcohol and take drugs to try to forget their inner pain, but this only makes them feel even worse.

The evil Jinn are sometimes called Devils, or Shayateen. Remember to avoid them and their ways at all costs because all they want is to ruin you and your good heart.

C. Why Were the Angels Worried?

There is another kind of creature Allah made. They are called **Angels**. They are made of light rays and can become many different shapes. They are the workers in the universe and they do whatever Allah tells them. Allah doesn't need any helpers, He just made the Angels anyway.

They are all good and they never do wrong. Angels are not male or female. They are almost like good robots that do whatever they are commanded to by Allah. We can't see them but sometimes they come around people in the shape of a person. Usually they only appear to Prophets and Messengers.

When Allah decided to make people, He said to the Angels, "*I am going to put a care-taker on the Earth.*" The Angels came closer to see what this new life-form would be like. (2:30)

When they found out that the new creatures, the humans, would be able to think for themselves, the Angels became worried. They thought that if someone could choose to think for themselves, they might think about doing bad things or even decide to hate Allah, the One Who made them!

People would be given physical bodies that could make changes on the earth and affect the smooth running of nature and the environment. They could choose to be good or bad. The Angels were worried and they asked Allah, "*Are You going to put a creature on earth that will cause trouble and kill? We always praise You and say Your Name is Holy.*"

Allah told the Angels, "*I know things that you don't know.*"

The Angels couldn't argue with that and so they just watched as Allah made the first human man and woman on earth. After that was done, Allah put them in a special garden to live. The name of the first man was Adam and the name of the first woman was Huwwa.

Allah gave the humans the ability to think and to make decisions. They could see their world around them and understand it and how to use it. They learned the name and usefulness of everything in their environment.

Then Allah commanded the Angels to tell Him about the world and how to use it. The Angels never learned about those things so all they could say was, "*We only know what You taught us.*"

Then the Creator, Allah, commanded Adam to explain everything to them about his environment and world. Adam told all about the birds, the plants and other things in a wonderful and complete way. The Angels were amazed.

Allah told the Angels to bow down to Adam to show their respect for him. The Angels bowed down and realized that the humans were no ordinary creatures. Humans had gifts that the Angels didn't have: the gift of choice and the power to think about the meaning of things. But while the Angels bowed, a Jinn named Iblis stood nearby and did a very bad thing. More about that later.

For now we can see that people are not alone in this universe. There are the plants and animals on earth that we have to take care of, and then there are the Angels and the Jinn. With all these different kinds of life-forms in the universe, it can get pretty interesting, can't it?

The Angels didn't know anything about the wonders of the Earth!

Questions to Answer

1. What does the word Universe mean?
2. In what order did Allah make the animals?
3. What is a Dinosaur?
4. Why are the dinosaurs all gone now?
5. What are Jinns and what do they do?
6. What are Angels and what do they do?
7. What is the job we people have on earth?
8. Why did the Angels have to bow down to Adam?
9. What does the word Shayateen mean?

Think About It

What makes one creature better than another?

Vocabulary Words

Instinct   Iblis   Arrogance

What to Learn

We are here to be tested and Shaytan wants us to fail our test.

A. Who is Better?

Allah made us human beings better than the animals because we can think and understand things. Do you remember how Adam was able to learn all about his environment and how to use it? Animals, on the other hand, live mostly by following their instincts. **Instincts** are actions that are already part of a creature's way of living from birth.

Birds are born already knowing how to build their nests, they don't have to learn it from someone, nor do they think about doing something different. Fish know how to swim and ants know they have to live in a nest.

Even every different kind of bee in a bee-hive knows its proper job. Some bees get honey from flowers, others feed the baby bees in the hive, others guard the nest while others flap their wings all day to air condition the entire hive! No one assigned the jobs or showed anyone how to do it. All those things are from animal instincts.

We human beings have to think about and learn everything we do. While it may seem like a weakness, it's actually a strength, because we can change our minds or find a better way of doing something at any time.

For example, when people thought that tents were better than living in caves, they made tents. When they thought about building houses, they made them, too. Today, we live in huge buildings made of stone, steel and lumber. One day we may live in underwater cities or on space stations!

Allah also made us better than the Angels because we could make choices about what to believe. The Angels always have to obey Allah while people can either obey Allah or forget about Him. We have the power of choice. But what about the Jinn? Were we made better than them?

Let's compare: the Jinn are creatures who could be either good or bad. That means they have the power to choose to obey Allah or not, just like we can. The Jinn are made from fire-energy, so they can move through walls and can even enter our minds and make suggestions in our thoughts. They sound pretty powerful, don't they?

But while the Jinn have a lot of powers, at the same time they have several serious weaknesses. The first is that they do not have earthly bodies like we do. They can't see the beauty in the world like we can and they don't understand how nature works.

Remember that Allah showed the Angels that Adam could understand the world around him while the Angels couldn't. The same thing is true of the Jinn. They are limited in their understanding.

The Jinn are all over the Universe but they don't see all that beauty as proof that they should obey Allah. That's why some of them can go bad even though they know for sure that Allah is their Creator.

We, on the other hand, can see the beauty of the world and the universe and understand that only Allah could have made something so vast and wonderful. Our connection to the earth is so close that we are even made of the same stuff as the earth. All the ingedients in clay and earth- with a little water mixed in- were used to make us!

Even though we can't see Allah now, we can choose to believe in Him from His proof. We see the universe for what it is while the Jinn just ignore it and go on their way. We were made better than the Jinn, too.

B. Why am I Alive?

Allah made humans for one thing only: to choose to serve Him. He could have made us like the Angels who have to obey and never go against His commands. But He wanted to make a creature that would choose to love Him. Isn't it more important that someone likes to be around you, rather than *having* to be around you?

Allah could have also made us like the Jinn who can go all over the universe and can be good or bad, but they can't see any beauty in the creation of Allah. They just live and do whatever they do.

People can love Allah or forget Him. They can obey Allah or not listen to His commands. They can be the best creatures in the universe or the worst. Allah said that He made us to be the best. The only thing is that if we don't try to be the best, we might go down to being the worst. (103:1-3)

We have a lot of responsibility on our shoulders. Our short time on earth is a test for each and every one of us. We are born, we grow up and then we die. In that time we learn about good and bad, we hear about Allah in one way or another, and we use our brains to think about life and what it means.

If we choose by ourselves to be good, believe in Allah and live by Islam, then we passed the test. After our bodies die, our soul inside of us gets released into the real world, the other world. There we will be let into the most fabulous place of all: Paradise. We will never die and we will never feel sad there.

But if we let ourselves do bad things, forget about Allah and reject Islam, then we failed the test, and in the other world our souls will be sent to a place to be punished. That terrible place is Hell-fire. Why do we deserve to be punished? Because Allah gave us a mind to think and all the proof in the world to believe in Him but we chose to follow bad ways. Let's try real hard to pass the test of this life and avoid Hell-fire.

> Once a woman was making a fire under a pot. As the flame grew hotter she moved her young son away from it. Then she went to the Blessed Prophet Muhammad and asked, "Tell me, is Allah the most merciful of the merciful?"
>
> The Prophet replied that He certainly was.
>
> Then the woman asked, "Is Allah more merciful to His servants than a mother is to her child?"
>
> The Prophet answered that He was many times more merciful.
>
> Then the woman said, "A mother does not cast her son into the fire."
>
> The Blessed Prophet then bowed his head and cried softly. A moment later he raised his head and looked at her saying, "Allah punishes only those of His servants who rebel against Him and refuse to say that there is no god but Him."
>
> (Ibn Majah)

C. The Proud Jinn.

Allah had ordered the Angels to bow to Adam and they all did without a word. The Jinn can go most places that Angels can and so many were there watching.

"*No way!*" thought Iblis, as he saw all the Angels bowing down to this new creature, the human man named Adam. "*I'm not going to bow down to that piece of dirt!*"

Iblis, who was a very hot-tempered Jinn stood proud and tall and didn't want to bow along with the Angels. Allah knows everything and He certainly knew that Iblis didn't want to join in the bowing. "*Why aren't you bowing along with the Angels?*" Allah asked him.

Allah knew the answer, of course, but He wanted to have Iblis admit the reason by himself. That way a guilty creature proves to itself that it is doing wrong. Iblis answered, "Y*ou made him from dirt while I'm made from fire!*" (7:12-13)

Obviously, Iblis thought that fire was better than dirt or clay so he didn't want to bow. He refused to accept that the humans were better than him also. He became arrogant and full of pride. **Arrogance** means that you think you're so great when you're really not.

Allah doesn't like arrogance and pride. He likes humbleness and kindness. He ordered Iblis to get away from there on account of his bad behavior. But Iblis wasn't going to go quietly. His arrogance made him do a foolish thing. "*I bet I can ruin almost all of them and make them thankless towards you!*" Iblis challenged.

Imagine that! A puny Jinn challenging Allah. "*Give me time to prove it!*" Iblis shouted.

Allah is not one to back down from anything. He made the universe and although He doesn't need to prove anything to anybody, He will let creatures try and challenge Him so they can understand why they deserve to be punished later on when they're judged. So Allah greed to allow Iblis to live until the end of time so he could try and carry out his threat.

Iblis's name was then changed to Shaytan, a word that means devil. He's waiting to influence you to do wrong and to make you forget Allah. He hates

Paradise is better than the best place on Earth

Hell-Fire is worse than the worst place on Earth!

us humans and won't stop until he has made you go bad. Only the people who come closer to Allah's ways are protected from him. Ask Allah to protect you from the rejected Shaytan everyday. (2:257)

Iblis, or Shaytan, as he is known, won't stop until he's taken all the love for Allah from the world and made it cold.

D. The Ultimate Plan.

In Allah's plan, the entire universe will be ended one day and He will gather the souls of all the creatures that ever lived together and judge their behavior. As we have learned, the good souls will go to Paradise while the bad souls will be punished in Hell-fire.

Allah had told Iblis, "*You will be given time but you won't be able to harm those who ask Me to protect them.*"

Iblis got even angrier as he promised, "*I will be waiting to pounce on them. I will attack them from all directions and You will find most of them don't have any thanks for You.*"

Allah made Iblis leave and ordered that he will be forbidden to return.

Allah declared, "***Get out of here! You are cursed and rejected. If any of them follow you then I will fill Hell-fire with you all!***" (Qur'an 7:18)

Only the people who come closer to Allah's ways are protected from Shaytan's plans. Ask Allah to protect you from the rejected Shaytan everyday.

Questions to Answer

1. What does the word, Instinct mean?
2. Why are humans better than the Jinn?
3. What advantages do people have over the animals?
4. Why did Allah create us humans?
5. Why did Iblis refuse to bow to Adam?
6. How did Iblis get the new name, Shaytan?
7. What was the challenge Iblis made to Allah?
8. Where will all the bad humans and jinn go in the end?

What Does Allah Say?

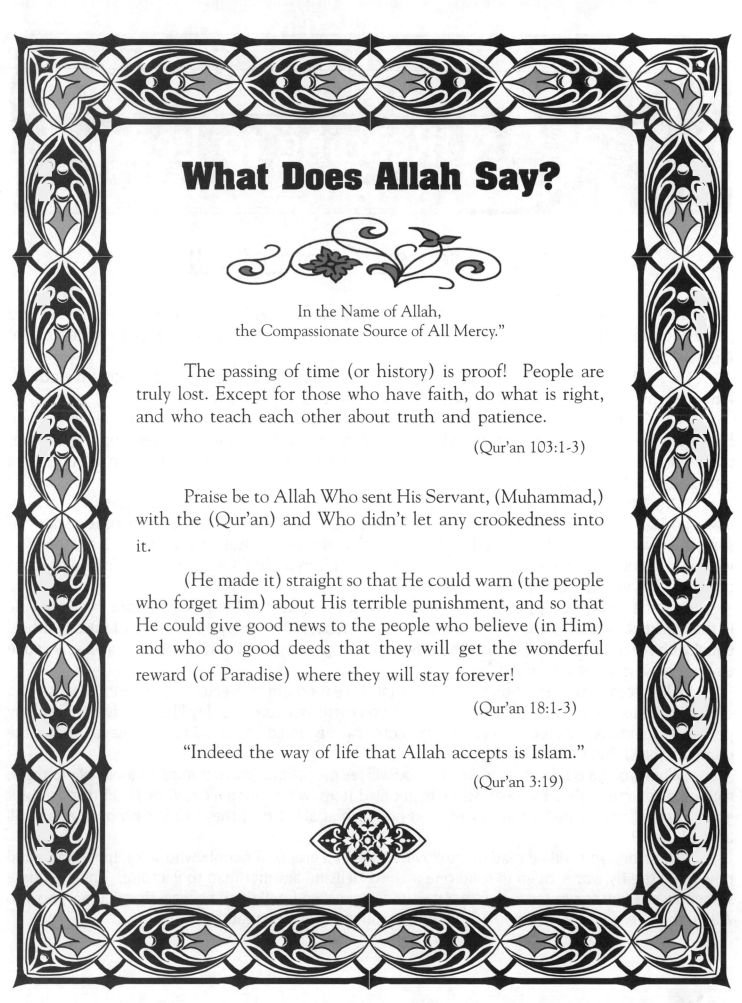

In the Name of Allah,
the Compassionate Source of All Mercy."

The passing of time (or history) is proof! People are truly lost. Except for those who have faith, do what is right, and who teach each other about truth and patience.

(Qur'an 103:1-3)

Praise be to Allah Who sent His Servant, (Muhammad,) with the (Qur'an) and Who didn't let any crookedness into it.

(He made it) straight so that He could warn (the people who forget Him) about His terrible punishment, and so that He could give good news to the people who believe (in Him) and who do good deeds that they will get the wonderful reward (of Paradise) where they will stay forever!

(Qur'an 18:1-3)

"Indeed the way of life that Allah accepts is Islam."

(Qur'an 3:19)

The Greatest Crime of All

Islam teaches that every man and woman was created by Allah to serve Him. Allah gave us a guide book called the Holy Qur'an to help us understand how we should follow His way while we're in this world.

In addition, Allah made a well-balanced universe filled with the signs of His creative power. Anyone who opens their eyes can't help but notice the detail and beauty within it.

The Shaytan, an evil creature, wants us to forget Allah and fail in the one job we were given. How does He do this? He tempts us to look at only things that make our bodies feel good. He makes us forget our spiritual life and our love for truth and convinces us to do nothing more than to waste time and look for things that seem fun.

One of the ways he gets us to forget Allah is to tell us that there is not just one Creator, but many gods. Instead of praying to a Creator we can't see yet, the Shaytan tells us to make a statue of something we know and to bow to it. He tells us all the forces in nature are gods. He'll say there's a wind god, a sun god or a tree god. He makes us think it's more fun if we can "see" our god or make our god with our own hands.

After a while, he may even tell us that other humans like ourselves are gods too! Many people in the world have fallen victim to this terrible crime. What is the name of this crime of making others equal with Allah? It is called Shirk. Shirk means making anyone equal with Allah or saying someone else has powers along side of Allah.

Allah told us that He is only One and that there is no other Creator besides Him. He is not a creature like us and He was certainly never born on earth as a human being like ourselves. But many people let themselves be fooled- even smart people can be fooled! Allah said He will never forgive the crime of Shirk. That's how bad it is.

When you go out in the world today you will see people praying to statues, or idols, of monkeys, round-bellied men called Buddhas, white men called Jesus, white women called Mary, bird gods, spirit gods, forest gods- some people say there is no Allah at all! Don't they see His proof in nature all around them?

The story you will be reading next will be about a group of people who worshipped idols and how one little fly was enough to send one man to Hell and another man to Paradise. The next time someone asks you to pray to a man or a tree or an animal god, tell them no way- that you only bow to Allah, the Creator of everything Who is not like anything in His creation.

The Idol Worshippers And the Fly

Salman al Farsi, who was a student of the Prophet Muhammad, was giving a speech in which he told a very interesting story. He said:

Once upon a time, two men had a unique experience with a fly. When they died, one of them entered Hell-fire because of it while the second one entered Paradise.

In days long ago, these two men were traveling in a far off land. On their way, their journey led them to a road where they happened to meet some idol worshippers. The people had placed their idol at the crossroads and were forcing everyone who passed by to make an offering to their idol. When the two men arrived at the junction, the idol worshippers said to them, "You must make an offering to our god."

The first man said, "I have nothing to offer."

"You can sacrifice anything." They answered. "Even a fly will do!"

The man agreed and started running after a fly and caught it. He then sacrificed it to the idol and the people around him were happy. And so, that man later entered Hell-fire because of his action. (For doing Shirk.)

When the idol worshippers told the second man to do the same thing, he declared, "I don't give any offerings to anyone or anything besides Allah."

The idol worshippers became angry and argued with him furiously. They finally became so mad that they grabbed him and killed him. And so, when he died, he entered Paradise because of his true belief in only one God.

Part A. Exercises.

Answer the following questions in complete answers. Use a separate piece of paper.

1. What does Shirk mean?
2. Where did each of the two men go to after they died and why?
3. What is one good lesson to learn from this story?
4. Who was Salman al Farsi?

Part B. Thinking to Learn

Explain why you think Shirk is the worst crime of all. Write at least 2 paragraphs.

7 How Do I Know the Rules?

Think About It

What would happen if everyone broke all the rules all the time?

Vocabulary Words

'Adl   Justice   Hudood
Hadith   Sunnah

What to Learn

A Muslim lives according to rules and laws and this is what Allah wants people to do.

All our good deeds and bad deeds will be weighed by Allah on Judgment Day! Do you have more good deeds or bad ones?

A. What is Justice?

If someone breaks a rule, should they be punished? What would happen if there were rules to follow but no one was punished for breaking them? Perhaps you have a rule in your class about standing in line and waiting your turn for things. What would happen if no one waited in line and instead rushed to the front? Everyone would be pushing and shoving and maybe someone would get hurt.

There are a lot of rules to follow throughout our lives. There are rules at home, rules at school and rules in our community. Why do people have rules? The simple answer is so that everyone can be treated fairly and have a chance to do things without being hurt or pushed away unfairly. Rules make the world fair and safe for everyone.

So if a person breaks the rules that are there for the good of people, should they be punished?

Absolutely! Because if they weren't punished then nobody would follow the rules. Punishment is the thing that lets people know that there is a price to pay for breaking the rules. If everyone follows the rules then they are rewarded with a smoother and easier time in their life. So we can see that a big part of life is about rewards and punishments for our actions.

There is an important teaching in Islam called **'Adl**, or Justice. **Justice** means that you get what you deserve. If you obey the rules then you deserve the benefits of safety and freedom. If you break the rules and make life harder for other people, then you deserve to be punished. Islam teaches that justice is the most important part of our daily life together on this planet. To be fair to everyone and to obey the rules is the way of a Muslim.

A Muslim Woman Judge Listens to a Case in Court

B. Who Made the Rules?

When you move around between your home, school and community, you will notice that there are a lot of laws and rules to follow. Rules about behavior in class, talking to adults, driving, chores at home-even homework has rules about not cheating and writing neatly! Where did all the rules and laws come from and who makes them? You would be surprised to know that there are a lot of sources for our rules in this life. Can you guess who the most important law-maker of all is?

There are two types of laws that we follow: laws made by people and laws made by Allah. Examples of laws that people made are simple to find. Almost all the laws that help us move around each other and live safely with each other are based on laws people made. These are the little, detailed laws. For example, a stop sign on a road is a law made by people. Laws about recycling garbage or paying taxes are also made by people.

What kinds of laws are made by Allah? Allah's laws are the big rules that help us behave well and know what to do with the most important parts of our lives. For example, Allah taught us not to steal, not to kill people for no reason, not to lie and not to cheat. You can have all the man-made laws in the world, but if people don't obey Allah's laws, they will never obey human laws.

The name for Allah's laws in Arabic is "Hudood." The word **Hudood** means "limits." Allah set the limits of how we behave and we try our best not to go beyond the allowed limits. Even though man-made laws may change over time, Allah's laws never change.

Sometimes people make rules that go against the laws of Allah. When that happens, whose laws should we obey, people's or Allah's? You guessed it, if a law made by people goes against a law made by Allah, then we have to follow Allah first. That is because Allah made us and gave His Messages to us with the best laws.

Can you imagine going against the One Who gave you life to begin with? That would be foolish indeed! (45:7-11)

C. What is the Sunnah?

How do we find out what Allah's limits, or laws are? Where do we look? Do you remember the name of the last book Allah sent to this world? That's right, the Holy Qur'an is the last message from Allah to people. In it we find all the main laws that Allah wants us to follow so we can live better lives.

There is also one more place we look into for rules we need to follow. Do you remember the name of the Prophet of Allah that brought the Qur'an to us? Yes, his name was Prophet Muhammad, peace be upon him. Allah told us in the Qur'an to follow the lifestyle, or **Sunnah**, of Prophet Muhammad.

Allah said, "*You have in the Messenger of Allah, (Muhammad,) a beautiful example to follow.*" (Qur'an 33:21)

The Prophet taught us many things to help us be better Muslims. The Prophet's sayings and doings are called **Hadith**. There are six main books that have the Prophet's Hadiths in them. You will see the names of those six books on this page.

To better understand how the Prophet's Sunnah are connected to the message of the Qur'an, let us look at the Islamic practice of prayer. Allah said in the Qur'an that Muslims must pray every day. "*Establish Prayer.*" (2:110) But Allah didn't tell us how to pray. He didn't give us all the details in the Qur'an.

That was the job of the Prophet. He said, "Pray like you've seen me praying." So he taught us how to pray to Allah. Do you see how the two go together?

When we put these two things together, the Book of Allah and the Sunnah of the Prophet, we have a complete guide for living our lives. A Muslim who wants to live by Allah's ways follows the Qur'an and Sunnah. It is the best way to live.

The Six Main Hadith Collections

Bukhari

Muslim

Tirmidhi

Abu Dawud

An Nisa'i

Ibn Majah

Questions to Answer

1. Why is it important for all people to obey rules and laws?
2. What does Islam say about Justice?
3. What will happen to all our good and bad deeds on Judgment Day?
4. What two types of rules are there?
5. What are the Hudood of Allah and what does that idea mean?
6. How do the Qur'an and the Sunnah work together?

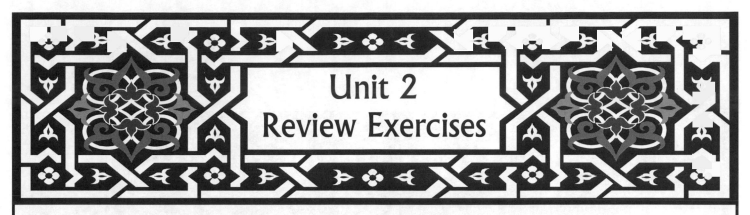

Unit 2
Review Exercises

Vocabulary Review

On a separate piece of paper, write the meaning of each word below. Remember to write in complete sentences.

1. Iblis
2. Shirk
3. Justice
4. Dinosaurs
5. Jinn
6. Meteor
7. Shaytan
8. Hadith
9. Angels
10. Sunnah
11. 'Adl
12. Hudood

Remembering What You Read

On a separate piece of paper, answer the questions below. Remember to answer as best as you can and write in complete sentences.

1. Who was Iblis and what did he do?
2. What does the word instinct mean?
3. Why were the Angels worried about the creation of human beings?
4. Why do Muslims follow the rules of Allah in their daily life?
5. What are the six main books of Hadith? List them all.
6. What was the main lesson in the story of the Idol-worshippers and the Fly?
7. What are the two places our soul can go to after we die and are judged?
8. How does the Sunnah complete our knowledge of Allah's commands?
9. What did Allah tell us about the example of the Prophet Muhammad?
10. Explain the place of 'Adl in our daily life.

Thinking to Learn

Read the following statement and explain whether it is true or false. Write in complete sentences on a separate piece of paper.

In Islam you only need to follow the Qur'an and nothing else.

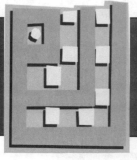

Unit 3

The Life of a Muslim

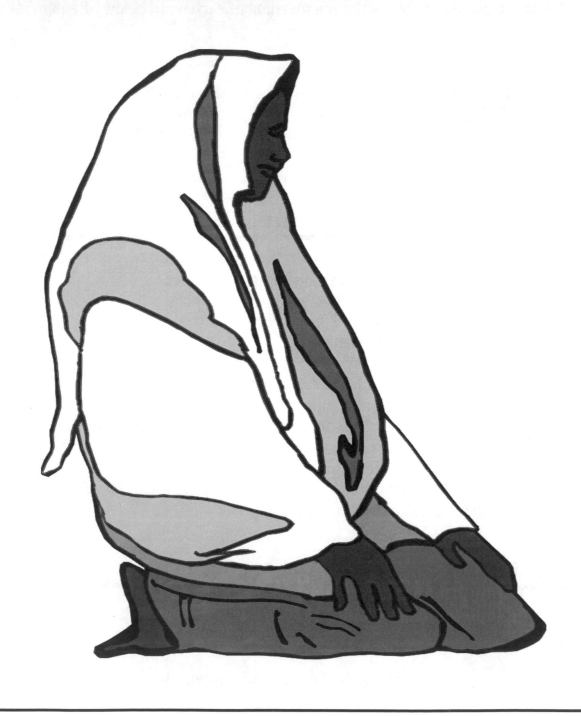

The Five Special Gifts

Think About It

If Islam means finding peace by surrendering to Allah, are there any dangers in life that may come between us and our peacefulness? What are some possible things that may disturb our peace?

Vocabulary Words

Pillar	Salat	Zakat
Shahadah	Saum	Hajj

What to Learn

Islam has a daily program for life.

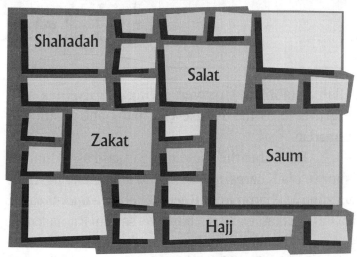

A. Our Shield Against Shaytan.

As we have learned before, Islam is a way of living life. It's not just a religion. We have also learned that our reason for being here on this planet is to choose to love Allah by ourselves and to obey His rules and laws. Shaytan wants us to forget Allah and to disobey Him. How can we protect ourselves against his evil plans and stay true to Allah in our daily life?

Allah thought of that and gave us a way to keep our souls safe from harm. He gave us five special practices to live by that help us to resist Shaytan. These five activities are called the Pillars of Islam. A **Pillar** is a strong pole, usually made of stone, that holds something up. The practices of Islam are like stone pillars because they hold up our way of life and make it strong and sturdy. Shaytan has a tough

time with people who shield themselves using the five pillars of Islam.

The first pillar is called the **Shahadah**. It's an important phrase that helps us to remember our Creator and the Sunnah of our Prophet. The second pillar is called **Salat**, or Prayer, and it helps to keep our mind and heart focused on goodness and honesty all throughout the day.

The third pillar is called **Zakat**, or Charity that makes pure. It is the act of giving money in charity to the poor so we can clean our hearts from greed and learn to help others.

The fourth pillar is called **Saum**, or fasting and it helps us to control our bodies. The last of the five pillars is called **Hajj**, or Pilgrimage. It is the once in a lifetime journey to Mecca where we join hands with other Muslims to make the world a better place. Say the name of each of these five pillars in order: Shahadah, Salat, Zakat, Saum and Hajj.

In a Hadith, or saying of the Prophet Muhammad, peace be upon him, he said, "Islam is founded on five things: Declaring that there is no god but Allah and that Muhammad is the Messenger of

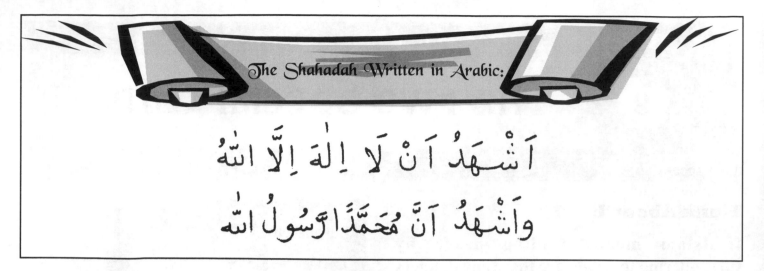

The Shahadah Written in Arabic:

اَشْهَدُ اَنْ لَا اِلهَ اِلَّا اللهُ

وَاَشْهَدُ اَنَّ مُحَمَّدًا رَسُولُ اللهِ

Allah, establishing prayer, giving charity, making a pilgrimage to the House (Ka'bah) and fasting in Ramadan."

In Arabic the same thing is said as, "Buniyal Islamu 'ala Khamsin: Shahadati an la ilaha ill Allah wa anna Muhammadar Rasul Allah, wa iqamis salati wa ita-iz zakati wa hajj il bayti wa sawmi Ramadana."

This Hadith is found in the two collections called Bukhari and Muslim. Can you memorize this Hadith in both Arabic and English? Try it!

B. The Shahadah: The Declaration of Islam.

The Shahadah is the key to entering Islam. No one is a Muslim unless they believe in what the Shahadah teaches. When a non-Muslim person says this one simple sentence, with full belief in their heart, then Allah counts that person as a Muslim right there.

Any sins that the person did in his or her life before that moment are automatically forgiven. It's like being born fresh and new as a baby! No bad deeds are on your record! What is this wonderful sentence a person says to enter Islam?

The words of the Shahadah are as follows: "Ashahadu an la ilaha ill Allah wa ashahadu anna Muhammadar Rasulullah."

In English it translates as: "I declare that there is no god but Allah and I declare that Muhammad is the Messenger of Allah."

If you never said this sentence in your life before- or never thought about the importance of what it says- then you had better do it right away! If you've said it many times before, and always knew its importance, then you love to say it whenever you get the chance. Let's everyone say the Shahadah listed above in Arabic first, then in English, together out loud right now.

The Shahadah, as you may have noticed, has two separate parts. The first part talks about Allah and how there are no gods except Him. "La ilaha illa Allah." "There is no god but Allah." This teaches us not to worship any idols or man gods.

It also teaches us not to be afraid of anything except displeasing Allah. The Blessed Prophet Muhammad said this one teaching is so important that if a person's last words were "La ilaha ill Allah," then they would go to Heaven. (From a Hadith in Abu Daud.)

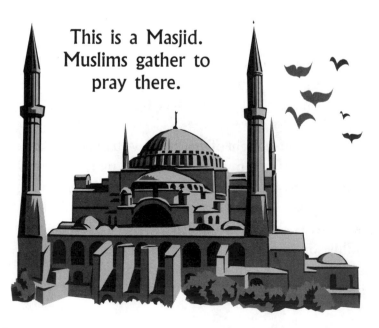

This is a Masjid. Muslims gather to pray there.

The second part of the Shahadah mentions that the Blessed Prophet Muhammad is the Messenger of Allah. "Muhammadar Rasul Allah." By saying this we remind ourselves that Allah sent many Messengers and Prophets to the world, and that Muhammad, peace be upon him, was the last one.

Because he was the last, his message is the most recent and most correct. This part of the Shahadah teaches us that we must follow the Prophet's Sunnah and that following his way is pleasing to Allah. The Shahadah is the starting line for a follower of Islam. It is our Declaration of Independence.

C. What is Salat?

Humans are strange creatures. We have powerful bodies and a brain that is faster than a computer, but people still stumble and make mistakes in their lives. Why? Because we have choice, we can sometimes choose to do things that don't make much sense, like telling a lie or breaking something for no good reason.

Sometimes it's hard to remember to be good. We can get so busy doing something like playing a game or doing a job that we forget who we are and why we're here. We might even start treating people badly or getting angry for no good reason. How can we remember the feelings of peace that Islam is supposed to put inside of us?

Thankfully, Allah gave us Salat. Salat is the Islamic term for prayer. Allah commanded Muslims to pray five times every day. Not whenever we want to, because then we might do them all at once and forget about Allah for the rest of the day, but when He told us to. Allah said, "*Prayers are a duty on believers at set times*." (4:103)

The five daily prayers are done at different times throughout the day so that we always get a reminder, every few hours, that we are Muslims and that we have a duty to Allah. Salat is like our alarm clock. When our minds and bodies begin to forget Allah, the Salat wakes us up and refreshes our heart and mind. The next time you make Salat, thank Allah for the wonderful gift He gave you and remember how it helps us.

From The Prophet:

The Blessed Prophet, peace be upon him, asked some people, "If there was a river at your door and you bathed in it five times a day, would there be any dirt left on you?"

The people nearby said, "No."

Then the Prophet said, "This is like the five daily prayers which Allah uses to clean out bad deeds." (Bukhari, Muslim)

D. When Do I Make Salat?

The five daily prayers all must be prayed at their proper times. Each prayer also has a name of it's own. The first prayer is called Fajr Salat. It is prayed early in the morning before the sun comes up over the horizon. The second prayer is called Zuhr Salat. We pray this one a little while after noon.

The third prayer is called 'Asr Salat and is prayed in the late afternoon. When the sun disappears beyond the horizon we pray the Maghrib Salat. The fifth and final prayer, called 'Isha Salat, begins when the last bit of light is gone from the sky at night and lasts until just before dawn in the morning.

The Blessed Prophet Muhammad said that doing the Salat was so important that if a Muslim gives up on his or her Salat, that they are no longer counted as a Muslim by Allah. "Giving up the Salat is the same as unbelief and shirk." (From the Hadith collection of Muslim.)

A believer in Allah always tries to do their Salat on time. If we do accidentally miss a Salat time, say because we were sleeping or just forgot, then the Prophet advised us to pray the missing Salat right away. Remember your Salat carefully as you learn how to do it and make sure you do it on time.

Questions to Answer

1. How do the five pillars of Islam help us against Shaytan?
2. What is the name of each of the five pillars and what does each mean?
3. What does each part of the Shahadah teach us?
4. What are the names of the five daily prayers?

9 How Do I Prepare for Salat?

Think About It

Before you go skating, you tie up your laces. Before going for a bike ride you check the air in your tires. Why do you always make sure you're prepared before doing something?

Vocabulary Words

Iman   Wudu   Ghusl   Niyyah

What to Learn

Before we pray we make sure we have prepared our bodies to present ourselves to Allah.

Always search for the forgiveness of Allah.

A. What is the Importance of Our Salat?

When we perform our five daily prayers, we're not just doing stretching exercises or aerobics. We don't stand up for prayer just because we want something to do either. We stand for prayer to Allah because Allah told us to. "*Establish Prayer,*" He said. (2:110) We need the Salat to help keep our hearts pure and free from bad thoughts. So we had better take it seriously.

When we are making Salat, we are presenting ourselves to Allah officially. Although we can't see Allah, He can see us. Do you remember Who Allah is? Allah is the power that created everything in the world and universe. We are like nothing compared to Him. We are less than nothing. If we don't take our Salat seriously then we are really insulting Allah.

The Blessed Prophet once remarked, "Allah will not count the prayer of a person whose heart is not in it." And since Allah said that giving up Salat is the same as not believing in Him, then we don't want to make a careless prayer that Allah won't accept. We might as well be doing nothing!

Our belief in Allah must be true, even as our Salat must be right. The word for belief in Arabic is **Iman** (Ee-maan). By concentrating on doing our Salat well, we show that our Iman is true and solid. We defeat the Shaytan completely. When we pray the right way then our Iman actually increases even more- making us come even closer to our Creator!

Salat is such an important part of our lives that we don't want to neglect it or waste it. As you learned before, by doing the Salat we get sins forgiven as if we were washing dirt from our bodies. Don't take the Salat as a mere game because it's really one of the most important things you will ever need in this life.

"Water makes everything pure." So said the Prophet Muhammad.

B. Preparing for Salat.

When the time for Salat has come upon us, we must make ready to perform it. The Blessed Prophet once said, "To offer the prayer in the first hour is to please Allah. To offer it in late hours is to ask Allah's forgiveness." (Tirmidhi)

What must we do to make ready for this important part of our day? There are basically two main things to prepare for Salat. Both of them involve your body. Let's see what those are.

Pretend that you heard the leader of your country wants you to go to his or her office today, would you go to see him in your sleeping clothes? Would you go only half dressed and present yourself before him? You would never do that because you would feel like a fool!

Well, can you imagine presenting yourself to Allah, the One Who is more powerful than all the leaders of the world combined, only half dressed or worse? You should feel doubly foolish! So one of the main requirements for Salat is that you cover your body and that you wear nice, clean clothes, knowing that you have an important meeting with an important Being.

Allah said in the Qur'an, "*Wear your beautiful clothes at every prayer and place of prayer.*" (7:31)

For a male, his body must be covered from below his knees up to his belly. Then he should wear a shirt that covers up his upper body. It is recommended to wear some sort of a hat, like a kufi or turban on his head as well.

Females also cover their bodies in prayer. Their whole body must be covered from the ankles to their neck and down to their wrists. In addition, females are asked by Allah to wear a Hijab, or head scarf, which covers their hair. This is to help the girl to realize that Allah only counts her heart and soul and not her good looks or beauty.

We always pray with our shoes off, unless we're on the road traveling. Wearing socks is allowed for prayer, but make sure they're clean and not really dirty.

Our clothes are one of the two major parts of getting ready for Salat. What is the other part about? As you will see, it's an even more important part of preparing to present ourselves to our Creator.

C. Getting Clean For Prayer.

What would you do if a person came to shake your hand and their hand was full of dirt? Would you shake it? Probably not. You would say, "Wash your hands first!" Only when the person coming to you was clean would you accept their greetings.

Like in our example before, would you go see the leader of a country with a dirty face and stinky body? "Never," you would say, "Never, Never, Never." So shouldn't we wash ourselves before standing before Allah and presenting ourselves for prayer? Of course!

How do we wash ourselves for prayer? There is a method called **Wudu**, or Ablution. This means washing up for prayer. It is a simple thing to do and only takes a few minutes to do. When we have our Wudu, as it is called, we are clean for prayer. Allah will not accept our prayer unless we are clean for it. If we don't want to be clean in front of Allah then our Iman, our belief, must be very weak indeed!

The Blessed Prophet once said, "A person who doesn't keep his promises has no Iman. And a person has no prayer if he is dirty, and whoever doesn't offer their prayer has no (Islamic) way of life. The importance of prayer in this way of life is the same as the head to a body." (Tabarani)

The Blessed Prophet also said, "The key to Salat is being clean." (Ahmad) In Arabic it is said as, "Miftahu as salati at tuhuru." Can you memorize that short Hadith in English and Arabic?

We need to make Wudu for Salat if any one of the following things happened: 1) We touched a lot of dirt or unclean things and are filthy. 2) We used the bathroom. 3) We had any bleeding or 4) passed gas. 5) We went to sleep or 6) vomited.

If strange liquids came out of our personal parts, then, in addition to the Wudu, we need to take a bath or shower. This is called a **Ghusl**, or shower. For this book, however, we will stick to how to make the Wudu. If you did Wudu and none of the above six things happened, you can continue to offer all your prayers until one of those things occur. Then a fresh Wudu is necessary.

D. How Do I Make Wudu?

Making Wudu is easy. All you need is clean water and yourself! Before you begin you must do something called making intention, or **Niyyah**. This means that you are going to settle in your mind what you're doing before you begin. You say silently to yourself, "Nuwaitul Wudu" which means, "I intend to make Wudu."

This is important because the Holy Prophet Muhammad said, "Actions will be judged by your intentions." So your Wudu will count if you intended to make it. What if you were watching television and while the show was going on, you ran to make your Wudu, but the whole time you were still thinking of the action on TV? You never settled in your mind what you were doing and thus might have even made mistakes. So make the proper Niyyah, or intention, for everything.

To continue with your Wudu procedure, say, "Bismillahir Rahmanir Raheem." Which means, "In the name of Allah, the Caring and the Kind." The Prophet advised us to start things by saying this.

The parts of Wudu shall be listed below as follows:

1. Begin by washing the right hand three times to the wrist. Then the left hand three times to the wrist.

2. Take water into the mouth with the right hand three times. Each time swish the water around and make sure that it covers everywhere. Use your right index finger to rub the teeth and gums. This helps prevent tooth-decay and gets awful germs out of your mouth.

3. Sniff water up and out of the nose three times with the right hand. This clears the nasal passages and allows clear breathing.

4. Take water into both hands and gently pour it over the entire face. Try not to splash it all over the place. The Blessed Prophet once warned that a person can waste water even if they were making Wudu by a river. Every part of the face must be wetted.

5. Next, wash the right arm up to the elbow three times and then the left. Leave your hands up in the air and let the water fall down off your elbows. This keeps most germs from coming back down onto your hands.

6. Wet the fingers with water and rub them from the front of the top of your head to the back of the head, palm down. Then run your hands back up to the front of your head.

7. Use your index fingers and thumbs to rub the ears clean.

8. Take the back of your hands and rub the back of your neck once.

9. Wash both feet with the left hand up to the ankle. Start with the right foot.

10. Say this phrase: *"Ashahadu an la ilaha ill Allah. Wahdahu laa shareeka lahu. Wa ashahadu anna Muhamadan 'abduhu wa rasulhu."* It means: *"I declare that there is no god but Allah; One, with no partners, and I declare that Muhammad is His servant and Messenger."*

11. Say this Du'a: *"Allahumma ja'alnee min at tawwabin wa ja'alnee min al mutahireen."* It means: *"Allah make me among the repentant and make me among the clean."*

Now you're ready to make your Salat!

Questions to Answer

1. Why should we consider our Salat important?
2. How should we dress for prayers?
3. What six things make us too dirty to pray?
4. What is the difference between Wudu and Ghusl?
5. Make the correct Wudu procedure in front of your parent or teacher.

What Does Allah Say?

In the Name of Allah,
the Compassionate Source of All Mercy."

Indeed, the prayer is a duty for the believers at set times.

(Qur'an 4:103)

Observe the prayers strictly.

(Qur'an 2:238)

Believers! When you are about to offer your prayers, wash your faces and hands up to the elbows and wipe your heads and feet up to the ankles.

(Qur'an 5:7)

Prayer is only for Allah.

(Qur'an 13:14)

Every creature in space and on earth bows down to Allah.

(Qur'an 13:15)

Skill Builder: Learning to Pray

The Salat procedure is a simple one to learn. It consists of a series of movements and phrases that are done and said in a set way. Each of the five daily prayers is said in a similar way. The only difference between them is that some have more movements than others. We say our prayers in Arabic because this is how the Prophet Muhammad taught us to say them. He even taught people who couldn't speak Arabic very well to say the prayers in Arabic. This helps to make all Muslims united in the world and keeps us connected to the original language Allah used for His last revelation to the world. As you learn how to pray, keep in mind that is is a holy act and is not to be taken lightly. It is you presenting yourself to Allah.

Part A. Where Do I Pray?

The Blessed Prophet taught us that the entire world is our Masjid. The word Masjid means place to bow down. Often times Muslims will go to a special building to pray together in groups. Those buildings are also called Masjids. In English the word for Masjid is Mosque. A Muslim prefers to use the word Masjid because it means a place of prayer. The word "Mosque" was invented by Spanish Christians over five hundred years ago and means "Mosquito" in their language. They boasted that they would stamp out every Masjid in Spain like swatting "mezquitas." Therefore, the term "Mosque" is offensive to us.

Sometimes Muslims will find themselves outside when prayer time comes. We can pray outside of a Masjid if we have to because the entire earth is our Masjid. The only places we are not allowed to pray in are dirty areas, such as muddy fields or the bathroom. The place must be clean. Muslims usually like to pray on prayer rugs or mats, but you can also pray on grass, cement, wood floors or anywhere else that is clean.

All Muslims face the direction of Mecca, in Arabia, when they pray. The direction of Mecca is called the Qiblah. We pray towards Mecca not because our Prophet was born there, but because there is a special building there called the Ka'bah. The word Ka'bah means, "a cube or square-shaped thing."

The Ka'bah is an ancient, or old, place that was chosen by Allah to be the main place for people to pray to Him. It is the place that an ancient Prophet named Ibrahim built so that all the people of the world would have a common place to come to when they wanted to really show how much they love Allah.

Every Masjid in the world is built facing in the direction of Mecca. When Muslims gather together to pray this is called making Salat in Jam'a. The word Jam'a means "group." When Muslims pray in Jam'a, one person will stand in front of the others and act as the leader of the prayer. Such a person is called the Imam, or leader. Everyone praying behind an Imam follows along with him or her.

Every prayer consists of two up to four cycles called Rak'as. One series of standing, bowing and prostrating (bowing on the floor twice) equals one ra'kah. Fajr has two rak'as. Zuhr, 'Asr and 'Isha have four rak'as.   Maghrib is the only regular Salat that has three rak'as. The prayer that will be explained on the following pages will consist of two rak'as.

In Fajr all Surahs are said aloud. In Zuhr and 'Asr Salats all Surahs are said silently. In Maghrib and 'Isha, the Surahs are said aloud only in the first two rak'as.

Part B. The Start of Salat.

Just like with Wudu and anything else important, we begin our Salat with Niyyah, or intention. This way we make it clear to ourselves what we're doing before we begin. While facing the Qiblah, properly dressed and in a state of Wudu, we say silently to ourselves, "Nuwaytus Salatul _____" What we say in the last space is the name of the prayer we are doing.

Then we begin the Salat itself by raising our hands to our ears and saying, "Allahu Akbar." Which means, "Allah is the Greatest." Females raise their hands only to their shoulders. Then we fold our hands over our lower chest. Females fold their hands over their upper chests. The right hand goes over the left.

Some Muslims like to pray with their hands hanging loosely from their sides. This is allowed also, but it is better to fold your hands in front of you, right over left, based on an abundance of Hadiths about it.

Step 1

Raise hands up and say, "Allahu Akbar."

Males raise their hands up to the side of their head. Females raise their hands just up to the shoulder level. After performing this beginning motion of the Salat, a person must think of themselves as cut off from the outside world until they are finished.

Step 2

Fold right hand over the left in front of you.
Then say, "*Subahanakal lahumma wa behamdika, wa tabaruka ismuka, wa ta'ala jeduka, wa la ilaha ghairuka.*"

(It means: "Glory to You, Allah, and praise by You. Blessed is Your Name, great is Your Highness and their is no god except You.")

Then recite,
"*Ow thzu billa himina Shaytan ir rajeem.*"

(It means: "I ask Allah to protect me from the rejected Shaytan.")

Part B. The Greatest Surah.

    While we are standing in that position, which is called, Qiyam, or standing up, we must take care not to look around or move our bodies. From the moment we said, "Allahu Akbar," the prayer started and we shouldn't do anything except what is allowed in the prayer until we finish. If we laugh, start to talk or walk around, then that Salat is broken and we have to start all over again.

    The very next thing we should say is what Allah called the greatest Surah, or chapter, of the Holy Qur'an. It is the one Surah that Allah gave us that has everything for us in just seven little verses, or ayahs. It is such an important Surah that if we forget to say it in our Salat then the whole Salat doesn't count. Here is the Arabic text of that Surah, which is called Al Fatiha, or the Opening, along with the English meaning. In the Salat we say it in the Arabic only.

Step 3

Surah al Fatiha is said in Arabic this way:

"Bismillahir Rahmanir Raheem
Al humdulil lahir Rabbil 'alameen,
Ar Rahmanir Raheem
Maliki yowmid deen
'Eyaka na'budu wa 'eyaka nasta'een
Ihidinas siratal mustaqeem
Sirat aladheena an 'amta alayhim,
Ghayril maghdoobi 'alayhim
Wa lad dawleen."

(It means: "*In the Name of Allah, the Caring and the Kind. Praise be to Allah, the Lord of the Universe; the Coaring and the Kind and Master of the Day of Judgment. You alone do we serve and to You alone do we turn for help. Guide us in the straight way. The way of those who You are happy with, not the way of those who Your angry with, and not the way of those who have gone astray.*")

Qur'an 1:1-7

After saying Surah al Fatiha, we say another portion of the Qur'an. It can be as little as three ayahs long or even a whole long Surah! Most people say short Surahs such as Al Ikhlas or Al Nas. In a third or fourth Rak'a of a prayer, only Fatiha is said before going into bowing. But as we are still in the first two rak'as, we must say more Qur'an here.

Next say a short Surah.
We chose Surah Ikhlas to say here but you can choose any one you want.

Bismillahir Rahmanir Raheem.
Qul hoowa Allahu ahad.
Allahu Sawmad.
Lam Yalid wa lam yulad.
Wa lam yakun lahu kufuwan ahad.

Which means: "In the Name of Allah, the Caring and the Kind. Tell everyone: "He is Allah the One. Allah is always forever. He doesn't have any children and He was never born, and there is nothing the same as Him."

(112:1-4)

Part C. The Ruku and Sajda.

Step 4

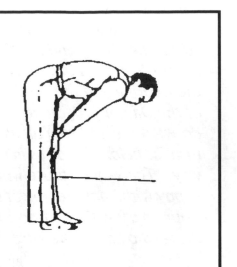

After completing the Surah, the next thing you do is say, "Allahu Akbar." Then you bend forward at the waist and put your hands on your knees. This is called Ruku. You say silently, "Sub-hanna Rabbial Owdheem," at least three times.

There are other similar phrases that are also allowed to say. Your parents or teacher will let you know about those. The basic phrase said here means, "Glory to my great Lord."

Step 5

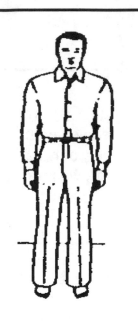

Then we say, "Sami' Allahu liman hamida," (Allah hears those who praise Him,) and return to a standing position. But our hands are left loose at our sides. We can also add the phrase, "Rabbana lakal Hamad." Which means, "Our Lord to You belongs all praise."

Step 6

Then we say, "Allahu Akbar and lower ourselves to our knees and make Sajda, or bowing on the floor. Our elbows must stay up in the air and our feet must be raised up so that the bottom our toes are on the ground. Place your hands on the floor on the side of your head. Your nose and forehead are touching the ground. Say three times, "Sub-hanna Rabbial 'ala." It means, "Glory to my Lord the Most High."

Step 7

Front View   Back View

Then we say, "Allahu Akbar," and sit up on our knees for a moment. Girls sit a little to their left side while boys keep their right foot raised up. Your teacher can show you the difference.

Step 8

Next say, "Allahu Akbar," and do one more Sujud and say the same phrase three times that you said before.

Step 9

Then say, "Allahu Akbar," and return to a standing position with your hands folded in front of you. That was one Raka', or cycle of prayer.

Repeat steps 3-8

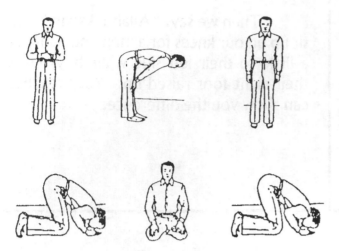

Step 10

Now pretending that we were doing Fajr Salat, which has two Raka's, we still have to complete another one. That is easy. All you have to do is repeat steps 3-8. But after saying Surah al Fatiha, choose a different Surah to say afterwards than what you said in the first Raka'.

So, for example, if we said Surah al Ikhlas in the first Rak'a, in our second Raka', after al Fatiha, we'll say Surah Nas, or which ever one we choose!

After the end of the second Sajda, instead of standing up after saying, "Allahu Akbar," we will return to a sitting position and stay there. (Note: If you were doing a 3 or 4 raka' Salat, all Qur'an reciting will be silent, said to one's self.)

Step 11

While sitting we will say a special set of supplications and phrases. The first phrase we say is this: "*Atay hiyatu lillahee wa salawatu wa tayyibatu. As-salam 'alayka ayyuhaan nabeeyu wa rahma tullahee wa barakatuhu, Assalam 'alayna wa 'ala 'ibad ilahas sawliheen.*"

Then you raise the index finger while saying the next phrase:

"*Ashahadu an la ilaha ill Allah, wahdahu laa shareeka lahu, wa ashahadu anna Muhammadan 'abduhu wa rasoolhu.*"

(*It means: "All purity, prayer and goodness belong to Allah. Peace upon you Prophet and Allah's mercy and blessings. Peace be upon all righteous servants of Allah. I declare that there is no god but Allah, He is One with no partners, and I declare that Muhammad is His servant and Messenger."*)

Step 12

Then you say the prayer called the Durood which is a meant to ask Allah to bless the Prophet. The words of the Durood * are as follows:

"*Allahumma salee 'ala Muhammadin wa 'ala aalee Muhammadin, Kama salayta 'ala Ibrahima wa 'ala aalee Ibrahima. Innaka hameedun Majeed. Allahumma barik 'ala Muhammadin wa 'ala aalee Muhammadin, Kama barakta 'ala Ibrahima wa 'ala aalee Ibrahima fil 'alameen. Inaka hameedum majeed.*"

(* Note: There are other valid ways to say the Durood.)

(It means: "Allah send blessings on Muhammad and on the family of Muhammad, just like You put blessings on Ibrahim and on the family of Ibrahim. You are worthy of all praise, the Majestic. Allah grace Muhammad and the family of Muhammad, just like you put grace on Ibrahim and the family of Ibrahim in the world. You are worthy of all praise, the Majestic.")

Step 13

Then you turn your face to the right and say, "Assalamu 'alaykum wa rahmatullah.

Step 14

Then you turn your face to the left and say, "Assalamu 'alaykum wa rahmatullah."

Your prayer is now finished and you can rise and go about your business. It is recommended to stay seated, however, and say some small phrases to remember Allah. Then personal requests to Allah for forgiveness or guidance can be made. (This is called making dhikr and then making Du'a.)

10 How Do I Praise Allah?

Think About It

If you love someone, what should you say to them? If you really need someone a lot, what should you tell them to thank them?

Vocabulary Words

Praise   Glorify   Dhikr
Du'a

What to Learn

A Muslim remembers Allah many times throughout the day and praises his or her Creator.

All living creatures pray in their own way!

A. Why Should I Praise Allah?

Islam teaches us that one of the best things we can ever do is to praise Allah. The word **Praise** means to say wonderful things about someone to show how great they are. This helps us to understand that we should never feel arrogant, like Iblis did, because the only One Who is great is Allah.

Allah says in the Qur'an that every creature in the world praises Him in its own way. If you will remember, all the plants and animals follow their instincts in their daily life. By living the way they are supposed to, these creatures are actually praising Allah. All the birds, squirrels, fish, bugs and trees praise Allah every moment of every day. They are all perfect Muslims. They are surrendered to Allah and they are at peace.

Allah gave us people Salat as a way to remind us to remember Him and to be good. It is also a way to get some of our bad deeds forgiven. In addition to Salat, there is another level of activity that can bring us closer to Allah. If we really love Allah and want to express our affection, then we should also say words of praise to glorify our Creator. The word **glorify** means also the same thing as praise.

Our last Prophet from Allah, Muhammad, may peace be upon him, told us this good news right from our Creator: Allah said, "*I am near My servant when he thinks of Me and I am with him when he remembers Me. If he remembers Me to himself, then I remember Him to Myself. If he remembers me in a gathering, then I remember him in a better gathering than theirs.*" (Bukhari)

So when we remember Allah, Allah will remember us. Wouldn't you like to have the Lord of the entire Universe mentioning you! I sure would!

The Blessed Prophet Muhammad taught us many beautiful phrases we can say to praise Allah. We can say them after our Salat is finished, or in the

No matter how busy your life gets never forget to make Dhikr because when you're gone from this world and no one remembers you, Allah will still know who you are.

morning, on a bus or anywhere we want to. We don't need Wudu and we can even use our own words if we want to. Many Muslims like to say words of praise that the Prophet taught because he said them in such a beautiful way. Let's learn a few of these words of praise, called **Dhikr**, (thzikr) and how they can help us.

B. Dhikr Sentences.

The Blessed Prophet once said, "Whoever says, 'Glory to Allah and His is all Praise,' one hundred times will get all his or her sins forgiven even if they were as much as the foam on the sea.'" In Arabic the phrase is, "Subahan Allah wa beehamdihi." (Bukhari)

Once the Prophet was talking to a man named Abdullah when he said to him, "Abdullah, should I point out to you a treasure from the treasures of Paradise?"

Abdullah replied, "Yes, Messenger of Allah. Please tell me."

The Prophet answered, "Say this phrase, 'There is no might or power except with Allah.'" "La howla wa la quwwata illa billah." (Bukhari)

The Prophet once said, "Here are some sentences that Allah likes the most. They are, 'Subahanallah' (Glory to Allah), 'Alhumdulillah' (Praise be to Allah), 'La ilaha ill Allah' (There is no god but Allah), and 'Allahu Akbar' (Allah is the Greatest). You can say them in any order you want." (Muslim)

"There is a phrase that is light on the tongue," said the Prophet, "but heavy in the balance, (the scale on Judgment Day). That phrase is, 'La ilaha ill Allah.'" "There is no god but Allah."

Praising and remembering Allah, or Dhikr, is so important that the Prophet once said, "When a group of people sit together and do Dhikr, the angels surround them, peace comes over them, Allah's mercy covers them and Allah speaks to the angels that are near Him (about the group.)" (Muslim)

Many Muslims remember Allah in large gatherings and do group Dhikr. Other people praise Allah alone or silently. Which ever way you like to do it, always remember Allah everyday with special words of praise. Allah said in the Qur'an, "*Remember Me and I will remember you.*" Let's make it our goal to think about Allah often and when we do, to say some words that praise and glorify him.

C. What is Du'a?

So far we have learned about Salat and Dhikr. There is one more way to make our connection to Allah strong and meaningful in our lives. This is called making Du'a. The word Du'a means to call on someone. Allah said in the Qur'an, "*When My servants ask about Me, I am indeed close. I listen to the request of every person when he or she calls on Me. So let people listen to My call also, and believe in Me so they can be rightly guided.*" (2:186)

How do we make Du'a? How do we call on Allah? It's also an easy thing to do and it doesn't

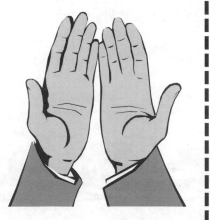

Hold your hands in front of you like this when making Du'a. It shows you are asking to receive something from Allah. Afterwards, wipe both hands on your face showing that you are washing the grace of Allah on you.

require Wudu either. All you need to do is raise your hands in front of you like you were going to receive something from someone and then ask Allah for whatever you like.

You can ask Allah in any language, not just Arabic and you can use your own words or some of the beautiful Du'as that Allah taught us in the Qur'an. What should we ask Allah for? Can you imagine a person going to Allah and asking for riches or lots of money and things like that? What would you say about such a person? You would probably say they're very greedy.

One of the main lessons that Allah wants us to learn is that this life and all the good things in it is very short. It won't last. So rather than run after wealth and endless fun, we should try to come closer to Allah. Like Allah said, "*What is with you will disappear but what is with Allah will last forever.*"

We should only ask for what we really need in this life and in the next life. We can ask for Allah's forgiveness for our bad deeds and sins. We can ask for Allah's help in a tough time or before we do a hard job. We can thank Allah for something good that happened and ask Allah to help us get through a bad time. We can even just talk to Allah about our feelings if we like to because like He said, He hears every Du'a we say and that He is near.

Here are some of the beautiful Du'as that Allah taught us in the Qur'an. Try to learn them in either Arabic, English or both and say them any time you would like. We must make Du'a and call on Allah because Allah doesn't like us to ignore Him in our lives. We need Him so let's not neglect the One Who

can help us more than anyone else in the whole world.

The following three Du'as are taken from the Holy Qur'an.

"Rabbana atina fid dunya hasanatin wa fil aakhirati hasanatin wa qeena adhabin naar." (Our Lord, give us the best in this life and the best in the next and protect us from the punishment of the fire.) 2:201

"Rabbana laa tuzigh qulubana ba'd ith hadaytana wa hablana min ladunka rahmatin innaka antal wahhab." (Our Lord, don't let our hearts go wrong no since You've guided us. Give is mercy from You because You are the One Who gives endlessly.) 3:8

"Rabbana inanaa amanna faghfir lana dhunubana wa qeena 'athaaban naar." (Our Lord, we believe, so forgive us our sins and save us from the punishment of the fire.) 3:16

There is another Du'a from the Qur'an that is very long but that is also very beautiful. You can find it in Surah 3, ayahs 26-27 and 29-30. Look them up and read them aloud and remember your Lord as much as you can!

D. How is Du'a Answered?

Allah has promised to hear our Du'as. How are they answered? Allah has said in the Qur'an that He will help us if we are sincere. If we say our Du'as with no sincerity, how can we expect to be helped? At the same time, if we live our lives every day and never remember Allah, or only call on Him when we're in trouble, do you think our Du'a deserves to be answered? Of course not! (11:9-11)

"*When trouble touches a person, he cries to Us (Allah) lying down, sitting or standing. But when We have solved his problem, he passes on his way as if he never called on Us in trouble!*" (10:12)

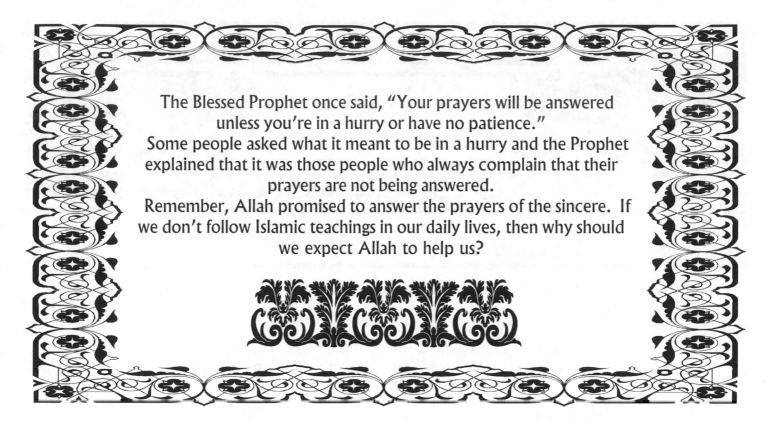

The Blessed Prophet once said, "Your prayers will be answered unless you're in a hurry or have no patience."
Some people asked what it meant to be in a hurry and the Prophet explained that it was those people who always complain that their prayers are not being answered.
Remember, Allah promised to answer the prayers of the sincere. If we don't follow Islamic teachings in our daily lives, then why should we expect Allah to help us?

Allah said, "*Tell people, 'If you love Allah then follow (the Prophet). Allah will love you and forgive you your sins because Allah is the forgiving and the Kind.' Then tell them, 'Obey Allah and His Messenger.' But if (people) turn away, then know that Allah doesn't love those who cover up (the truth).*" (3:31-32)

If we are sincere and we call on Allah in both good times and bad, then we become more deserving of Allah's special favors. At the same time, we must not ask for things that are only for our own greed. What would you think if someone came to you asking only for money and other similar stuff all the time?

Everything happens for a reason and only Allah knows the reason. Allah has said He will answer the call of the sincere, but how is the answer given to us? (41:49-52)

Allah said that He will help us in ways that we don't even expect. "*...You don't know that maybe Allah might bring out a new situation.*" (65:1) "*...For those who fear Allah, He always prepares a way out.*" (65:2)

This means that He will answer our sincere Du'as but that we don't always see how this is done. Perhaps most of our Du'as will be answered without our ever knowing it. (35:2-3) Remember to never stop calling on Allah and to keep on the look out for how He answers your prayers.

Questions to Answer

1. What is the difference between Dhikr and Du'a?
2. Why should we remember Allah in our daily life?
3. How do we hold our hands when making Du'a?
4. Write down and memorize one Dhikr phrase.
5. What is one thing Allah said about Dhikr?

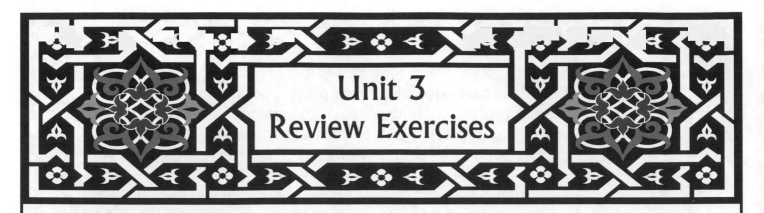

Unit 3
Review Exercises

Vocabulary Review

On a separate piece of paper, write the meaning of each word below. Remember to write in complete sentences.

1. Dhikr
2. Qiyam
3. Wudu
4. Zakat
5. Ghusl
6. Pillar

7. Qiblah
8. Raka'
9. Du'a
10. Shahadah
11. Salat
12. Niyyah

Remembering What You Read

On a separate piece of paper, answer the questions below. Remember to answer as best as you can and write in complete sentences.

1. What are the two parts of the Shahadah and what does each teach us?
2. List all the five pillars of Islam and what they mean in English.
3. What are the names of the five daily prayers?
4. When does each of the five daily prayers get performed?
5. List six things that break our Wudu.
6. What is a Masjid and why is it important?
7. Why must we remember Allah often?
8. What should we ask Allah for and how is our Du'a often answered?
9. How does Zakat make us cleaner inside?
10. Find one ayah from the Qur'an or a Hadith, other than what you see in this book, about Salat and write it down with the reference.

Thinking to Learn

Read the following statement and explain whether it is true or false. Write in complete sentences on a separate piece of paper.

A Muslim only needs to pray five times a day and can forget Allah the rest of the time.

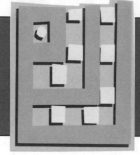

Unit 4

Meet New Muslim Friends

11 An Eid With Nadia

Think About It

Which kind of holiday is better: one where everyone gets things, or one where everyone gives to those in need? Explain.

Vocabulary Words

Eidul Fitr	Taqwa	Miskeen
Tatar	Tarawih	Ramadan
Khutba		

What to Learn

Ramadan brings the Muslim community together to serve Allah

A. Living in Poland.

Assalamu 'alaykum! Peace be with you! My name is Nadia Hamidovic and I'm a Muslim from a little country called Poland. I know it's hard to think of there being Muslims from this Eastern European country, but our history here goes back over 600 years!

I live in a small town called Bohoniki. Most of the people around here are farmers or merchants. My dad, whose name is Selim, owns a local grocery store. Although there are a lot of non-Muslims living around here also, most of us in town are Muslims.

My ancestors were called Tatars by the Europeans, but we just like to call ourselves Muslims. The **Tatars** were a Muslim tribe which came from a place called Crimea. When the Mongol empire was very powerful about 700 years ago, the Tatars were a part of their army.

The ancient Christian kingdom of Lithuania, which controlled Poland then, signed a treaty of peace with the Mongols of the Golden Horde in 1319 CE.

A lot of Muslims were soldiers in the Mongol army. Soon many Muslims came to Eastern Europe to help defend the Lithuanians against an invading German army called the Teutonic Knights. And so the Muslims were also helping to defend Poland as well.

After that, thousands of Muslims began living in Eastern Europe. Since then, Muslims have been here and were always welcome to stay in this land. There's less than ten thousand of us today but we are a growing community and every once in a while some non-Muslims convert to Islam.

I learned all about our history from our Imam in my Friday night Islamic studies class. We meet in a very old and very beautiful Masjid made of wood and stone called the Bohoniki Masjid.

We just finished fasting in the month of Ramadan and had a big celebration. Let me tell you

what we did this month and how we spent our holiday. Come on, let's go to the Masjid and talk some more.

B. Ramadan Means Fasting.

We'll sit up here on the second floor. This is where the sisters pray. We can see the Imam from the edge of the balcony down there on the first floor. Don't get too close to the railing!

Now, about **Ramadan**. My father told us a couple of months ago a lot more about this special time. It's the name of a month in the Islamic calendar. Living in this non-Muslim country we usually use the Christian calendar, but my father says it's better to use the Islamic one. That's because the Christian calendar was actually invented by idol-worshippers.

All the names of their months and days, like January and June or Monday and Saturday, are named after idols and false gods from an ancient people called the Romans. The Christians just copied whatever the idol-worshippers did. That's not good.

In Ramadan, my dad said, Muslims fast all day long. Fasting is called Saum in Arabic. Sometimes you can call it Siyam as well, which means the same thing. Do you know what fasting is all about? It's when you show your love to Allah by trying to control your bodies as much as you can.

The Shaytan uses the desires and wants of our bodies to try and trick us into living in a bad way. For example, I know a girl who eats junk food all the time. She can't stop and always complains about being tired or feeling sick. The Shaytan is using the "sweet tooth" to control that person and make them weak and lazy.

My Imam taught me to memorize the ayah in the Qur'an where Allah says to fast. It goes like this: "Ya ayyuhal ladheena aamanu. Kutiba 'alaykum as siyamu kama kutiba 'alal ladheena min qablekum la'alakum tataqoon." It means, "You who believe. Fasting is written for you even as it was written on those before you so you can learn to have Taqwa."

The word **Taqwa** means to be aware or conscious of Allah. In other words, when we have Taqwa we always remember we are Muslims and we avoid doing bad deeds. Can you memorize that important ayah about fasting too? Try it!

When we fast in Ramadan, we don't eat or drink any food from before the first light in the morning until after the sun has gone down in the evening. My mother, Mu'mina, told me also that we aren't even allowed to fight or argue during the day. You won't believe how hard it is to follow that rule with two younger brothers around!

The first few days are kind of hard for all of us. Just think: you were eating and drinking all you wanted and then suddenly the food is off-limits; the water is locked up. It's a big change. My uncle sleeps all day in the beginning of Ramadan. My dad says that's being lazy, but at least he's fasting.

C. How I Spent My Time in Ramadan.

Every night in Ramadan my family and a lot of other people went to the Masjid at night for special prayers called **Tarawih** Salat. Theses prayers are done after Isha Salat and they last for over half an

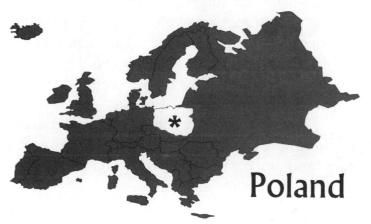

Poland

hour! I always stand next to my best friend, Aliya, in the women's rows up here on the second floor balcony. I love staying up late!

The Tarawih Salat is a bunch of two raka' prayers done one after another. One of thirty sections of the Qur'an is read each night. Since Ramadan is either 29 or 30 days long that means we finish the Qur'an reading in one month.

Each morning my whole family gets up about an hour before dawn begins to take a small breakfast called Suhoor. It's our last chance to eat for the rest of the day and we pay close attention to the time when we have to stop eating. When Suhoor time is over we make our Niyyah for fasting and then pray Fajr. After that I go back to sleep for a few hours.

My mother stays up and reads her Qur'an for a little while, but since I have school to go to, I need to be well rested. After school I go to the Masjid where some of my friends are and we read the Qur'an together in a circle. Each person takes turns reading a few ayahs at a time. Then we read the translation of the meanings afterwards. This is followed by group Du'a. This is how I spend most days in Ramadan.

D. Important Lessons.

Our Imam told us that during Ramadan the Shayateen are locked up in chains so that it's easier for us to do good deeds. Every good deed done during Ramadan, he told our class, gets ten extra good deeds added to it. He also said that the Blessed Prophet taught that, "Whoever fasts the month of Ramadan with Iman and sincerely looks to please Allah and get His reward will have all his or her previous bad deeds forgiven." (Ahmad)

At the same time, we're supposed to control our tongues and feelings, too. I learned that the Prophet said, "If a person doesn't avoid lying and following lies, then Allah doesn't count it if he or she gave up their eating and drinking." (Bukhari)

That means that we don't only learn the lesson of controlling our bodies in Ramadan, but we also learn to control our behavior. If we don't try to, then Allah doesn't count our fasting.

The Holy Qur'an is read and studied all throughout the year.

Probably the biggest lesson of all is for us to feel sorry for the poor. I know there are some people in town who don't have as much as I do. When I'm fasting and feeling hungry in the day, I see them sometimes and I feel bad knowing that I can eat as much as I want after sunset, but they will have only a tiny meal.

My dad always pays his Zakat in this month to the Masjid so they can help feed the poor people. My dad says a Muslim always feels sorry for the **Miskeen**. That's the word for poor people in the Qur'an. Zakat is the money every Muslim must give for the sake of Allah so the poor can be helped. My dad says its two and a half percent of all his money at the end of the year.

The Masjid volunteers collect the Zakat money from all the Muslim families and use it to run a soup and bread kitchen all year round in the big city of Warsaw. There is a big Masjid there and it helps a lot of Miskeen people. We sometimes invite the poor Muslims around our own town to share in our evening meal, called Iftar. They are so happy and they ask Allah to bless us.

Before eating Iftar we make a Du'a that goes like this, "Allahumma laka saumtu wa 'ala riz qeeka aftartu." It means, "Allah I fasted for you and I break my fast with what you gave me."

E. The Big Holiday.

When the last day of Ramadan was ended, all of us were very excited about the holiday that comes afterwards. In Poland we call that day Ramadan Bayram, but the real name of it is **Eid ul Fitr**. This means the Holiday of Breaking the Fast.

Everyone dresses in their best clothes and goes to the Masjid at about eight in the morning. My mom bought me a new dress for Eid and I was so happy! My two little brothers got some toys as presents and they were jumping for joy.

At the Masjid we all do a special kind of prayer called the Eid Salat and afterwards we listen to the Imam give a speech called a **Khutba**. This year he talked about how Muslims must remember the lessons they learned in Ramadan all throughout the year. He said that now that we can control our bodies and our tongues that we should be stronger Muslims and more kind to people.

He said not to forget the Qur'an the rest of the year and to remember that there are always people less fortunate than us who need help. When his Khutba was finished he said, "Eid Mubarak!" which means, "Blessed Holiday!"

Everyone stood up and started hugging and wishing each other a happy Eid. The rest of the day we were visiting relatives and going to parties and it was the most fun I had in a while! If you want, you can come and stay with our family for Ramadan next year. Insha'llah, if Allah wills, we'll meet again. Assalamu 'alaykum!

Questions to Answer

1. How did Nadia's ancestors get to be in Poland?
2. What does a Muslim do in Ramadan?
3. Why is it better to use the Muslim calendar rather than the Christian one?
4. List three lessons we are to learn from Ramadan.
5. Write down one Hadith about Ramadan.
6. Memorize the Ayah, 2:183, about fasting that is given in this lesson on page 58 in both Arabic and English.

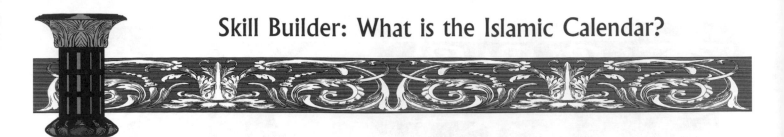

Islam has its own calendar. For Muslims to practice Islam fully, they must learn to use their own way of dividing the months and years. The following lesson will highlight the importance of our calendar as well as how to use it.

Part A.   A Lost Day in India.

There is an interesting story about the importance of calendars. A long time ago, a country from Europe called England invaded and took over a great land in Asia called India.

For almost two hundred years the Indian people were like the slaves to the English. In time, they began to worship the ways of their masters and tried their best to copy them in everything that they did.

To keep the Indians under control, the English encouraged them to forget their own calendar, culture and in some cases, even their own language! But even though many Indians tried their best to look and act English, the English never accepted them as equals. The English thought the Indians were lower than them and not very civilized, no matter what they did. This made many Indians feel bad and they tried to show the English that Indian history and culture was great and full of glory as well.

Once an English writer was traveling around India and visiting the palaces and lands of local Indian rulers. The rulers had no real power, of course, because the power and the guns were with the English. But the English let them stay in their palaces on the condition that they control the local people for them. The Indian rulers did a good job of this and hurt many of their own people, even as they tried to act as English as they could to get more favors and honors from their masters.

This English writer wanted to see for himself if there was anything great about India. He went to the palace of a Muslim ruler, called a Nizam, and sat with him for tea. The Nizam wanted to impress the Englishman about Indian history and glory and started bragging about how powerful his ancestors were and how great their kingdom was.

The English writer listened for a while and then asked the Nizam a simple question: "What day is it today?"

The Nizam smiled at this chance to impress an Englishman and almost sang out the date according to the Christian calendar.

"No," the English writer said, "What's the date according to your Muslim calendar?"

The Nizam was silent. He didn't know what the Islamic date was. He bowed his head in shame and the English writer left, knowing why it was so easy for his tiny country to control the huge land of India.

Part B. Keeping Track of Time.

Every society or civilization has invented its own calendar to keep track of the days, months and years. The Hindus, Jews, Buddhists, Aztecs and others have all invented their own calendars. Muslims have also made a calendar of their own.

Muslims who live in non-Muslim countries are usually forced to use the calendar of the people there, but we can also use our own along side of theirs. In countries and lands that were settled or conquered by Europeans, the people use what is called the Gregorian Calendar. It is named after a man named Gregory who took an idol-worshipper's calendar and changed it around a little bit for use by Christians. He did this in the year 1582 of the Christian calendar. All the names of the days and months are named after idols and false gods.

The starting year of the Christian calendar is based on the year they think that a man named 'Esa, or Jesus, was born. (We Muslims believe that 'Esa was a Prophet while most Christians call him God.) Everything before that first year they label as BC, or Before Christ, and everything afterwards they call AD, or Anno Domini, which stands for "the Year of our Lord." This goes along with the Christian belief that Prophet 'Esa was actually Allah, and the son of Allah too, being born on earth. What is the name of the terrible crime the Christians are doing here? Shirk.

Because the Christian calendar is actually an idol-worshipping calendar with a starting year based on a Shirk idea, we Muslims don't like to use it. We have our own calendar and way of keeping track of time.

Just like other civilizations, we have twelve months in our yearly calendar. But our months are not named after idols, like the Christian calendar is. Also, our calendar is more accurate than other calendars. The calendar the Christians use has months with many different numbers of days. Some months have 28 days, others have 30 or even 31 days. Every once in a while their calendar needs to be corrected and they add days to it. This is a result of the poor way in which the Roman idol-worshippers made their calendar long ago.

The Islamic month is calculated by the orbit of the moon around the earth. It takes about thirty days for the moon to make one complete cycle around the earth. You can see how the moon at night slowly changes over the month with a crescent moon, a quarter moon, a half moon, a full moon, and then it goes down to no moon at all! When the first sliver of the returning moon is seen, then, it's called the new month! An Islamic month can have either 29 or 30 days in it depending on when the new moon is seen.

The week in the Islamic calendar has seven days. It's easy to remember their names because their names are just numbers, except for the day of Jum'ah. Jum'ah is the same day as Friday in the Christian calendar. The name Jum'ah means "gathering" and it's the day Muslims gather in the Masjids to hear the weekly Khutba.

The Islamic year doesn't begin with the birth or death of someone, like in other calendars. Our calendar, whose starting year was decided by the Muslim ruler, 'Umar ibn al Khattab, has, as its beginning year, an event called the Hijra. This was the great journey made by the Prophet Muhammad from Mecca to Medina. Everything before that starting year is labelled BH, or Before Hijra, while every year afterwards is labelled AH, or After Hijra. Remember, our calendar is called the Hijri calendar. In the Christian calendar, the Hijra happened in the year 622.

C. Finding the Date.

To find out the year that something happened from one calendar system to the next, there is an easy math formula you can use. To find out the Islamic Hijri year when you only have the Christian Gregorian year, do this: Take the Gregorian year and subtract 622 from it. Then divide 33 by 32. Next, multiply the first number you got by the second number. Then you have the approximate Islamic Hijra year!

Example: Pretend the Christian Gregorian year is 1999. Subtract 622 to get 1377. When we divide 33 by 32 we get: 1.03125. Multiply this number by 1377 and the Islamic Hijri year is 1420!

We Muslims must learn to use our own calendar and stick by it because Allah said in the Qur'an, "The number of months in the sight of Allah is twelve. This was decided by Him on the day He created space and the earth. Four of them are holy. This is the correct way to use them so don't do wrong against yourselves (in the calendar)..." (9:35)

Allah decided this type of calendar and Muslims live throughout the year by it. The month of Ramadan, Hajj and other times of the year are important to us. To help practice using our own calendar, we should have an Islamic calendar in our classroom and home and use it to check the date. Every time we look for the date on the non-Muslim calendar, we should check the date on the Islamic one as well.

When we talk to each other and the day of the week is mentioned, we should use our names for them, and not the idol-worshipper's names that the Christians just copied. When we write the date on our homework we should write the Islamic date and year first and put the non-Muslim one underneath it, or better yet, not at all!

To help in learning our own calendar, you will find a list of the Islamic months and days in this skill builder exercise. Learn them and use them because this is the best way for a true believer in Allah. Good luck and good learning! By the way, what's the date today?

Islamic Months and Their Meanings

1. Muharram: "The sacred month."
2. Safar: "The void month."
3. Rabi ul Awwal: "The first spring."
4. Rabi ath-Thani: "The second spring."
5. Jumada al Ula: "The first dry month."
6. Jumada ath-Thani: "The second dry month."
7. Rajab: "The revered month."
8. Sha'ban: "The dividing month."
9. Ramadan: "The month of great heat."
10. Shawwal: "The hunting month."
11. Dhul Qa'dah: "The resting month."
12. Dhul Hijjah: "The month of Pilgrimage."

The Days of the Week

Sunday: Al Ahad
Monday: Al Ithnayn
Tuesday: Ath Thulatha
Wednesday: Al Arba'a

Thursday: Al Khamees
Friday: Al Jum'ah
Saturday: As Sabat

Part A Exercises.

Answer the following questions in complete answers. Use a separate piece of paper.

1. What point did the Englishman want to make to the Nizam who was busy bragging about past Muslim achievements?

2. What does this example mean for Muslims today?

Part B Exercises.

1. Describe the features and history of the Islamic calendar?

Part C Exercises.

1. Calculate the approximate Islamic year from the non-Muslim year we are currently in. Show all your math work.

12 Saira: A Girl of Mecca

Think About It

What if there was a place on earth where there was no hatred and bad influences? What would such a place be like?

Vocabulary Words

Baytullah   Kiswah   'Umrah
Ka'bah   Laylatul Qadr

What to Learn

All Muslims Want to Go to Hajj.

A. Living in Mecca.

Assalamu 'alaykum wa ahlan wa sahlan! Peace be to you and you're welcome here! My name is Saira Abu Zayan and I live in Mecca, in Saudi Arabia. Sometimes I think this is the busiest city in the whole world because so many Muslims come here all year round. Come, let's sit together and talk about my home town.

Everyone comes here to visit the **Baytullah**, or House of Allah. No, it's not the place where Allah lives. It's the holy shrine that Prophet Ibrahim and his son, Isma'il, built thousands of years ago to unite people in the worship of Allah. It is also called the **Ka'bah**, or Cube, because it's shaped like a box. Although it's made out of bricks, they put a pretty black cloth over the whole building called the **Kiswah**. It has verses from the Qur'an in gold thread all around it.

On Fridays I go with my parents to the big Masjid that's built around it. They call it the Masjidul Haram. *I just call it the Masjid where you had better behave yourself.*

We listen to the Imam of the Ka'bah during Jum'ah time because that's when he gives the Khutba. My mother and me sit with all the other women while my dad sits with all the men. On Fridays there are thousands and thousands of Muslims there.

Last week I met a girl my age from Canada. She was here on 'Umrah with her parents. **'Umrah** means a small pilgrimage where you come to remember Allah. It's like a mini-Hajj. Her name was Sadia and she was real nice. I invited her and her whole family to come to our house for dinner one night and everyone had a good time. I think Sadia and me will be good pen pals.

Most people come here during the month of Hajj, though. It's at that time when I think the whole city is going to burst with people! Last year two million people came and stayed for a whole week! Why do they all come during that month? Because doing the main Hajj, or pilgrimage, is a duty that every Muslim man and woman must do at least once in their life if they can make it. Allah says so in the Qur'an. (See the Qur'an, 2:196-200)

Since I live here, I get to perform the 'Umrah several times a year and I've done the main Hajj four times already! It's so much fun being with all those other Muslims and joining together to serve Allah.

B. Where Did the Hajj Begin?

The Hajj was started by Prophet Ibrahim, peace be upon him. He had two wives, one named Saira and the other was Hajira. They all lived in Palestine. The two women couldn't get along so Allah told Prophet Ibrahim to bring Hajira and her son, Isma'il, to a barren valley in the Arabian wilderness. The valley was called Becca at that time.

After Ibrahim left, Hajira and Isma'il ran out of food and water. The only reason that Ibrahim left them there was because Allah said He would take care of them. When they started getting really thirsty, Hajira ran around looking for water. She ran up and down two hills called Safa and Marwa and found nothing.

Then, when she went back to Isma'il, who was lying down tiredly, she saw a bubbling spring gush out of the ground near where he kicked the dirt. That spring is called the well of Zam Zam. The Angels made it come up for them.

After that, Hajirah and Isma'il had all the water they needed. They traded water with passing caravans for food and soon people began settling down in the valley. When Ibrahim returned for a visit a few years later, he was so happy that he wanted to build a special shrine for Allah there.

But before he began, he had a dream one night that he was sacrificing his son. Allah gives revelation to His Prophets through dreams also. When Prophet Ibrahim told his son what he saw in his dream, Isma'il told his father, "Do whatever Allah commanded you to do."

Ibrahim didn't want to sacrifice his son, of course, but he also didn't want to disobey his Creator. So he took Isma'il out to a place to sacrifice him and was about to do it when an Angel came from Allah and told him to stop; that he already proved that he would do it and that he could let Isma'il get up.

The father and son were so happy and then they saw a ram, which is a kind of animal, stuck in some bushes nearby. They sacrificed that instead and gave the meat to the poor. Then Ibrahim and his son built the first Ka'bah together.

C. Why is Mecca so Special?

My father introduced me to my Qur'an teacher when I was six years old. She's a really nice lady and she always tells me stories and answers my questions. When I asked her about why everyone comes here to Mecca, she read to me the prayer that Prophet Ibrahim made to Allah.

He had said, "*My Lord, make this city a place of peace and feed its people with fruits, those who believe in Allah and the Last Day.*"

Then, while he was building the Ka'bah with his son, they both asked Allah, "*Our Lord, accept*

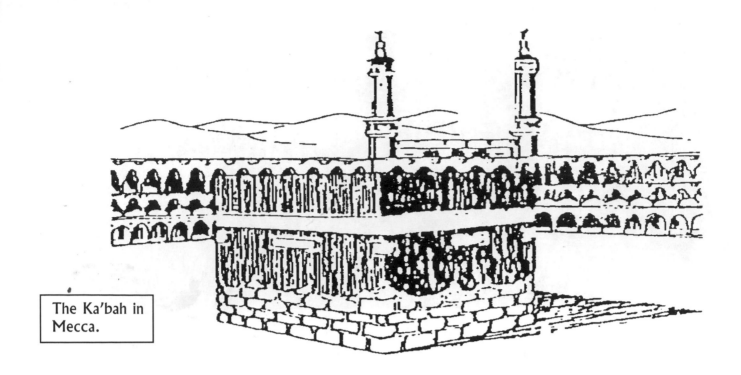

The Ka'bah in Mecca.

this from us because You are Hearing and Knowing. Our Lord, make us Muslims and make our descendants Muslims. Show us where to perform our rituals and turn towards us because You are the Forgiving and Merciful." (2:126-128)

My teacher explained that this is the one place in the world where only Allah is worshipped like He should be worshipped. There are no idols, no statues of man-gods and no bad things like drugs or alcohol allowed. The Ka'bah was made by a beautiful Prophet long ago for the benefit of all people who surrender to Allah. People who come here will find peace.

I learned that all the things people do on Hajj go back to an important part of the history here. When people walk around the Ka'bah seven times and praise Allah saying, "Labbayk Allahumma Labayk," they are following the tradition of Prophet Ibrahim.

When they go up and down the hills of Safa and Marwa, they are remembering Hajira and her struggle and when they sacrifice the animals at the end they are recalling the obedience of Isma'il.

The other parts of the Hajj also have a lot a meaning. We drink the water of Zam Zam and stand on the plain of Arafat to remember Judgment Day. My favorite part is called "Stoning the Shaytan" where we get to throw rocks at some stone pillars that represent the Shaytan. When I was taught the full

meaning of what we do in the Pilgrimage, I asked my dad to go on another one right away.

D. The Prophet Muhammad and Hajj.

Allah's last Prophet to the world, Muhammad, peace be upon him, was born right here in Mecca in about the year 571 CE (53 BH). When he lived here, idol-worshippers were in control of the city. They prayed to statues and man-gods and never cared about doing good or right. They knew the Ka'bah was built by a Prophet of Allah but they thought that idols were better to pray to than Allah.

The Prophet Muhammad never liked the idols and thought they were wrong. When he was forty, Allah chose him to be His last Messenger and began revealing the Qur'an to him. The very night when the revelation started falls in the month of Ramadan. They call that the Night of Measurement, or **Laylatul Qadr**.

The idol worshippers didn't want to listen to the Prophet when he told them about Allah. They even hurt him and his followers. Finally the Prophet had to leave Mecca with the other believers and live in a city called Medina. Medina is about one day's drive from here by car.

After that the idol worshippers came and attacked the Muslims three times. But they were never able to win against the Muslims who were getting bigger in numbers all the time.

Finally, the Prophet was able to march a huge army back here and take over the city without a battle. He even forgave all the idol-worshippers and took no revenge on them. This made most of them become Muslims right there. They were so impressed by his kindness.

Then the Prophet ordered all the idols that were in and around the Ka'bah to be destroyed. He prayed to Allah for guidance and then taught the people how to perform Hajj the correct way; the way that Allah wants it to be done. After the Prophet passed away the Muslim world kept growing so big that the Hajj became a huge annual event.

When I look out of my window on the street below I see Muslims of every race and color. They're dressed in all kinds of clothes and everyone says, "Salam" to each other and smiles, even though they don't know each other's language. When the Hajj is over we have a big holiday called Eid ul Adha. I get a lot of presents from my realtives and parents that day!

If you ever get the chance to come to Mecca for a Hajj, then make sure you look me up and come for a visit. I would love to have you as my guest because the Prophet Muhammad taught us that if we have guests in our house and serve them that we get a lot of Thawwab, or rewards, from Allah! Help me get more rewards by spending time with nice people like you. Until I see you here, Assalamu 'alaykum!

Questions to Answer

1. What is the Ka'bah and why do people visit it?
2. What is the difference between Hajj and 'Umrah?
3. Who was Ibrahim and how is he connected to the Ka'bah?
4. Who were Hajira and Isma'il?
5. List three things people do on Hajj?
6. How did Prophet Muhammad make the Hajj and the Ka'bah for Allah again?

Ayesha: A Muslim American Girl

Think About It

If you're going to study Islam, what is the best place to learn in?

Vocabulary Words

Musalla	Mu'adhan	Fard
Ta'leem	Kiraman Katibeen	
Musalla		

What to Learn

The Masjid is a natural place for a Muslim to learn in and visit.

A. Welcome to My Masjid!

Assalamu 'alaykum! Peace be with you! How are you doing? My name's Ayesha Ali and I live in a city called Boston in America. My Ummi's a store manager and my Abi works for the city. Why don't you come and hang out with me for a while. I'm going to the Masjid for Sunday School. You can come to!

This is Masjid al Qur'an. It's been here a long time and a lot of Muslims come here. We have a really nice **Musalla**, or Prayer Area. On Fridays it fills up all the way. There's a small Islamic bookstore here also. Whatever books we need for Sunday School we can get there. They have other stuff as well. Last week I bought a necklace that says "Allahu Akbar" on it and some nice-smelling oils.

As we enter the Masjid the Prophet told us we should say, "Allahumma af tahli abwaba rahmatika." That means, "Allah, open up for me the doors of Your mercy." I always say it and you can learn that little Du'a as well!

My Abi and Ummi go home after dropping me off. When I'm not around that's when they say they can get all their household chores and errands done. My Abi comes to the men's study group on Thursday nights and my Ummi comes to a study class they call a Ta'leem of Fridays. The word **Ta'leem** means learning and knowledge. She and the other women study Islamic teachings and the Qur'an. When I'm older I'll start going with her.

Let me show you around. Our Masjid has two floors. The **Musalla,** or praying area, is on the first floor and the classrooms are up here on the second floor. I'm in class 'C' because of my age level. My teacher is sister Shakeela Shabazz. She's a really smart sister and I like her a lot. She really knows what us kids are thinking.

Well, class is going to begin in a few minutes. I see my friends Aziza, Safia and Rochelle. Come on in with me and after class we can talk some more. Sister Shakeela won't mind because she always tells us that Allah loves big gatherings where His name is mentioned, so the bigger the better. I believe her.

B. The Angels Are Watching Us.

That seemed like such a short class! It's really true that time flies when your having fun. I especially liked the part where sister Shakeela was telling us about how the Angels are sitting on your left and right shoulders. What did she call those two Angels? Oh yah, the **Kiraman Katibeen**. That stands for the Noble Writers. (See 50:17-19)

The one on the right records all your good deeds and the one on the left does what? Yep, you guessed it. All your bad deeds go in that one's book. On Judgment Day they're going to give your books to Allah for review and you better have a thicker book from the Angel on the right!

I think Angels are so cool. Allah has them everywhere! Do you remember the part about the two Angels standing by the door of the Masjid on Fridays? They write down the names of all the people who come to Jum'ah Salat. But when the Imam is about ready to start his Khutba, the Angels fold their books away and go inside to listen. I guess that means that a Muslim should be on time for Jum'ah!

I also thought it was neat when the sister explained why Muslims line up in rows when they pray in Jam'a. She mentioned the Hadith of the Prophet from Bukhari where he said the Angels line up in rows in front of Allah and that they fill in all the spaces in each row until they're full. That's why we line up that way too.

Oh, I see it's almost time for Zuhr Salat. I need to make Wudu and then we can go in the Musalla for prayer. I'll see you in there in a minute. Don't forget to say that little Du'a I told you about before you walk in the Musalla!

C. Waiting for Prayer.

Okay, I'm ready, let's say the Du'a and go inside. The brothers line up there in the front rows near the Imam. Then they fill up the rows one at a time going back. We sisters start from the very back rows and fill them up first and then move forward. The older the sister, the closer she should be to the last row in the Masjid. My Ummi says it's the best way for us to be organized because it keeps the men and women from looking at each other.

Both my parents are converts to Islam. My Abi became a Muslim in the 1960's when there was the Nation of Islam movement. Most of my parent's older friends also came into Islam that way. I guess it wasn't really a true Islamic movement, however, because they had a lot of unIslamic teachings. But after a few years, most of the Muslims discovered what real Islam was and entered the universal world of Islam.

Have you ever heard of Malcolm X? He was the most famous one who helped everyone else see the real truth. Warith Deen Muhammad carried the trend on after him and helped lead a lot of Muslims, including my Abi, into real Islam.

My Ummi became a Muslim about two years before I was born. She met Abi at a Muslim convention in Philadelphia and they got married a few months after that. Then I came along and the rest is history.

Hey, do you see that brother coming in over there? That's brother Jamal. He's the **Mu'adhan**, or prayer caller. He calls the Adhan. He has such a beautiful voice. My cousin Lateef is also learning how to be a Mu'adhan and he might be chosen to call the Muslims for Salat on Sundays in a few months. Brother Jamal has that honor every Friday, though, and he deserves it too. Let's listen to the words of the Adhan. My Ummi says when we hear the Adhan we should repeat the words we hear silently to ourselves.

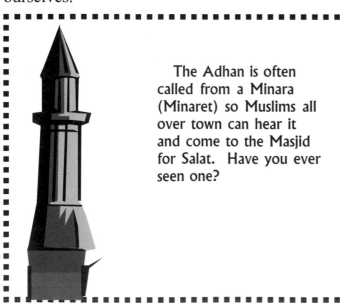

The Adhan is often called from a Minara (Minaret) so Muslims all over town can hear it and come to the Masjid for Salat. Have you ever seen one?

Allahu Akbar, Allahu Akbar.
Allahu Akbar, Allahu Akbar.

Ashahadu an la ilaha ill Allah.
Ashahadu an la ilaha ill Allah.

Ashahadu anna Muhammadar Rasul Allah.
Ashahadu anna Muhammadar Rasul Allah.

Haya alas Salah. Haya alas Salah.
Haya alal Falah, Haya alal Falah.

Allahu Akbar. Allahu Akbar.

La ilaha ill Allah.

(It translates like this:)

Allah is the Greatest. Allah is the Greatest.
Allah is the Greatest. Allah is the Greatest.
I declare there is no god but Allah.
I declare there is no god but Allah.
I declare that Muhammad is the Messenger of Allah.
I declare that Muhammad is the Messenger of Allah.
Come to Prayer.
Come to Prayer.
Come to Success.
Come to Success.
Allah is the Greatest.
Allah is the Greatest.
There is no god but Allah.

D. The Sunnah Salat.

That was nice. Let's do our Sunnah Salat. That's the name for any extra prayer you do outside the five **Fard**, or required, prayers to get extra rewards from Allah. You do them by yourself. Since It's Zuhr time now, we do a four Raka' Sunnah prayer individually. It'll just take a few minutes.

There, now we just wait until the Mu'adhan gives the Iqamah, or call to line up in the rows. It's similar to the Adhan except they add an extra phrase that says, "Qadi qamatis Salat." "Stand up and

How Many Raka's in Each Salat

Fajr	Zuhr	'Asr	Maghrib	'Isha
2 Sunnah	4 Sunnah	4 Sunnah	3 Fard	4 Sunnah
2 Fard	4 Fard	4 Fard	2 Sunnah	4 Fard
	2 Sunnah		2 Extra	2 Sunnah
	2 Extra			3 Extra
				2 Extra

establish the Salat now." Oh, there's brother Jamal getting ready to give it. Okay, he's finished, let's line up with the other sisters. The brothers are also lining up.

Alhumdulillah, now that our four raka' Zuhr Salat is finished, we can pray one more Sunnah prayer. This one is two raka's only. Oh, by the way, do you know how many raka's are in each of the five Fard prayers and how many Sunnah raka's we pray before and after them? I'll tell you.

For Fajr you do two raka's Sunnah and then the two raka's Fard for the Fajr itself. There are no Sunnah prayers after Fajr Salat. Then we just did Zuhr, you know, four Sunnah raka's, the regular four raka's Fard of Zuhr and then a two raka' prayer after it.

For 'Asr time you can do two or four raka's Sunnah before and then the four Fard raka's. There are no Sunnah Salats after 'Asr or before Maghrib. Maghrib is three raka's. You can do two Sunnah raka's after it. For 'Isha you do four Sunnah, four Fard and then as many Sunnah Salats as you want afterwards.

That's not too hard to remember, but if you want to get it all organized for your own learning, you can have this checklist I wrote that lists everything in five different rows. I learned all the names and raka' numbers a few years ago when I first started Sunday School, so I don't need this page in my notebook anymore.

Well, I've got to go to class again for the afternoon session. It was nice meeting you and I hope you drop by again for a visit. Take care! Assalamu 'alaykum!

Questions to Answer

1. What is a Musalla?
2. What is a Mu'adhan?
3. Who are the Kiraman Katibeen and what do they do?
4. What is a Sunnah Salat?
5. What should we say when we enter a Masjid?
6. Why do Muslims line up in rows in group Salat?

14 Ahmad of Malaysia

Think About It

How should a person treat a guest?

Vocabulary Words

Halal   Haram   Dhabiha
Ummah

What to Learn

Muslims have manners for eating and serving guests.

A. A Banquet in Kuala Lumpur.

Assalamu 'alaykum! My name is Ahmad Dato and I'm from Kuala Lumpur in beautiful Malaysia. There's really a lot to do and see here so why don't you come along with me to my house where we can have lunch and then go out and see the city!

My home is a two-story bungalo where I live with my parents and my three younger sisters. I think my parents are in the kitchen getting the food ready so we have a few minutes to wait. This would be a good time to go and wash our hands. You know the Prophet Muhammad always taught us to wash our hands before eating, as well as afterwards. We can use this sink over there in the bathroom.

That's my mom coming out of the kitchen with a tray of cut up vegetables and fried yams.

Assalamu 'alaykum, mother. These are my new friends. Can they stay for lunch? Thank you!

You know a Muslim kid is always supposed to respect his or her parents and ask them about things.

I learned a Hadith about it that goes like this, "Innal laha harama 'alaykum 'uquq ul ummahaat." It means, "Indeed Allah has forbidden you to disobey mothers." (Bukhari)

Oh my, look at the dishes my father is bringing! There's pan fried dumplings, chick peas fried with potatoes and red pepper shrimp! I never realized how hungry I was until this moment.

Al-humdulillah!

Do you know the Du'a we should say before eating? After all, Allah is the One Who made this good food possible by letting my parents get good jobs so they could buy food. The long Du'a is, "Allahumma baraklana feema razaqtana wa qeena athabin naar." That means, "Allah bless us in what You provided for us and protect us from the punishment of the fire." Let's say it together.

There is a shorter Du'a that you say afterwards. It's simply saying, "Bismillahir Rahmanir Raheem." I know you know what that means already! Let's say it now all together. Okay, let's eat!

Do you Know These Foods?

Haram

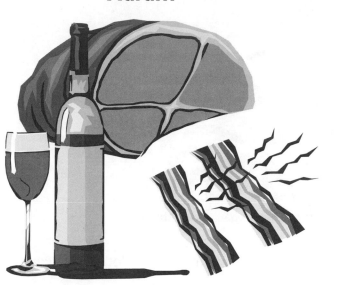

Halal (Only Dhabiha prepared meat)

B. What are Halal Foods?

Here, try some of this chicken stir fry that my mom just brought out. It's really good. Oh, don't worry, all the food is Halal. A Muslim only eats food that is **Halal**. That word means "Allowed by Allah." Almost every food in the world is Halal for us Muslims to eat. All fruits, vegetables, grains and seafood are Halal. That's good because I love shrimp!

As far as land animals and birds are concerned, most of them are Halal too, if you prepare them in the right way. How do you prepare them in a Halal way? That's easy. When the butcher slaughters a cow, chicken or goat, they must first say a "*Bismillah*." Then they have to cut the neck of the animal so quickly that it doesn't feel any pain.

Most of the meat prepared by non-Muslims is done in a bad way. They make the animals scared and then put them through pain and torture before killing them.

There's another thing that makes our meat better: we make sure all the blood drains out of the animal right away. The non-Muslims just leave the blood in the meat where it rots and spreads diseases.

So a Muslim eats meat prepared in the Halal, Islamic way. This is called **Dhabiha** meat. Any animal that isn't prepared in the right way according to Islam is Haram for us to eat. **Haram** means "Forbidden by Allah." Our Creator knows what's best for us so we should follow His rules.

Do you know which kinds of animals are absolutely Haram for us to eat no matter what? The main one is pigs. We aren't allowed to eat them at all. We also don't eat dogs, lions or other animals that hunt others. We eat the meat of plant-eating animals. We don't eat the meat of meat-eaters.

The Prophet Muhammad, of course, didn't even eat much meat at all. Most of the foods he ate were very simple. He ate dates, milk, bread, honey and other small things. Even when he was the ruler of all of Arabia and could have had anything he wanted, he still ate only a little and even slept on an old mat made of hard fibers called reeds.

I read that once he was sleeping when his friend, 'Umar, came into his house. The Prophet rolled over in his mat and 'Umar saw the red marks on his back from sleeping on the rough reed bed. 'Umar felt very sad that the man he loved so much was sleeping in such an uncomfortable place.

Just then the Prophet woke up and 'Umar cried out, "Messenger of Allah, why don't you order us to make a big bed for you or to spread a comfortable blanket over your mat?"

The Prophet said, "Koon fid dunya ka anaka ghariboon ow 'abirus sabil." "Be in the world as if you were a stranger or drifter."

The Prophet looked at 'Umar and said, "What do I have to do with this world? I'm like a traveler who stops to rest under a tree, and then I move on."

That was a good way of saying that we're not in this world to look for comfort all the time because we're all going to die and leave this life after a few years. We try to follow the Prophet's example in my house, too. None of us has a big fancy bed and we make sure that we never bring in expensive decorations in our home. We also never throw food away. Simple living is how the Prophet taught us to be.

Now that we've finished eating, we should say two small Du'as to thank Allah for the food He let us have. First we say, "Alhumdulillah" if anyone asks us how we liked the food. Then we say, "Alhumdu lil lahil lathee at'amana wa saqana wa ja'alana min al Muslimeen." That means, "Praise to Allah who fed us, gave us drink and made us among the Muslims."

C. Our Brotherhood and Sisterhood.

Oh no, you don't have to help us clean up from lunch. You're our guest and we love to serve you. Don't you remember what the Blessed Prophet said? He declared, "Laa yu'minu ahadukum hatta yuhibba le akhihe maa yuhibbu linafse." That means, "Your Iman isn't complete until you love for your brother what you love for yourself." So let us take care of you.

If you really want to do us a favor, please, just ask Allah to reward us. Say, "Jazzakullah."

I know it's getting late. I think I hear the Mu'adhan giving the Adhan from the Masjid. Let's listen and repeat the words to ourselves. Okay, do you have your Wudu? Great. Let's go!

My parents encourage me to go to the Masjid everyday for Salat, at least two or three times. My dad tries to pray all the five prayers in the Masjid. He said the Blessed Prophet promised that praying in a group is twenty-five times more rewarding than praying alone. Imagine that, you get that many extra rewards for your angel on the right to record. I wonder if his fingers ever get tired!

remind us of that fact. While stepping out with our left foot, into the unpredictable world, we say, "Allahumma in nee as-aluka min fadlika." That means, "Allah, I'm looking for Your blessings." And don't we ever need them!

Well, it was wonderful meeting you and I'm glad you stopped by. Islam teaches us that every Muslim is a brother and sister to every other Muslim. Our whole Muslim community, or **Ummah**, is meant to be like a big family. I'm glad I got to know you as a part of my family too. Come and see me again! Assalamu alaykum!

Do you remember what Du'a to say when we enter the Masjid? We also should enter with our right foot to symbolize that we like goodness. Remember the Angel on the right! Okay, I see the people lining up for prayers inside. Let's hurry.

Alhumdulillah, that was a nice prayer on a bright sunny day. It's great to be a Muslim because we really get reminded that life is beautiful. No matter what troubles come our way, Islam teaches us to put them in perspective. You know, to understand that no matter what happens to us, Allah is greater than all those problems and that our main duty should be to live free from worry. We tell our worries to Allah and He removes them, if we're sincere believers.

While we're leaving the Masjid, there is a beautiful Du'a that the Prophet taught us to say to

Questions to Answer

1. What do we say before eating?
2. What is Halal meat?
3. List two things that are Haram to eat.
4. How is a Muslim to act towards mothers according to the Prophet?
5. What do we say after eating?
6. What does Islam say our relationship is towards other Muslims?
7. What does the word Ummah mean?

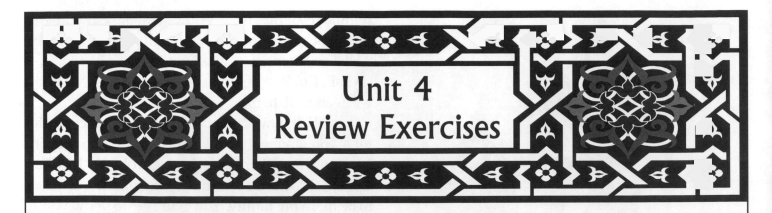

Unit 4
Review Exercises

Vocabulary Review

On a separate piece of paper, write the meaning of each word below. Remember to write in complete sentences.

1. Eidul Adha
2. Dhabiha
3. Ramadan
4. Hajj
5. Halal
6. Ta'leem

7. Taqwa
8. Haram
9. Baytullah
10. Miskeen
11. Adhan
12. Musalla

Remembering What You Read

On a separate piece of paper, answer the questions below. Remember to answer as best as you can and write in complete sentences.

1. What are three things we do on Hajj?
2. How are Muslims supposed to consider other Muslims??
3. What is Iftar and Suhoor?
4. What are the origins of the Hajj?
5. Describe three things about Angels from this Unit.
6. What are Sunnah Prayers?
7. Describe three manners Muslims follow for eating.
8. What are two things Angels do?
9. Choose one of the four children you met from this unit and describe three valuable things you learned from him or her.

Thinking to Learn

Read the following statement and explain whether it is true or false. Write in complete sentences on a separate piece of paper.

Ramadan is only about Fasting.

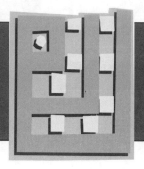

Unit 5

Prophets of the Past

Think About It

Why do you think Allah sent so many Prophets to the world?

Vocabulary Words

Huwwa   Ahl al Kitab

What to Learn

A Muslim believes in all true Prophets from Allah.

A. There Were Many Prophets.

As you learned before, Allah sent a Prophet or Messenger to every nation on earth. Allah said, *"Wa Immin ummatin illa khala feeha natheer."* *"Every people had a Warner (Prophet) among them."* (35:24)

Do you remember the words for Prophet and Messenger? The words are Nabi and Rasul. Do you also remember the name of the first man on earth?

Adam, being the first man, was also the first Prophet. He didn't get any books or written revelations to pass on to his children and their children, though, because he lived at a time when writing was not invented yet.

Adam and his wife, **Huwwa**, lived in a beautiful garden. The Shaytan came and fooled them into disobeying Allah. The only rule that Allah had given them was to not eat the fruit of a certain tree.

The tree wasn't magical or anything, but it was a simple rule that was given to them to follow. The Shaytan told them that if they ate from the tree that they would live forever. When they ate from the tree,

however, they realized it was a mistake and they felt ashamed.

For breaking that rule, Allah told them to leave the garden and go out into the harsh, wild world and live there. Allah didn't stay angry at them for a long time, however. After a while He taught Adam and Huwwa how to ask for His forgiveness. They were so happy to be forgiven!

(Prophet Muhammad once said that if we ask forgiveness for a sin it's as if we never did the bad deed. That's how much forgiveness Allah has for us if we would just ask for it.)

Allah told Adam and Huwwa that He would send Prophets and Messengers to their descendants and that whoever listened to His guidance would be saved. Whoever would choose Shaytan for a friend, however, would lose in the end.

Adam and his wife were sent out in the wild and untamed wilderness. How do you think they felt?

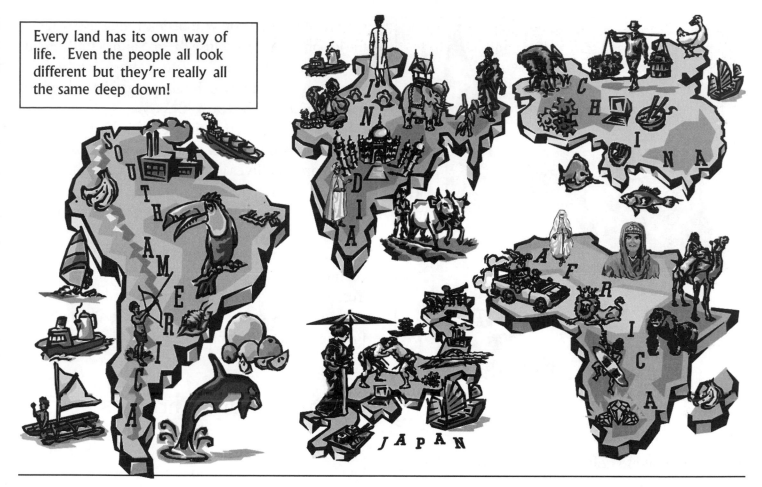

Every land has its own way of life. Even the people all look different but they're really all the same deep down!

After that ancient time, people spread out all over the world. After thousands and thousands of years, people eventually began to look different as well. Some people's skin became darker, while others became lighter. Some groups of people grew taller while others stayed the same. Why does this happen?

Have you ever seen a big family group together? Have you noticed that most of them look sort of the same? This happen with large groups of people also. If a bunch of tall people went off on their own for a thousand years, when you bring them all back you would find they are all taller than everyone in your own group.

Allah said, "*You people! We made you from a single man and woman and then made you into races and groups so you can get to know each other. The best among you is the one with the most Taqwa.*" (49:13)

So people started to look different, but they were all still the same humans that Allah created with a soul inside and feelings of wanting to find their Creator. Allah sent a Prophet to them all.

There were Prophets in Africa, Asia, the Americas, Europe, the Middle East and even Australia! In fact, the Blessed Prophet Muhammad, peace be upon him, said that there were over one hundred thousand Prophets sent to this world! That's a lot of guidance from Allah!

Allah said, "*We sent every Messenger before you with this revelation sent by Us to him, that is: there is no god but Me, so serve Me.*" (21:25)

B. Who Were Some of the Prophets?

If Adam was the first Prophet and Muhammad, may he be blessed, was the last, who were the Prophets in between? Allah's book, the Holy Qur'an, tells us the stories and names of only a few. Only twenty-five Prophets are mentioned by name. Why is this so?

Can you imagine how thick and heavy the Qur'an would be if it included the names and stories of every Prophet! It would be huge!

80

Allah said to all the Messengers, "All you Messengers! Do all the best things and do what is right because I know everything you are doing. This brotherhood of yours is a single brotherhood and I am your Lord so have awareness of Me." 23:51-52

History of the Rasuls

The purpose of the Qur'an is not to just give us a history lesson or to entertain us. It is a book that is supposed to help people learn to live Allah's beautiful way of life.

Any Prophets and their stories that are mentioned are for us to learn from. They are examples of how to avoid sin and move towards goodness. Their stories are lessons for us!

Allah said, "*We have told you the story of some of the Messengers and others We have not told you.*" (4:164)

There were many major Prophets and many minor ones. In other words, some Prophets and Messengers had bigger jobs and more important missions than others. But we hold them all as equals because they all brought Allah's true guidance to the world.

Allah said, "*To those who believe in Allah and His Messengers, and who don't think one Messenger is better than another, We will soon give them their rewards because Allah is the Forgiving, the Kind.*" (4:152)

Some of the major ones that you will be learning more about in a higher grade level are: Nuh and Dawud. Other minor ones that you will also learn about in the future are Suleiman, Yahya, Hud and Zakariyya.

In this book, you will be learning the stories of the Prophets: Yunus, Musa, 'Esa, Salih, Muhammad, Ayyoub and Ibrahim. You have already read something about Prophet Ibrahim, may he be blessed, in the making of the Ka'bah.

Every Prophet mentioned in the Qur'an has an interesting story to tell. The main thing we must learn from their lives is how they came to obey Allah and how they remained strong in the face of ignorant people who wanted to make them become rebels against Allah like them.

Do you remember who is the one who wants to corrupt, or make bad, all the people in the world? Yes, the Shaytan is coming for each and every one of us and it was only Allah's guidance through His Prophets that helped many people lead good and true lives.

C. The Jews and Christians.

Some of the Prophets mentioned in the Qur'an are also known to the Jews and Christians. This is because they also remember the names of some of the Prophets from old times. They say the names a little differently. For example, we say 'Esa while the Christians name him, Jesus. We say Musa while the Jews call him Moses.

They know those names because Allah sent many Prophets to their ancestors, or fore-fathers long ago. But they didn't listen to Allah even though He sent them so many chances.

The Prophet Said:
"My example in comparison to the other Prophets before me, is that of a man who built a nice house, but left out one brick in a corner. His neighbors come and look at the house and say it's so beautiful, but then they say, 'If only that last brick was there in its place!' I am that brick and I am the last of the Prophets." (Bukhari)

"Every Prophet was given some type of miracle which the people could strengthen their Iman with. But I was given the revelation (of the Qur'an) which Allah revealed to me. I hope I will have more followers than any other Prophet on the Day of Resurrection." (Bukhari)

In fact, the Jews made up a lot of false and bad stories about Allah's Prophets to make fun of them. They also made up their own books and said that it's a revelation from Allah. But many people, (even other Jews,) have proven that their books are made up and not from a true Messenger of Allah.

The last Prophet sent to the Jews was named 'Esa. He lived about 2,000 years ago. But when the Jews refused to listen to him also, other people named Greeks and Romans accepted some of this Prophet's message, but not all of it. They took the name "Christians" to call themselves, even though Prophet 'Esa never gave this name to them.

Soon these "Christians" twisted and changed 'Esa's teachings so much that they started worshipping 'Esa, himself, as Allah! They did a terrible crime! Do you remember what it's called? It's called Shirk.

Listen to what Allah is saying in the Holy Qur'an:

"*He is Allah and there is no god but Him. He knows what is secret and in the open. He is the Caring and Kind. He is Allah and there is no god but Him: the King, the Holy, the Bringer of Peace, the Faith-Giver, the Protector, the Exalted, the Irresistible and Supreme. He is too glorified for the partners they give to Him.*"

"*He is Allah the Creator, the Evolver and Giver of Shapes. All the most beautiful names are His. Everything in space and on earth praises Him because He is the Exalted and Wise.*" (59:22-24)

Doesn't it sound awfully wrong to worship a man instead of Allah!

Because the Jews and Christians did get written books from Allah in the past, Allah calls them, "**Ahl al Kitab**" or, "People of the Book."

No man could have made the world and the universe!

But because they made so many mistakes in their beliefs and lost their books, Allah told us to tell them, "*You People of the Book, agree to come to a common understanding with us, (Muslims,) that we serve no god except Allah, that we don't make any partners with Him and that we don't make any of us a lord besides Allah.*" (3:64)

Then Allah informs us, just in case they don't listen, "*But if they turn around (and ignore you), then tell them, 'We declare that we are surrendered to Allah. (We are Muslims).*'"

As you learn the stories of the Prophets in the coming lessons, try to find the wisdom and examples that we can learn from so that we don't make the same mistakes that other people did in the past. Remember, all true Prophets are from Allah and Adam was the first while Muhammad was the last. May Allah put peace and blessings on them all!

Questions to Answer

1. Why did Adam and Huwwa have to leave their wonderful garden?
2. How did people start to look differently from each other?
3. What is the purpose of the stories of the different Prophets in the Qur'an?
4. Why do the Jews and Christians know the names of some of the old Prophets too?
5. What mistakes did the Jews and Christians make about their Prophets?

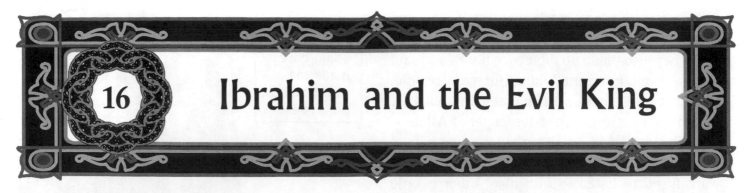

16 Ibrahim and the Evil King

Think About It

Why is it wrong to pray to a piece of stone?

Vocabulary Words

Azar   Suhoof   Mesopotamia

What to Learn

The environment and nature are signs of Allah's power and can make our Iman stonger.

A. Meet Ibrahim!

Ibrahim was born thousands of years ago in a far away land called **Mesopotamia**. That ancient land is in the Middle East. Just a little north of Arabia and a little to the right. Can you find it on the map on this page? His city was near two big rivers called the Tigris and Euphrates.

Ibrahim's people were mostly farmers but the city also had a lot of merchants and skilled artists who made beautiful jewelry, pottery and clothes. There were also people who could make beautiful statues out of stone. People would buy those statues and then call them their gods! Ibrahim's people were idol-worshippers. To make matters worse, Ibrahim's own father, **Azar**, was an idol-maker!

Ibrahim didn't have a hard life as a child. His father made good money from his idol-making business and Ibrahim was even able to learn how to read and write. His father probably hired tutors to teach him because the schools were only for the children who were chosen to be priests or business secretaries.

Ibrahim was a curious child, like most. But as he grew older, he didn't want to spend all his time playing. He also wanted to learn more, to know more about what is right and wrong. One day he was thinking about the statues his father made. Maybe he saw a slab of stone come into his father's shop one day, saw his father carve a face on it, and then saw a man come and pay gold and start praying to it.

Ibrahim thought about it and one day said to his father, "*Are you taking an idol for a god? It seems to me that you and your people are making a big mistake.*" (6:74)

Azar just got mad and told Ibrahim to be quiet.

The Ancient Middle East

The Fertile Crescent

Palestine

Mesopotamia

Egypt

Arabia

Ibrahim saw the three most powerful things in the sky: the Stars, moon and sun. He believed they were greater than the idols and so thought they must be gods. But when he realized that they were just moving objects that didn't do anything else, he understood that Allah could never be a mere thing.

B. The Truth Comes Out!

Ibrahim wanted to know the truth so he decided to go and look for it. He already knew that idols were powerless pieces of stones, so he would never worship them. Now he wanted to know who and where Allah is?

He went out of his house one night and walked in the fields around his home. Perhaps the only sounds in the darkness were crickets or startled birds. Imagine a warm, soft wind blowing slowly across the endless fields of wheat and how the young Ibrahim felt. Suddenly, he looked up in the darkened sky and saw a bright and beautiful star on the horizon.

"That's it!" he cried. "That's got to be my Lord!"

Ibrahim thought that the star must be Allah because it was clearly more beautiful and powerful than a stone idol. Ibrahim stared at it for a long time, but then a strange thing happened. The star began to slowly fall in the sky until it was hidden below the horizon. Ibrahim's Lord was gone!

When Ibrahim realized that the star was just another thing that comes and goes, he gave it up and said, "I don't love things that go away."

A little while later, the full moon came out and cast its grayish light over the plains and nearby river. Ibrahim felt as if he was looking at it for the first time. It was so beautiful and bright! "That's it!" he cried. "That's my Lord!"

But the same thing happened soon after. The moon fell below the horizon and just disappeared. Ibrahim decided to give that up as well. He went home and went to bed feeling more confused than ever.

When he woke up, he walked outside and saw the same fields where he had walked last night in search of his lord. Then a thought came to his mind. He turned his head to look at the sun but his eyes started to hurt so he looked away. "Surely this must be Allah!" he said.

He ran around all day thinking about the wonderful gifts that the sun's light brings. Perhaps he was even happy. But then, as the day passed, he noticed the light was getting weaker and weaker as the sun was setting. When the sun disappeared behind the horizon he realized that Allah must be something greater than stones, stars, moons and the sun.

He realized that if all those things were so strong and powerful, then the One who made them must be totally more powerful than that. No person could ever go and just see such a powerful Lord. (See Surah 6:76-79)

As a reward for finally understanding the truth, Allah sent a revelation into Ibrahim's heart that he was right and that he should tell his people the truth so they could give up idols and serve only Allah, their true Lord. At last Ibrahim had found Allah.

C. The People Get Angry.

Ibrahim started to tell everyone what he found out. First he went to his dad and told him that he shouldn't pray to useless stone statues. He invited his father to believe in the unseen Allah Who made the entire world. But Azar just got angry and threatened to throw stones at him if he didn't keep quiet. He told his son to go away and stay away from him for a long time as a punishment.

Ibrahim looked at his father and said, "*Peace be on you. I will pray to my Lord to forgive you because He is gracious to me.*" (19:47)

Then Ibrahim began his mission and started to tell everyone about Allah. His people didn't want to listen to him because they were used to seeing the idols every day. They thought that by putting food in front of the idols that rain would come or that a baby would be born or that good luck would come. Only a very few listened to the young man. How could he prove to the people that idols were false?

After a while, Ibrahim thought of a plan. There was a big holiday coming up when all the priests and people would go out in the fields for religious rituals and prayers to the gods of the field. The main temple, which had all the most important idols, would be empty. Ibrahim knew what to do.

When the holiday came and the temple was left unguarded, Ibrahim went inside with a big ax. He smashed all the idols and threw them to the ground. But he left one big one standing untouched. The biggest one of all was left alone. Then Ibrahim hung the ax around its stone neck and left.

When the priests returned and went into the temple, they saw the idols smashed into a million pieces! They cried out in terror: "Who did this to our gods! Help! What happened?"

Some people said they knew of a young man who might have done it. So some soldiers went and arrested Ibrahim and brought him to the temple. The chief priest asked him, "Did you do this to our gods?"

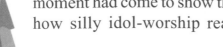

Ibrahim smiled. Now the moment had come to show the people how silly idol-worship really was.

Ibrahim waited while the people decided what to do.

"Who me? The big one probably did it. Ask the (broken idols) who did it if they can talk."

The people and priests became confused for a minute. "You know they can't speak." the chief priest told him.

So Ibrahim shouted out, "So why do you worship, in place of Allah, things that can't do any good or bad to you?"

The people became angry and shouted, "*Burn him! Protect your gods!*" (21:51-68) But the people could not kill him because only the king could order a man to be killed. So Ibrahim was arrested and taken to the king, whose name was Nimrud.

D. Nimrud Learns a Lesson.

Ibrahim was brought into Nimrud's palace. It was a huge building filled with rooms, hallways, treasures and guards. Ibrahim stood before the king but refused to bow down. Nimrud was curious at this young man. What made him so brave? Didn't the boy know that Nimrud could order his death in a moment? He decided to have some fun and test this prisoner.

After finding out who he was and what he did, Nimrud told Ibrahim to explain himself. Ibrahim didn't lie or deny anything. When Nimrud told him that he could have him killed in a second, Ibrahim responded, "*My Lord is the One Who gives life and death.*"

Nimrud got angry and said, "*I decide who lives and dies!*"

Ibrahim answered, "*Allah makes the sun rise from the East. Can you make it rise from the West?*" (2:258)

Nimrud knew he couldn't do that. His real weakness was brought to light. He was just a man who had no real power, even if he could cause a little pain here and there. The real power was with Allah. But Nimrud was arrogant. He became even more angry because he felt like this young man made him look like a fool. He ordered Ibrahim to be thrown in a fire and burned to death!

The guards took poor Ibrahim away and a big fire was made in the city so everyone could watch the young trouble-maker being punished. Everyone came to watch. When the fire was ready, Nimrud, the priests and the people all watched as Ibrahim was brought and thrown into the hot fire.

But a miracle from Allah happened! Allah had other plans for Ibrahim and He wasn't going to let some ignorant people get in the way of His plans. The fire instantly became cool. There were flames, but there was no heat. Ibrahim stood there in the middle of the fire and didn't get burned at all! (21:69)

Can you imagine how amazed everyone was! Many people ran away, the priests cried to their idols

and Nimrud stood frozen in amazement. Nobody bothered Ibrahim as he got out of the fire and just walked away. Wouldn't it have been funny if a guard went to touch the fire and suddenly it became hot again!

After that, everybody knew that Ibrahim couldn't be hurt. But the people just thought he had magic protecting him. They still didn't believe in Allah. Ibrahim received the message to leave his country and take whoever would follow him with him. Allah was sending Ibrahim to Palestine, a land far away, where he and his followers could serve Allah and not be afraid.

Later on, Allah revealed a special revelation to Ibrahim which he quickly wrote on leather scrolls. This revelation is named after the word for scrolls in Arabic, the **Suhoof**. His message was lost long ago, however, but his name is still remembered to this day for his bravery and courage in the face of danger. May Allah put peace upon Ibrahim and bless all of his descendants who follow in his wise footsteps. Amin.

Questions to Answer

1. What were Ibrahim's people like?
2. Why did Ibrahim want to look for the truth?
3. How did Ibrahim realize that Allah was not a thing we can see?
4. What happened in the temple and why?
5. How did Ibrahim show the king he was foolish?
6. How did Allah save Ibrahim?

Think About It

What would you expect a person to do if he or she lost everything they ever had?

Vocabulary Words

Sabr

What to Learn

A Muslim accepts that life will be sometimes easy and sometimes difficult.

A. What is Sabr?

Sometimes bad things happen to good people. Other times, people who are bad always seem to have an easy time, even though they don't deserve it. Some people will be rich while others will be poor. Sometimes a rich person will become poor or a poor person will become rich! Life is sometimes strange and it may even seem unfair at times.

Allah made this world as a testing ground. As you learned before, Allah wants us to choose to love and obey Him. The Shaytan wants us to forget Allah and do wrong. In our world our lives are always influenced by what happens around us and we can let ourselves go towards good and bad.

Even such things as accidents, being rich or poor or happy or sad are part of the test. None of us knows what will happen to us tomorrow. Every sunrise brings a new day full of possibilities and challenges. Allah said, "*We give people their different situations of good and bad by turns.*" (3:140) The key is not what happens to you, but what you do about it.

The Blessed Prophet Muhammad once said, "It's amazing that there is good in everything that happens to a believer (in Allah) and it's only that way for a believer. If something nice happens to him, he is thankful. If something bad happens to him, however, he has Sabr, and that is best for him." (Muslim)

The word **Sabr** means "patience and not giving up." We can't control what happens to us most of the time so we understand that life might not always be easy. But Allah said in the Qur'an that He will not give someone a test that is too much for them to handle. (23:62)

If a test comes and a terrible thing happens, we can handle it- if we want to. We can also give up, get mad at Allah and feel hopeless. But if we had Taqwa and some Iman, we would understand that life in this world is only a short time for us. We would step up to the challenge and come closer to Allah in our hearts, asking His help and strength.

No matter what happens, the sun still rises over the world every day.

Allah said, "*Innal laha ma' as Sabireen.*" "*Indeed Allah is with the people who have Sabr.*" (2:153) He has promised a wonderful reward in Heaven, or Jannah, for those who have Sabr in this life.

The Blessed Prophet Muhammad once said, "If a bad situation comes over you, never say, 'What if I would have done something else, would something different have happened?' Instead you should say, 'Allah has planned and Allah has carried out His plan.'" (Muslim)

The Prophet you will be learning about next had a bigger test than you could ever imagine. So many bad things happened to him and so many heartaches came to him. The Shaytan worked real hard to get this Prophet to give up on Allah. But as we shall see, this Prophet gave a beautiful lesson for us in how to have Sabr no matter how terrible life gets.

B. The Contented Prophet.

Prophet Ayyoub lived a long time ago. His village was somewhere in northern Arabia, near Palestine. He was respected among his people and had a nice home and family. He wasn't wealthy but he had an easy life and was very happy.

Prophet Ayyoub would give Allah's guidance to his people and some would listen while others would not. But they never bothered the respected, older man and his life was not too difficult. He was a contented Prophet.

Once, as if to demonstrate his easy lifestyle,

Prophet Ayyoub was taking a bath when suddenly a swarm of golden-colored locusts fell on him. They were not harmful insects and they could actually be sold to the townspeople for money. Ayyoub began scooping them up in his robe when Allah said to him, "Ayyoub, haven't I made you rich enough so that you wouldn't need what you see here?"

Prophet Ayyoub smiled and answered back, "Yes, Lord, but I can't do without Your blessings (that You let come my way.)" (Bukhari)

As we learned before, life can change in an instant. As Allah said, "*No person knows what will happen to them tomorrow.*" (31:34) And the same is true for Prophet Ayyoub. Allah was going to let him be tested.

Prophet Muhammad once taught that when Allah loves a person, He tests them. And when He really loves a person, He *really* tests him. Why is this so? Allah said in the Qur'an, "*Do you think you can say, 'I believe,' and not be tested in your Iman? We tested those before you and Allah will certainly show who is true and who is false.*" (29:2-3)

The purpose of a test is to prove whether we really believe in Allah or not. If we get mad and feel hopeless after a hard test, it means we don't see anything good beyond our own little life in this world. We didn't put our hopes in Allah and the next life.

Think about it: if you love Allah and don't let the things of this world bother you too much, whether good or bad, don't you deserve to get the greatest reward for not following your body's desires and the Shaytan? Of course!

The Blessed Prophet once said, "Whenever a Muslim is afflicted by any kind of hardship, whether it's a terrible sickness, anxiety (worry), sadness, harm, a natural disaster or even a cut from a thorn, Allah wipes out some of his or her smaller bad deeds." (Bukhari, Muslim)

Let's see what happened to Prophet Ayyoub and how he handled the situation.

C. Disaster Strikes!

One day everything was normal, the next day the world was turned upside down! It was a sunny Wednesday morning when Prophet Ayyoub awoke and went out to start his day. But beginning on that strange day, his farm animals started to get sick and died, one by one. The rain also stopped from that day so his crops soon whithered and died.

This is bad because in those days people used animals for food and work and a person's crops were their life. Basically, Prophet Ayyoub lost all his income. Imagine how bad he must have felt. He had a family to feed and people who depended on him.

But if that wasn't bad enough, his wife and children also began to get sick and die. How horrible it is to see your family members dying and you can do nothing to save them. That is the worst thing that can happen to any of us. Imagine all the loss and pain he felt!

Then, as if that wasn't enough, his house and lands were destroyed. Maybe by a fire or flood, but however it happened, he lost everything. He lost it all. Imagine him standing there, alone, seeing his house gone, his family gone and his income gone. A year before he was on top of the world and now he seemed to be on the bottom. Even his neighbors refused to help him. Maybe they were afraid his bad luck would spread to them.

Then the Shaytan came around. You know how he works. The Jinn are invisible and can whisper bad thoughts into our minds. The Shaytan began telling Prophet Ayyoub horrible things that must have been like this: "See what Allah did to you. See how much Allah's love is worth! Forget about Allah and go get a job and try to get rich so this can never happen to you again."

The Shaytan caught Ayyoub when he was weak from sadness and disaster. Wouldn't many people listen to those terrible lies and forget about Allah? After all, how much pain can one person bear? Prophet Ayyoub was confused about what to do. Maybe he wandered in confusion for weeks or even months. His health went down and he looked miserable.

But do you remember what Allah said? He said He won't put a test or burden on someone that is more than they can handle. The choice is up to us if want to rise up to the challenge and remain firm in our Iman. Prophet Ayyoub realized this and decided he would never leave Allah and he asked Allah for help.

Prophet Ayyoub lifted his hands up and cried, "*The Shaytan has hit me with sorrow and suffering!*" (38:41)

Then he prayed to Allah, "*Sadness and misery has caught hold of me, but You are the Most Merciful of the Merciful!*" (21:83)

Prophet Ayyoub lost everything and his land became a dry desert!

Ayyoub was tested with the worst situation any of us could ever imagine. He could have let himself go crazy or become an unbeliever, but instead, he strengthened his Iman and took the lesson from his suffering that this world is only temporary and that the real life is yet to come. He turned to Allah.

D. After Difficulty There is Relief.

The Shaytan realized he was powerless against this true Muslim. He was totally surrendered to Allah no matter how bad his life got. The Shaytan decided to move on and bother somebody else. The Holy Qur'an talks about tests and how hard they are. At the same time, no test lasts forever. Eventually, as Allah says, "*There is ease after a hard time.*" (94:5) And Prophet Ayyoub was going to get his time of rest.

Allah revealed to him, "*Kick the ground. A spring will be uncovered where you can bathe and drink.*" (38:42)

The cool water felt like a life-saver to him. It was his sign that his life was going to become good again. Prophet Ayyoub picked himself up and started over more full of purpose and Iman than ever. He went to his people and told them about the wonderful lessons of Sabr that he learned.

Eventually, he was able to rebuild his house, get more farm animals and he got married again and had more children than he had before! But this time he never took for granted what he had but was always thankful to Allah and aware of the fact that this life was more temporary than most people even realize.

Allah told him, "*Take some grass in your hand and slap it. Then don't break (your promise.)*" (38:44)

The grass was supposed to symbolize all the lessons of this life for him. Can you figure out how? And Allah was telling him not to forget again that this life is really short and only a place of tests and trials.

Allah tells us to consider Prophet Ayyoub's example and to learn from it. Allah said about him, "*Indeed, We found him full of Sabr. He was excellent in Our service and he always turned to Us!*" (38:44)

Can we learn the lessons of Prophet Ayyoub? The next time something good happens, remember Allah and be thankful. Don't just remember Allah in your hard times.

The next time something bad happens, no matter how horrible it is, remember that this life is only short and try to come closer to Allah in your heart and call out to Him with all your worries and fears. He promised to hear every cry.

Allah said, "*Have Sabr, because the promise of Allah is true. Ask forgiveness for your sins and glorify Allah at night and in the morning.*" (40:55)

We must try to have Sabr and move forward as best as we can. Read the Qur'an for more strength because the Qur'an gives us the stories and examples of how we can learn to handle whatever comes our way.

Questions to Answer

1. Why do people sometimes have hard or difficult times?
2. What does the word Sabr mean?
3. What is the Prophet Muhammad's advice for what we should say when something bad happens?
4. Why was Prophet Ayyoub tested?
5. How did Prophet Ayyoub handle his test and what did he get afterwards?

What Does Allah Say?

In the Name of Allah,
the Compassionate Source of All Mercy."

And your Lord says, "Call on Me. I will answer you. But those who are too arrogant to serve Me will find themselves in the humiliating Hell-fire.

(Quran 40:60)

Shaytan threatens you with being poor and asks you to do wrong. But Allah promises you forgiveness and bounties. Allah cares for all and knows everything.

(Quran 2:268)

Every soul will taste of death and you will be paid back only on the Day of Judgment. Only the one who is far from the fire and entered into the Garden will have achieved the real goal. The life of this world is only about things and illusions.

(Quran 3:185)

If Allah touches you with a hurt, no one can remove it. If He decides to give you a good thing, no one can keep it away. He brings these things to whoever He wants to and He is the Forgiving and Kind.

(Quran 10:107)

18   Salih and the Camel

Think About It

Why should people not be greedy and cruel?

Vocabulary Words

Thamud   Al-Hijr

What to Learn

A Muslim never tries to control a natural resource so much that other people can't share in it.

A. Who Were the Thamud?

In Northern Arabia there is nothing but dry land and deserts. There is very little rainfall in most of the region and life is hard for the people who live there. The only places where a lot of people can live together are the small patches of fertile land surrounding the scattered water wells.

Over three thousand years ago, a mighty group of people called the **Thamud** controlled this land. Their soldiers guarded every well and they kept all the other people away from the water. If they did let some people bring their flocks of animals to drink from the well, they charged them a lot of money for the service.

The leaders of the Thamud grew very wealthy from this. No matter how hot the weather was or how much the common people, passing caravans and shepherds needed water, they only gave any if they were paid nicely. To protect their wealth and power, the Thamud kept an army of many soldiers and built a lot of castles and forts that they carved right into the rock walls of nearby cliffs and mountain-sides. They thought they were the strongest people around.

The Thamud controlled all the water wells in the hot dry land of northern Arabia.

B. The Hopeful Son.

Among the Thamud a boy was born. That was not a strange thing in itself because babies are born all the time. But this special boy, who was named Salih, was going to have a mission that would change his people's way of life forever.

We can well imagine that he had an easy life growing up. His family were members of the ruling tribe and he never went without food or water or whatever else he needed. He probably received a good education and many people thought he would make a fine leader one day.

But then, something happened. Allah doesn't tell us in the Qur'an how Salih came to be interested in the truth. Perhaps he saw the misery and sadness of the poor people who were not allowed to water their animals on hot days. He must have felt bad for them. Or maybe he didn't believe in the idols his people were worshipping and decided to look for the real power behind everything in the world, just like the young Ibrahim did. But however he found the truth, Allah chose him and made him a Prophet with a mission to stop the evil ways of the Thamud.

Salih, who was by now a strong young man, began his mission right away. He had to get his people to give up idols and to let others use the wells. At first, he started going around his city and telling people, "*Serve Allah! You have no gods except Him. Won't you be aware?*" (23:32)

During one gathering of people, probably in the street or market place, he stood up and declared loudly, "*My people! Serve Allah! You have no god except Him! He is the One Who created you from the earth and settled you on it! Ask His forgiveness (for your bad deeds) and turn to Him, because my Lord is always near and ready to answer.*" (11:61)

Clearly, his people were amazed! Salih was from among them. He had an easy life because of the Thamud being cruel to other people. Now this young man was speaking out against the very way of life that made them wealthy?

The leaders of the Thamud heard him and said sadly, "*Salih! You were one of us! Our hopes (for the future) were on you up until now. Are you telling us not to worship what our own fathers worshipped? We have doubts about what you are calling us to.*" (11:62) They even called him crazy and a liar! (54:24-25)

C. The Great Debate!

The Prophet Salih continued his mission, even though the powerful leaders of the Thamud said they didn't believe him. In fact, everyone started talking about Salih, whether for good or bad. Some people, mostly the poor, accepted the message of Salih, while the arrogant and wealthy rejected him.

One of the bad people said, "*(Salih) is just a man like the rest of you. He eats the same food as you do and drinks the same drinks you do. If you obey a man like yourselves you'll certainly be lost. Is he saying to you that after you've died and become dust that you will be made again? That promise is way off. There is nothing but our life in this world! We die and live but we will never be raised up again!*" (23:33-37)

Prophet Salih didn't give up. He wanted to confront the main crime of the Thamud: their total and selfish control of the wells. He told his people, "*I am your Messenger who you can trust! So be aware of Allah and obey me! I'm not asking for any reward from you. My reward is only from the Lord of the Universe.*" (26:143-145)

Salih then told them to stop keeping people away from the wells and to let everyone come and have equal turns to use the water. He told them not to follow the ways of the arrogant. But they laughed at him and said, "*You've got a magic spell on you! You're nothing more than a mortal like us. Bring us a sign if you're telling the truth!*" (26:152-154)

So Salih brought a camel to the people one day and announced, "*This camel has a right to go to*

Prophet Salih went from place to place teaching and calling people to Allah.

The camel was a test. It would go to the wells and the Thamud leaders were supposed to let it take a turn to drink. This was to show them that everyone should get a fair turn.

the well for water and you also have a right to use the wells, but on set days in turns. Don't hurt her or the punishment of a mighty day will come over you." (26:155-156)

D. The Terrible Crime.

Salih's plan was simple. He called people to Allah and gained many followers. At the same time he exposed the great wrong of the Thamud and ordered them to give everyone the right to use the water wells. When they challenged him for a sign he brought out a special camel and told them to take turns with the camel for water. That would be their test.

The leaders, however, had plans of their own. They went to the poor people who believed in Salih and tried to put doubt and fear in their minds. Once they asked a group of poor people if they really believed in Salih and his revelations from Allah. When the poor people said they did, the arrogant leaders cried out, *"We reject whatever you believe in!"* (7:75-76)

The leaders of the Thamud also had a plan for dealing with Salih's special camel. One day they told Salih, *"We see a bad sign in you and in your followers."*

Salih answered them, *"Your 'bad sign' is with Allah and you are a people being tested."* (27:47)

The leaders of the mighty Thamud could take it no longer! They shouted and cursed in anger and one of them took out a long sword and ran at the special camel standing nearby.

Before anyone knew what was going on, the evil man cut the legs of the poor camel and it fell down in pain, crying and bellowing. It would never walk to the wells, or anywhere else, again. (54:29)

Prophet Salih and his followers were horrified. Such cruelty! The leaders of the Thamud just laughed and they congratulated the man who did it. They went away cheering and calling out to people about what they had done. Then they dared Salih's Lord to punish them. Prophet Salih stood up and called to the evil Thamud people, *"Go and enjoy yourselves in your homes for three days, and then the promise (of punishment) will be fulfilled!"* (11:65)

The people of the Thamud were getting tired of Prophet Salih and they wanted to do away with him and all his talk about honesty once and for all!

But for the moment, they seemed to go unpunished! There were no lightning bolts from the sky and no angry Angels coming to get them. They laughed and called Salih a total liar.

E. The Plot of the Evil Nine Brothers.

Prophet Salih became the victim of a cruel campaign of gossip and name-calling. The Thamud sent their people everywhere to tell people that Salih was false and that the camel test was a joke. Salih heard about all the talk and cried out, "*My Lord! Help me. They're accusing me of being a liar.*"

Allah sent him the message, "*In just a little while they will be very sorry.*" (23:39-40)

Now in the same city there lived a family of nine brothers. Every one of them was bad and they liked to cause trouble and hurt people.

One day, after hearing everything that went on between Salih and their leaders, they got together and said to each other, "*Let's make a promise by god that we will attack Salih and his family at night. Then we'll say in the morning that none of us were anywhere near (Salih's) house and that we don't lie.*" (27:48-49)

They wanted to kill Salih and get rid of him and his whole family once and for all! But Allah wasn't going to let that happen. He sent a message to Prophet Salih that very day that he should gather all his followers and leave the cities of rock and stone. So Salih did as he was commanded and left the city with everyone who would listen.

It was the third day after the camel had been attacked and the Thamud people must have thought that now Salih would really be proven a liar. Everyone was going along with their normal routine: the soldiers were keeping people away from the wells and charging a lot of money to use it, the priests kept praying to idols and the Thamud people and their leaders were busy eating, drinking and having fun with their wrongly made money.

Then a strange vibration, called a tremor, shook the land and cliff walls where their cities were carved. After it passed with no real damage, maybe the people just rolled their eyes and went about their daily lives. But then suddenly, out of no where, a massive earthquake struck all at once!

The force of the quake sent people to the floor like a pile of sticks and rocks were falling

The land of Al-Hijr is now a dry wasteland. A few ruins of stone buildings carved into the cliffs is all that remains of the mighty Thamud.

everywhere. Women and children were screaming, animals were rushing to get away and the men cried out in terror! The quaking wouldn't stop and everything was breaking apart!

When it was all over, many people lay dead and buried under tons of rock and rubble. The castles were wrecked, the shops destroyed and all the leaders were dead. The power of the Thamud was broken! With their cities destroyed, the few survivors scattered and fled in the morning.

Allah puts it this way: "*The mighty blast overtook the evil people and they lay on their faces in their homes before the morning as if they had never lived and prospered there. The Thamud rejected their Lord and so the Thamud were removed!*" (11:67-68)

Thousands of years later, when the Prophet Muhammad was traveling in the area where the Thamud used to live, now called **Al-Hijr**, he noticed that his companions had taken some water from an ancient well and were using it to drink and make bread from.

When he saw them doing that he ordered them to pour the water on the ground and to feed the bread to the camels.

The only well he let them use was one he found a little ways onward that he said was the same well that Prophet Salih's camel drank from. All other wells in that land were bad. (Bukhari) This was the end of the arrogant Thamud.

Questions to Answer

1. Who were the Thamud and what were they known for?
2. Describe one argument Salih used to convince the Thamud that idols were false.
3. What did the Thamud people think of Prophet Salih. Explain.
4. Why did Prophet Salih bring the test of the camel to them?
5. What did the Thamud do about the Camel?
6. Who were the nine brothers and what did they want to do?
7. How did Allah deal with the Thamud in the end?

Think About It

Why should a person do the job that they were assigned?

Vocabulary Words

Nineveh   **Gourd**

What to Learn

We shouldn't let anger make us give up a task too easily.

A. The Great City of Sin.

Almost three thousand years ago there existed a beautiful city named **Nineveh**. It was located on the banks of the Tigris river in Mesopotamia and was a huge, bustling metropolis of over 100,000 people. It was surrounded by farms and towns and had contacts with cities all over the region.

Although it was in the same land that Prophet Ibrahim was from, this was not his home town and we are now, in fact, a thousand years past his time in our story. This city was ruled by kings and had a very powerful army. Idol-worship was the religion most people followed and there was a lot of sin and bad deeds done by the people there every day. Cheating, stealing, murder, gambling, drunkenness and bad living was what most people did.

The kings and rulers used their power to gather great wealth and they wasted money on building huge palaces for themselves and having endless parties and ceremonies. Even though there were many poor people, the government didn't do anything to help them and they lived in misery and neglect. Although it was a great and powerful city, it was also based on fear and oppression.

B. The Prophet Who Ran.

In this land, Allah chose a Prophet to call the people away from the ways of Shaytan and towards goodness. As we have seen before, Allah always gives people a chance to hear the message of truth so they could become good, moral people. He would never destroy a city or make a civilization end without sending them His warnings. If the people listened and gave up their hurtful and evil ways, then Allah would let their community and culture continue for a while longer.

The mighty city of Nineveh!

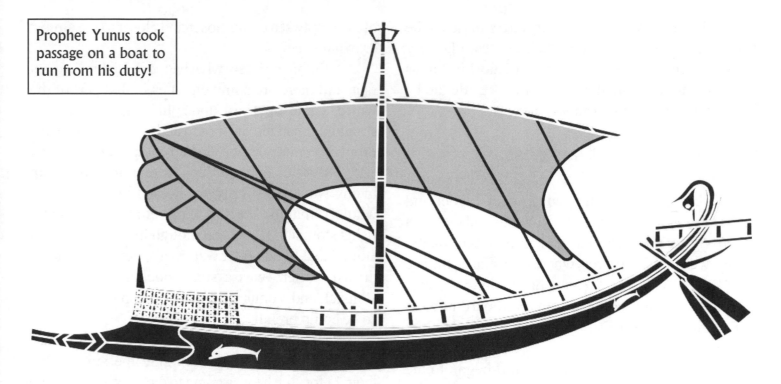

Prophet Yunus took passage on a boat to run from his duty!

The man Allah chose was named Yunus, the son of Matta. He entered the city and began to preach to the people about giving up idols, serving only Allah and living a good and clean life. Perhaps a few people followed him, but almost everyone else ignored him. He must have felt like he was talking to a brick wall! Everywhere he went: in the markets, in the restaurants, in the homes of people, nobody cared about what he was saying.

After trying to teach them and convince them of the truth for some time, Prophet Yunus got angry at them and shouted that he hoped the wrath of Allah would come on them. Then he ran away from the city and made his way south to the coast where the Tigris river emptied into the vast sea called the Persian Gulf. This large body of water is between the present day countries of Iran and Arabia.

He didn't know where he was going and he didn't know what he was going to do, but he just gave up on his mission too early and he didn't want to go back to Nineveh. He thought it was a hopeless cause and just hoped that Allah would destroy them and get it over with.

But Allah is more merciful than that and wanted to make sure that everyone heard the message before taking any action. By running away, Prophet Yunus was trying to make Allah's decision by himself. (21:87) Allah would soon show him what he had to do.

C. The Great Fish.

Prophet Yunus bought a ticket for a boat ride from some sailors and boarded the ship on a nice, sunny day. Prophet Yunus watched as boxes and baskets full of trade goods were loaded until it seemed that the boat would burst from all the cargo. After a little while, the ship's captain ordered the boat to set sail and out into the great sea they went.

After a few hours of sailing, however, the sky started to fill with dark storm clouds. In those days, ships were not as big as they are today and a big storm could make a boat sink- especially one full of valuable cargo.

Everyone on board became afraid. After a little while, the winds grew and the waves rose higher and higher. Water began spilling onto the deck and the storm became more and more violent. The sky was dark, the sea was raging and the wind was beating into the faces of the sailors.

Back then there was a superstition among people about storms at sea. They believed that if a storm came, it was because someone on board was bad luck. To find out who brought the bad luck with them, everyone would have to cast lots, or do a random drawing. Whoever came up with the unlucky marker was then thrown overboard to die so that the angry sea would become calm again.

Imagine the fear on everyone's mind as the sailors and people all threw their stones, like they were rolling dice. As his fate would have it, Yunus was the one who had the bad marker. Little did he know what was going to happen next!

D. A Cry From Darkness.

As the storm whipped up ever higher and higher waves, the sailors grabbed Yunus and took him to the edge of the deck. The dark gray-green colored waves were crashing everywhere for as far as the eye could see. What must Yunus have been thinking! Suddenly the sailors threw him overboard into the sea and watched as he struggled against the swirling waters.

After a few minutes the wind began to die down and the storm mostly went away. Imagine how happy everyone was on the boat! The captain ordered people to start bailing out the water in the bottom of the boat and he ordered the sails to be raised so they could be on there way.

Imagine poor Prophet Yunus as he struggled to keep his head above water! He saw the ship sailing away and knew he was done for! But Allah had still other plans for him! From out of the deep, dark depths of the sea something moved. A shadow upon the face of the empty sea came closer and closer to the almost drowning man.

Before he knew what happened to him, a giant fish, and there are some big ones in that part of the world, came up from under him and sucked the struggling man into its mouth and down into its belly, Prophet Yunus was gobbled up completely!

But this fish didn't chew on him or hurt him in any way. He simply swallowed Prophet Yunus whole! Imagine the shock of being inside a giant fish's stomach! But even though he was now in an animal that lived under water, Prophet Yunus didn't drown. There was a small pocket of air in the stomach and Yunus struggled to keep his head in it so he could breath.

He spent a long time in there and lost all sense of place and direction. Imagine the smell! He thought for sure he was going to die. But after a while of suffering he realized that there was only One who could save him. The One Lord that he had disobeyed and ran away from. He knew he was being punished for his failures and was being taught a lesson.

Prophet Yunus cried out to Allah for forgiveness. He said, *"La ilaha illa anta. Subahanaka! Inne koontu min adhawlimeen!"* *"There is no god but You! Glory to you! I was greatly wrong!"* (21:87)

Prophet Yunus cried out from inside the giant fish. How do you think he felt?

Allah heard his cries for forgiveness and forgave him. Allah has promised to forgive all sins if we just ask for His forgiveness sincerely. But how would Prophet Yunus ever get out of the belly of a giant fish! That was the easy part.

The mighty creature swam as fast as it could towards the sea shore and in one mighty heave, it spit the helpless man out of its belly and into shallow water. Prophet Yunus must have been amazed as he struggled to stand up in the low water.

Perhaps he was squinting his eyes from the bright sun which he hadn't seen in a while, maybe even days!

As he struggled up onto the beach, we can imagine him looking back at the sea and seeing the last signs of the great fish, perhaps a tale rising above the water. He was so thankful to Allah! But from his severe experience he was sick and needed to rest. As he lay on the hot sand he felt weak and tired. But Allah knew he needed help until he recovered.

Out of the ground and moving fast, Allah caused a thick and leafy plant to grow bigger and bigger until its leaves completely covered him in shade. Perhaps the fruit of this plant, a **gourd**, also provided food for him. Prophet Yunus knew he would live and he knew what he had to do. (37:145-146)

E. A City is Saved.

When he was strong enough to travel, he headed back towards the city of Nineveh. He managed to get a red camel somehow and wrapped himself up in a wool cloak. As he journeyed towards the sprawling city, he passed through some low mountains called the Harsha tracks and he cried, "At your service, My Lord!" (Bukhari)

He washed up on a lonely beach.

When he finally entered the city a few days or weeks later and began to preach, he was more convincing, kind and humble than he was before. People saw the change in him and were attracted to such a wonderful and nice man. Many people listened to him and began to be won over by his teachings.

Because so many people gave up idol-worship and decided to live a better lifestyle and to be nicer to others, Allah decided not to let the city be destroyed. Because many believed, He allowed their civilization to continue on for a long time after. (37:148)

Prophet Yunus achieved his mission and never forgot the great lesson he learned about Who he really depended on for his life. He always remained thankful to Allah and never stopped helping people and doing good for the rest of his days.

The Blessed Prophet Muhammad once remarked that if a Muslim makes Du'a to Allah using the same Du'a that Prophet Yunus said while in the belly of the fish, then Allah will remove his or her worry and distress and accept the Du'a. (Tirmidhi. Also see 21:88)

May Allah bless all the Prophets and Messengers and help us to learn form their noble examples. Amin! Let it be so.

Questions to Answer

1. Why was the city of Nineveh going to be punished?
2. Why did Prophet Yunus just give up early in his mission?
3. When Yunus ran off in a ship, how did Allah teach him a lesson?
4. What is the Du'a that Yunus made in the belly of the fish for forgiveness?
5. How did Prophet Yunus get out of the fish?
6. What happened to Nineveh?

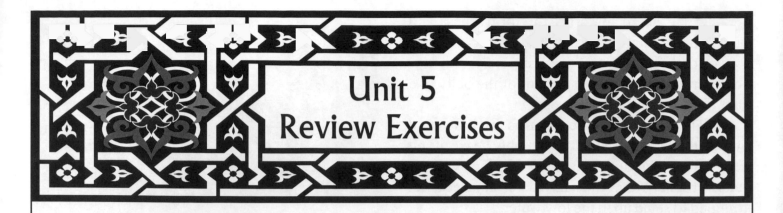

Unit 5
Review Exercises

Vocabulary Review

On a separate piece of paper, write the meaning of each word below. Remember to write in complete sentences.

1. Ahl al Kitab
2. Azar
3. Sabr
4. Nabi
5. Thamud
6. Mesopotamia
7. Huwwa
8. Nineveh
9. Christians
10. Al-Hijr
11. Rasul
12. Suhoof

Remembering What You Read

On a separate piece of paper, answer the questions below. Remember to answer as best as you can and write in complete sentences.

1. Describe how people became different races and ethnic groups.
2. What does Islam say about Jews and Christians?
3. How did Christians begin practicing shirk?
4. How did Ibrahim come into the truth about Allah?
5. Describe three things that happened in the story of Prophet Ibrahim.
6. How did Prophet Ayyoub react to his testing?
7. Describe briefly the story of Prophet Salih and the Thamud.
8. How did Prophet Yunus come to understand that he had to complete his mission?
9. Which of the Prophet's stories in this unit is your favorite and why?
10. What is the special Du'a that Prophet Muhammad said would always be answered?

Thinking to Learn

Read the following statement and explain whether it is true or false. Write in complete sentences on a separate piece of paper and give examples to support your answer.

We can't learn any lessons from the story of Prophet Ayyoub.

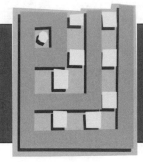

Unit 6

Three Prophets, One Way

Think About It

Why would a group of people see something that is true but then do something else?

Vocabulary Words

Pharaoh   **Bani Isra'il**   **Taurah**

What to Learn

The Jews rejected Prophet Musa and Allah has been very angry with them ever since.

A. The Great Prophets.

Allah raised up thousands of Prophets and Messengers around the world. As you learned in previous units, the Qur'an mentions the stories of some of them but not all of them. This is because the Qur'an is a book of lessons, not just a listing of everything that ever happened in the world.

Allah tells us parts of the Prophets' stories to help us understand how to live by Islamic teachings. Do you remember the main lesson we were to learn from the story of Prophet Ayyoub? We were meant to see how Sabr is a part of our life. Prophet Yunus taught us about not getting angry and not trying to run away from our duty. Prophet Ibrahim helped us to see that we can stand up against wrong with no fear and that we should always look for what's right. Prophet Salih taught us about fairness and sharing.

The people called Jews had a lot of Prophets sent to them by Allah in ancient days, just like many Prophets were sent to other people.

In those days of long ago, the ancestors of the Jews were called the **Bani Isra'il**. That is a way of saying that they were the descendants of a Prophet named Ya'qub, whose nick-name was Isra'il.

During the time of Prophet Ya'qub, all the Bani Isra'il people moved from Palestine to Egypt. They did this because there was a drought in Palestine and Ya'qub's son, Prophet Yusuf, was a powerful man in Egypt. You will learn more about Prophets Yusuf and Ya'qub in a higher grade level.

At first, the Bani Isra'il lived in peace in Egypt, but after many hundreds of years, the Egyptians turned the Bani Isra'il into slaves. Also the Bani Isra'il forgot about Allah, for the most part, and followed local idol-worshipping ideas.

Then Allah sent an important Prophet to Egypt named Musa, peace be upon him. It was Prophet

Musa's job to rescue the Bani Isra'il from slavery and to teach them how to be true believers in Allah.

B. The Baby is Saved.

When Musa was born, about three thousand years ago, his people were slaves in ancient Egypt. The **Pharaoh**, (*fair-o*) who was the ruler of that land, made the Bani Isra'il work all day building huge towers and temples. One day, when the Egyptians realized that a lot of slaves were being born, they became afraid that it would be harder to control so many people and that they may rebel against their masters.

The Pharaoh thought up an evil plan to prevent this. One day he ordered his soldiers to go and kill all the baby boys from the slave families so there would be fewer slaves in the future. When the soldiers were going from house to house and doing their evil work, Allah sent a message to one poor mother to take her baby, named Musa, and put him in a basket. Then she had to take him to the Nile river and let the basket float away.

The mother did as she was told and off the baby Musa went down the river in a basket. Then a strange thing happened. The basket floated right into one of the river-side palaces of the Pharaoh. An important woman who lived there found the baby and decided to keep him. Musa was going to be raised as an Egyptian in the house of Pharaoh!

Musa's mother was later chosen to be the slave-caretaker of the baby and she was so happy he was safe. But she could never tell anyone that she was the baby's real mother or he would be killed. As the years passed, she secretly taught Musa as much as she could about who he really was and thanked Allah for keeping her son alive. She even told him about a younger brother he had, named Harun. But Musa had to live in the Pharaoh's house and he was brought up like a member of the royal family.

C. The Accident that Turned Musa's World Upside Down.

Musa grew to be a strong young man. But one night, while he was walking in the city, he saw one man beating another. One was a slave and the other was an Egyptian. Musa tried to stop the Egyptian from hurting the slave but he accidentally killed the Egyptian man. After he found out about it, Pharaoh wanted to arrest Musa and punish him so Musa had to run away from Egypt into the nearby Arabian desert.

After weeks of traveling in the hot, dry sun, Musa came into a land called **Madyan**. He found a water-well there and was about to go to it and drink when he saw a bunch of strong men watering their animals. They were also keeping away the sheep of some helpless young women. When Musa asked the women why they were afraid to challenge the men, they explained that their father was too old to protect them.

So Musa took buckets and went to the well and brought water for their animals all by himself. The women were so happy that they came back after a while with an invitation for Musa to come and visit their family for dinner.

Later that evening Musa came to the home of Prophet Shu'aib, although Musa didn't know anything about Prophets at that time. The old man welcomed Musa and was very impressed with his good character and manners. He asked Musa to marry one of his daughters and to stay on a while and work for him. Musa agreed and a beautiful wedding took place.

D. A New Prophet is Raised.

About ten years later, Musa decided to take his family and go out on his own. He gathered up his animals and belongings and headed out into the wilderness. After several days of traveling, he made camp in the shade of a mountain called **Tur**. As he watched the sun set, he noticed a light flickering way up on the mountain.

He told his family to wait there while he went to see what it was. When he climbed up into the mountain, he found a fire burning hotly on a desert bush. He came closer to it but then a voice called to him saying, "*Musa! I am Allah! The Lord of the Universe!*" (28:30)

Allah then told Musa that He was making him a Prophet and that he had to go on a mission. He had to return to Egypt and preach to the Pharaoh and also to rescue the Bani Isra'il.

Musa was afraid but when the light of Allah's revelation comes upon a person, everything makes sense and they instantly know what the real truth of life is. The new Prophet, Musa, asked if his brother could help him, and Allah declared that Harun would be a Prophet, too.

Musa made sure his family was safe and then began the long journey back to Egypt. He found his brother, Harun, in the slave village and told him what had happened.

Harun explained that the Bani Isra'il were still all there and that life was even harder for them. So Prophet Musa secretly began to teach the Bani Isra'il about Allah, because most of them didn't know anything about Him or about living a good way of life. He told them to trust him and that Allah would save them.

E. The Showdown.

When it was time, Prophets Musa and Harun decided to go to the palace of Pharaoh. They told Pharaoh to believe in Allah and to give up his evil ways. Musa held up his hand and it glowed brightly. This was a sign given to Musa by Allah to help him convince the Egyptians. The Pharaoh was surprised to see Musa and told him that he would never give up his idols or power.

Musa then commanded the Pharaoh to let the Bani Isra'il leave Egypt with him. Pharaoh, who must have been amused, said that he would never let them leave. Over the course of the next several weeks, Musa and Pharaoh were locked in a battle of the soul. Musa would bring Allah's revelations and signs to Pharaoh while Pharaoh would just laugh.

In one contest, Pharaoh had his wizards turn a bunch of sticks into squirming snakes. Musa threw his staff on the ground and it became a giant snake that ate all the little ones up! All the wizards saw that and were so amazed that they begged to become followers of Prophet Musa. But still, Pharaoh didn't believe.

Then Prophet Musa called upon the punishments that only Allah can bring and a lot of disasters fell upon Egypt. There were floods, plagues, polluted waters, bug attacks and many other things. Finally, after the last disaster, Pharaoh agreed to let the Bani Isra'il go.

But when Prophet Musa was leading the thousands of Bani Isra'il away from Egypt and towards northern Arabia, the Pharaoh went back on his word and called out his army to go after the escaping people. Allah saved the Bani Isra'il by making a way for them across a large body of water called the Red Sea. When the Pharaoh and his army tried to cross the sea also, Allah caused the water to drown them.

Musa led the Bani Isra'il to freedom. He succeeded in his first mission. Now that the people were safe, Musa tried his best to teach them about goodness and moral living, but in those early years all the Bani Isra'il did was grumble and complain. They gave Prophet Musa so many problems and even started to make false idols to worship.

During this time, Allah revealed a message to Prophet Musa called the **Taurah**. It was to be the book of guidance for the Bani Isra'il. It had all the teachings they would need to purify their hearts and live their lives in a moral and good way. But the Bani Isra'il disobeyed those teachings in the same way they disobeyed Prophet Musa. As a punishment, Allah ordered that they wander in the deserts of Northern Arabia for forty years.

Because of their bad ways, Allah gave them many extra rules and laws to follow as a punishment. But after Prophet Musa passed away, they continued their disobedience against Allah and even disobeyed the teachings of the Taurah. (16:118)

Even though Allah sent many Prophets to correct them, the Bani Isra'il almost always did what they wanted to instead. They even killed some of Allah's Prophets if they didn't like them. They lost the Taurah and wrote a different book to replace it, saying it was from Allah, but it wasn't. They were truly wrong-doers.

In time, they changed the name they called themselves to the word, "Jews," or "Yahudi," and taught that Allah loved only them. They went far out of bounds and failed to become a good example to other people around them.

But Allah wasn't going to let them wander totally away without sending them one last chance. This is because Allah is merciful to all people as much as possible. A Messenger was going to be sent to them with so many big miracles that they could never deny them. But as we shall see, the biggest miracles of all are sometimes rejected by people the most.

Questions to Answer

1. How did the Bani Isra'il get into Egypt?
2. Why was Musa put into a basket?
3. Why did Musa have to run away from Egypt?
4. What happened to Musa in Madyan?
5. How was Musa able to lead his people to freedom?
6. Why did Allah begin to punish the Bani Isra'il?

21 The Mission of Prophet 'Esa

Think About It

What kind of child does every parent want?

Vocabulary Words

Zakariyya   Miracle

What to Learn

Prophet 'Esa was a true Messenger of Allah but people changed his teachers after he left the world.

A. One Last Chance.

About two thousand years ago Allah decided to raise up one last Prophet to call the Jews back to the true way of life. If you will remember, He had already given them the great Prophet Musa, but they disobeyed him. Allah also gave them the Taurah, but they lost it and made up another one. Finally, Allah sent them a lot of other Prophets to keep calling them back towards Islam (surrender to Him) but they fought against most of them as well.

To make matters worse, the Jews even invented a new religion, Judaism, in which they taught that Allah was only for them. They made so many rules that were not from Allah such as not being able to eat milk and meat together or not being allowed to break meat-bones at dinner. The Jews even made it forbidden for their own women to touch any religious books or scrolls, saying that women were too dirty! That wasn't fair! Allah was going to give them only one last chance to enter the right path.

B. The Special Girl.

In the land of Palestine, there were many Jews, Arabs, Syrians and Greeks all living together. The masters of the land, however, were people named the Romans. They controlled a mighty empire that stretched from Europe and North Africa into the Middle East.

In a small village in Palestine lived a young girl named Maryam. She was being raised by a Prophet named **Zakariyya**, because her own father had died. Prophet Zakariyya taught her the real truth about Allah and she was a very good student. She was so pure and obedient that even Prophet Zakariyya wished for a child as good as her.

One day Allah sent a feeling to her heart that she had to go away from her village and learn more about truth and goodness. When Maryam felt the message she obeyed it instantly and left her family and headed eastwards. She found a place to stay in a far away village and began her prayers and studies right away. Some time later Allah sent an Angel to her to give her some fantastic news.

The Angel appeared in front of her, looking like a perfect man. He told her that Allah had chosen her and was going to give her the gift of a holy son. Maryam was afraid at first, but the Angel made her feel better by saying that Allah chose her above all the women of the world for this special mission.

Maryam asked how she could have a child when she was not married and the Angel told her that Allah can do whatever He wants. He would just put the baby in there. "*When Allah decides something,*" *the Angel said,* "*He only has to say, 'Be' and it is.*" (3:47)

Then the Angel explained that the child would be named 'Esa (Jesus) and that he would grow up to be a Messenger from Allah. He would get a book called the Injeel and would have the mission of calling the Jews back to Allah once and for all.

Maryam was so happy and a few days later she noticed she was pregnant. After a few months she went out into the wilderness to await the birth of the baby. But it was hard to have a baby all alone and there was no one there to comfort her. She felt a lot of pain and cried out when the baby started kicking. She threw herself at the foot of a tree and didn't know what to do. She cried in despair.

Allah comforted her by making a little stream of water come out from the ground near her, and by letting fresh dates fall from the tree into her lap. A voice from out of no where said kind words to her and she began to feel better. When the baby was born, she wrapped it up in cloth and went back home to her own village with it. Baby 'Esa was born with no father. That was the first miracle in a long line of miracles for this special Prophet and Messenger. A **miracle** is a special thing that happens to show people Allah's power.

C. The Mission Begins.

When Maryam returned home, her relatives accused her of doing bad things and said she was not a good girl. When Maryam started to cry, Allah gave the baby the next miracle. The baby started to talk! It told everyone that he was a new Prophet and that he had a mission to bring the truth back to the Jews.

Everyone was amazed so they left Maryam alone and no one bothered her again. She raised her son in the best way and taught him to be kind to all people. He loved his mother and never disobeyed her.

When 'Esa became a young man, Allah sent him the revelation that it was time to start his mission. Prophet 'Esa began going around the land of Palestine, calling the Jews back to Allah. He taught that them that their ancestors were wrong for making too many rules and that their hearts had become dead. Only by obeying him and following his message from Allah, called the Injeel, could the Jews ever hope to return to Allah's way.

The mighty Roman empire controlled most of Europe, North Africa and the Middle East.

So many people came to listen to Prophet 'Esa, or to argue with him, that he asked Allah to make the job easier on him. Allah told him to find helpers who would travel with him and be his friends. Prophet 'Esa gathered many helpers and they moved from village to village teaching people how to live a good and moral life filled with Taqwa and Sabr. A lot of people believed in Prophet 'Esa's message but they were mostly the poor people.

When they heard about this man named 'Esa, some of the Jewish leaders began to get very angry. They were powerful because all the Jews had to follow them in religious matters. If people gave up Judaism and went back to pure spiritual teachings, then the leaders would have no more power. They had many secret meetings and made a plan to get rid of Prophet 'Esa.

Meanwhile, Prophet 'Esa brought his message to so many places and he performed many miracles. He healed the sick, cured the blind and helped feed many people, all with Allah's help. He even was able to have a dinner table full of food appear in front of his helpers when they asked to see another miracle.

But the plan of the Jewish leaders was about to be sprung on Prophet 'Esa. The Jews asked their Roman masters to arrest 'Esa and torture him. They told the Romans that 'Esa was trying to make the Jews rebel against them, but that was a lie, of course. The Romans captured him and beat him so badly that his face was all red and bloody. They tried to make him admit to being an enemy of Rome so they could kill him.

But Prophet 'Esa just kept telling them he was sent by Allah to call the Jews back towards goodness and true belief. When the Romans told the Jewish leaders that they had no problem with 'Esa, they told more lies until the Romans finally agreed to kill him. But another miracle from Allah happened. When the soldiers were taking Prophet 'Esa to the place of execution, confusion came over the men and Prophet 'Esa disappeared.

He was gone! But where did he go? Amazingly, Allah instantly transported 'Esa away from there and took Him to a hidden place in the Akhirah. Allah wasn't going to let them kill His great Messenger.

The Roman soldiers then grabbed someone else from the crowd that looked like 'Esa and continued on to do their evil deed. No one knows for sure. But Prophet 'Esa was not killed and he was not nailed to a wooden stake called a cross. He did not die. But the Jews thought they killed him and to this day the Jews and Christians say he died. But the truth is that Allah saved him for a special plan to come later.

D. The New False Religion.

The Jews thought they had killed Prophet 'Esa and went around celebrating. So what did the helpers of Prophet 'Esa do next? They wanted to continue the teachings of their beloved friend so they went around trying to spread his message even more. They gained some more followers among the Jews but not many.

Some groups even started teaching that Prophet 'Esa was Allah, Himself. What is that crime called? It's called Shirk!

The Christians who were promoting shirk were the most successful in spreading their ideas so most non-Jews who came in the new religion eventually became worshippers of 'Esa, and not Allah. Although Prophet 'Esa never told people to worship him. On the Day of Judgment, Prophet 'Esa will reject all those Christians who worshipped him. Imagine the looks on their faces when that happens!

About three hundred years after Prophet 'Esa was gone, the Christians made a holy book for themselves that they called the Bible. In it they put a lot of writings that different people made up and they even included the false books that the Jews had written long before. Even though it was not anywhere near being the true words of Allah, many Christians began believing it was.

As the years passed, the Christians argued with each other about what the teachings of their religion were and they eventually broke up into many different groups. Those groups have fought so many terrible wars with each other over the last thousand years and done so many horrible things in the name of their religion that every Christian country in the world has made it a law that the teachings of Christianity have to be separate from the government.

The message and the teachings of Prophet 'Esa became lost forever just a few years after he was gone from the world. But Allah wasn't finished yet and He would send one last, great Messenger with a book and a mission that would be for everyone in the whole wide world.

Finally, some of the followers of Prophet 'Esa started preaching to the Greek and Roman people in their land. Many of them came to believe in the new message and declared themselves to be followers of 'Esa, also. A Roman idol-worshipper started calling these new people, Christians, and so the followers of Prophet 'Esa had a name of their own.

But because Prophet 'Esa's revelation, the Injeel, was never written down, many people started making up their own teachings. After a few years, there were many different groups of Christians who had different beliefs and holy books from each other.

Questions to Answer

1. Describe three things that were wrong with the Jewish religion.
2. Why did Prophet Zakariyya have to take care of Maryam?
3. What did the Angel announce to Maryam?
4. How did 'Esa defend his mother while he was still a baby?
5. How did the leaders of the Jews react to Prophet 'Esa?
6. Why have Christians broken up into so many different groups?

22 The Birth of Muhammad

Think About It

Why is life so hard for an orphan?

Vocabulary Words

Monastery

What to Learn

The Prophet had very humble beginnings.

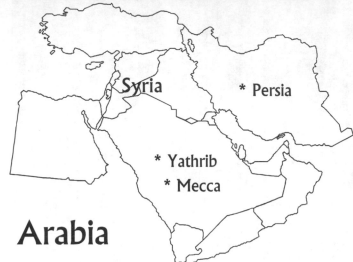

Arabia

A. Water and Abdel Muttalib.

Mecca was an important town in the land of Arabia because of the Ka'bah. The Ka'bah was where all the desert tribes kept their idols and statues that they worshipped. Every year many pilgrims and merchants would come to worship their gods and spend their money.

Abdel Muttalib was a wealthy merchant in this city in about the year 560 CE (60 BH). He was in charge of bringing water for all the visiting people every day. He and all his sons worked very hard to do it. What made it even harder was that the nearest wells were far outside the city. His family was tired from all the work and they wished it would get easier.

Then one day Abdel Muttalib discovered the lost well of Zam Zam. He knew it existed because of all the legends and stories about it, but it had been lost in a sandstorm or something many generations before and no one had been able to find it again.

Now, with the water so close, all he had to do was relax and count his money. Mecca and all the thousands of people who came to visit every year would have all the water they needed.

He was so happy that he decided to get his youngest son, Abdullah, married as a way to celebrate. He searched Mecca to find a beautiful wife for his son and finally chose a woman by the name of Ameenah.

Abdullah was twenty when he married her and the young couple lived together happily for a while. Soon it became Abdullah's turn to go on a business trip to Syria. Imagine his wife waving to him as he set off in the early morning with a caravan of horses and loaded camels. She must have been very sad. But what was on her mind more was that she was expecting a baby.

A few weeks later, when he was returning from his trip, Abdullah and his friends stopped over in a city called Yathrib to rest. But there he became sick and he soon passed away. When the news reached Ameenah in far away Mecca, she cried and wept for days. Abdullah's father, Abdel Muttalib, tried to make her feel better by telling her that maybe her baby would be like a young Abdullah to them. She vowed to never marry again.

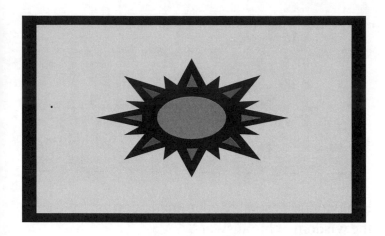

One night while sleeping, Ameenah had a dream in which she was told to name her expected child, "*Muhammad*," which meant Highly Praised. Although it was a strange name among the Arabs, nevertheless, when the baby was born in about the year 571 CE, Muhammad he was named.

Ameenah and Abdel Muttalib were happy at the birth. The baby Muhammad was such a beautiful child. Even though Ameenah was a widow and had no one to support her, Abdel Muttalib told her not to worry and that he would take care of her.

B. The Two Women Who Needed Each Other.

After a few months, nurse-maids from the countryside came to Mecca to find children to take care of for money. It was a custom in those days for city mothers to send their young children to be raised by country women, who would teach them to be strong and rugged.

None of the country women went to Ameenah's house because they thought she was too poor to pay. At the same time, one country mother named Halima didn't get anyone willing to let her take a baby because she seemed small and weak.

Abdel Muttalib brought the two women together. Ameenah was happy her child would experience country living and Halima was happy she would not go back empty handed. For as long as Muhammad stayed in the tent of Halima good fortune smiled upon her family.

The baby Muhammad stayed with Halima's tribe, the Banu Sa'd, for five years with only a few visits to his mother in Mecca. When he was finally returned to the care of Ameenah, she saw how strong and well-mannered her son was and felt happy inside.

The years apart had been hard but now they were together again. As it happened, however, only a few months later, while returning from a trip to visit relatives in Yathrib, Ameenah fell sick and passed away.

Muhammad's grandfather took charge of the young boy, who was now an orphan, and promised to care for him. But the sadness of losing both his parents was going to have a lasting effect on the boy who would one day grow to be a father himself.

C. Muhammad as a Child.

Muhammad was an orphan, that means he didn't have a father or mother. In Arabian society he would have been considered a worthless child without a family. But Muhammad's grandfather loved the boy dearly out of the memory of his beloved son, Abdullah.

But Abdel Muttalib was very old and had few days left to him. When he was weak and near his death, he made his son, Abu Talib, promise to care for the young Muhammad. And so, when his grandfather passed away, Muhammad went to live with his uncle. Muhammad, who was around ten years old, lost someone close to him again.

Abu Talib kept his promise and let Muhammad into his home. He soon became impressed with the boy's manners and good character. Whenever it was dinner-time, a large spread of food would be placed on a sheet on the floor and everyone would sit around it and eat.

All the other children used to jump up and down and grab at the food, because this was how children behaved at that time. But as Abu Talib's maid reported, Muhammad used to sit still and take whatever food was given to him. He had good manners and spoke clearly and nicely.

When Muhammad was about twelve years old, Abu Talib was planning to make a business trip to Syria. In those days, merchants would load camels and horses with goods and travel from city to city to

buy, sell and trade in the markets. The journey from Mecca to Syria was almost always a good way to make a lot of money.

Abu Talib at first didn't think about taking the young boy, Muhammad, along with him. It would be a hard journey and there would be no time to deal with a child. But after Muhammad asked repeatedly Abu Talib gave in and agreed to let him come along on the condition that Muhammad's job would be to take care of the animals.

The caravan set out a few weeks later and began the long journey northward to Syria. After a few weeks of hard traveling, the group of about twenty camels and men arrived in a town called Basra. There they decided to rest and make some business deals.

Just outside of town was a Christian **monastery,** or religious house, where there lived a priest by the name of Bahira. That morning, Bahira had watched the caravan pulling into town and he was startled to see that a cloud seemed to follow over them, shielding them from the sun.

He had read in one of his religious books that clouds only make shade over a Prophet, so he felt sure someone special was in that caravan. He sent an invitation to the tired men to visit the monastery for dinner and asked that everyone should come.

When all the merchants arrived, the priest asked if all of their group was present. They answered that everyone was there except for a boy who was left behind to watch the animals. Bahira requested that he be invited as well and so someone went to fetch the young Muhammad.

After he arrived and joined the dinner party, Bahira watched the boy carefully and noted his behavior. He asked Muhammad questions and saw the wisdom of his answers.

After a little while, Bahira took Abu Talib aside and said, "*This (boy) is the last Prophet.*"

When Abu Talib asked him how he knew this, the monk replied, "*The signs of the last Prophet are written in our books, and the clouds only cast shade over a Prophet. When you were approaching, I saw a cloud shadowing your caravan, and I had no doubt that the last Prophet foretold in our holy books was with you. For this reason I invited you, in order that I might meet him.*"

A few minutes later, Bahira asked and was told about Muhammad's sad family history which further convinced him of Muhammad's special status. Then he asked for the boy to come near him and lift his shirt up. The monk found a birthmark on his back, just between the shoulders.

Bahira looked at the spot, which was about the size of a small egg, and declared, "*Now I am certain that this is the last Prophet for whom the Jews and Christians await...*" He then told Abu Talib to take special care of him and to keep him safe.

Abu Talib quickly finished his business in Syria and returned home with his caravan. After this, Abu Talib kept a closer eye on his nephew.

Questions to Answer

1. Why was Abdel Muttalib happy that he rediscovered the lost well of Zam Zam?
2. Who did Abdullah marry?
3. Why did the baby Muhammad have to go and live with his uncle, Abu Talib, after only a few years of life?
4. What happened with Bahira?
5. Describe how you think events in Muhammad's early childhood must have affected him?

The Early Years

23

Think About It

What would you do if a real Angel from Heaven came and spoke to you?

Vocabulary Words

As Sadiq   **Al Ameen**   **Hira**

What to Learn

Allah chose one last Prophet to the world. His name was Muhammad.

A. Muhammad's Early Manhood.

By the time Muhammad grew into a young man in his early twenties, everyone in town had come to like him because of his good manners. People started calling him the most truthful and honest person around. He could be trusted in whatever he said. He never told lies. He was often called **As Sadiq**, or the Truthful One.

Other young men his age used to spend their time dancing, drinking wine and doing bad things. Muhammad never joined in these kinds of activities. Instead, he spent his time working for his uncle in the pastures outside Mecca.

Abu Talib was not a rich man, so he needed all the extra help he could get. For many years Muhammad was a shepherd watching his uncle's sheep.

Muhammad never liked idol-worship and never bowed to any statues. When he was a boy at the Banu Sa'd, he lived the Bedouin lifestyle which had little time for fancy idols. So from his earliest age he never developed the taste for believing in gods of wood or stone.

His years as a shepherd taught him that the world was a wide and beautiful place which could never be created by an idol. Imagine how many nights Muhammad must have looked out over the endless horizon and watched as the sun set, filling the sky with reds and purples. Muhammad knew idols were not real.

In his spare time, Muhammad tried his hand at trade and business. He would take some extra goods that his uncle gave him and enter the marketplace to make deals. He was always fair and honest in his dealings with others and always displayed good manners. Soon people gave him another nickname: **Al Ameen**, the trustworthy.

His honesty was soon to pay off in a big way, because, as we will see, regardless of how a person succeeds in their business dealings, if one is kind, fair and well-mannered, this is more valuable than any amount of gold or silver.

B. Who was Khadijah?

Abu Talib heard that a lady by the name of Khadijah was looking to hire someone to take a caravan of merchandise to Syria. Khadijah was a wealthy widow who came from a very good family. She was married twice before to rich men who had died, each one leaving her all their money.

Many of the leading citizens of Mecca had asked for her hand in marriage but she refused them all, thinking that they didn't want her as much as her money. Thus she decided to spend her time in the trading business and was very successful.

Abu Talib, who was always interested in ways to help his nephew, went to Khadijah's house and told her that he knew of a good person who would make a fine leader for her next caravan.

Khadijah, who had heard of the honest young man before, agreed to put Muhammad in charge of her next caravan. And so, when the caravan was ready, Muhammad guided it out of Mecca in the direction of Syria.

Khadijah sent her servant, Maysara, along to secretly watch how Muhammad conducted himself. While in Syria, Muhammad made many very good bargains and deals. He was always honest and generous to those he worked with. Then he made ready to return to Mecca with huge profits and valuable trade goods.

Maysara came to love and respect Muhammad for his fairness, kindness and good manners. When the caravan was only a few hours from Mecca, Maysara suggested that Muhammad ride ahead and be the first to tell Khadijah all about the successful trip.

Muhammad agreed and arrived on horseback in front of Khadijah's house at about noon. She saw him arrive and came down from her balcony to meet him. She listened carefully as Muhammad told her all the details of the trip. He was soft-spoken and gentle in his speech and Khadijah was happy with his dealings. After he finished, Muhammad returned home to his uncle's house.

Maysara arrived with the caravan a short time later and told Khadijah all that he saw. He talked about Muhammad's honesty, humility and good morals. Maysara finished by saying, "*Among all the young men of Mecca that I know well, there is no one comparable to Muhammad.*"

After a few days, Khadijah began to have feelings of love for Muhammad. She was almost forty years old and had refused to marry any of the nobles of Mecca. Now she wanted to marry a man much younger than herself, whose words and style had captured her heart.

Khadijah spoke to her close friend, Nafisa, about her thoughts. Nafisa told her not to worry and that she, herself, would take care of the matter. The next day she went to Abu Talib's house and asked to see Muhammad. After talking to him for a little while, he agreed that he would like to marry Khadijah.

The marriage was not delayed. Within three months of his return from Syria, Muhammad and Khadijah were married.

C. The Light of Revelation.

Fifteen years of happy marriage passed with Khadijah. The couple had four daughters: Zaynab, Ruqayyah, Umm Kulthum and Fatimah and one son, but the baby boy, who was named Qasim, passed away as an infant. Another much later son, Abdullah, would also not survive.

As he grew older, Muhammad began to feel restless. He had been an orphan, had known loss and was well aware of the lack of fairness that his society had towards the less fortunate. Many poor people in Arabia were robbed, cheated or made to suffer for no reason. There were no real laws and a weak person was always in danger of being bullied by the strong.

Muhammad was a man who believed in goodness and he had a searching heart. Ever since he was a young boy he had disliked the worship of idols. Perhaps his time as a shepherd reinforced his opinion that the Creator was not a piece of wood kept in a house.

The Arabs knew that Allah, the Supreme Ruler of the Universe, existed. But they thought Allah was far away and didn't pay much attention to people. They believed that you had to have a mini-god of your own to help you out. So, the Arabs made gods out of sticks, stones, bones and other things. They kept their biggest idols inside the Ka'bah. Muhammad knew these ideas were foolish and ignorant.

One day while he was walking around town, Muhammad saw some really sad poor people and he felt so sorry for them. Nobody was helping them.

When he came home, Khadijah asked him why he seemed so sad. When he told her what he saw, he also added that he wished he could have helped them, but he didn't have much money on his own.

Khadijah thought of a way to heal his noble heart and called the leaders of Mecca together and declared to everyone that she was giving total control over all her wealth to her husband, Muhammad.

After this, Muhammad was able to help the poor whenever he wished, though he never abused or wasted the wealth Khadijah gave him. But something was still missing in his heart. Something still felt empty inside.

After a while, Muhammad began remembering the peace he experienced in the open fields, tending his uncle's sheep when he was young. He was now forty years old, though, and couldn't really be a shepherd again, so he looked around for some place where he could be alone and think about the meaning of life.

He had heard of a small cave high in a mountain outside the city named the Cave of **Hira** and thought immediately to go there. He found it suited his purpose and made a regular habit of hiking up the mountain to spend long hours pondering over why he was alive and what life was about.

Then, in the year 610 CE, during one of his extended stays on the mountain, an hour came where his thinking and meditating became more urgent than he ever remembered. A new energy entered his mind and a strange feeling came to his heart.

Although the cave was dim and cold, heat and warmth seemed to fill the space around him. Suddenly, without warning, a blazing light filled the cave and dazzled his eyes. Out of nowhere and everywhere a voice called to him, "READ."

Muhammad was quite startled. All he could think of saying was, "*I can't read*," for it was true, he didn't know how to read or write. Then he felt a pressure squeezing on his chest until he thought his lungs were going to be crushed.

Again the voice commanded, "READ." Muhammad cried out, "*But I can't read*." The squeezing happened again and Muhammad thought for sure he was going to faint. The voice boomed out louder, "READ."

In order to save himself from more pain, Muhammad cried out, "*What should I read?*" This time there was no painful squeezing. No pressure on his lungs.

The voice merely continued, "*Read in the Name of your Lord Who created humans from something that clings. Read, because your Lord is Most Generous. He taught humans by the pen things they didn't know before.*" (96:1-5)

Muhammad repeated those words and then all was still. The light was gone and everything was quiet. He didn't know what happened to him. He became scared. He rushed from the cave and stumbled down the dark trail that led back to town.

Suddenly, he heard that voice again, coming from above; from the skies, from all around! He looked up and saw a vision of a perfect man, filling the space between the earth and the sky. He was saying, "*Muhammad, you are the Messenger of Allah and I am Jibra'il.*"

A moment later, the vision disappeared and Muhammad ran straight home to his wife. He burst through the door and cried out. "*Cover me!*" he begged her. She felt him shiver and held him long into the night. Her heart ached for him and she didn't know what to do.

D. The First Believer.

Muhammad thought about what had happened to him. But there were no more messages, no more strange experiences, so he thought that perhaps it was all a dream or something. Then, after several months went by, out of nowhere, Muhammad saw the same Angel he had seen before.

He was as high as the sky and seated on a floating chair. Muhammad became frightened again and rushed home to his wife. He begged her to cover him up and he fell asleep after some time. A few hours later Khadijah noticed that Muhammad was trembling.

When he woke up he spoke the words which the Angel Jibra'il planted into his dreams.

"*You who are wrapped up! Arise and warn! Glorify your Lord and keep your clothes pure! Avoid the idols. Don't give (in charity) with the expectation of receiving anything back. For your Lord's sake be patient.*" (74:1-7)

Khadijah was worried and asked Muhammad to rest a little longer. But he replied, "*Khadijah, the time for resting is over. Jibra'il has asked me to warn people and call them to Allah and to His service. But who shall I call? Who will listen to me?*"

Khadijah thought for a moment and then smiled. She told her husband that she was the first to accept the invitation. She would accept the call of Allah. Thus, Khadijah became the first person to accept Islam.

Soon thereafter a new revelation came to the Prophet Muhammad commanding him as follows:

"*You, covered in a cloak, stand in prayer at night, but not all of it. Half of it or a little less or more. Read the Qur'an in a slow voice. We will soon send you a heavy Message. Indeed the rising by night is the most powerful for controlling (the soul), and the best for forming words (of praise). Indeed you are busy in the day with ordinary duties. But remember the name of your Lord and devote yourself to Him completely. He is the Lord of the East and the West. There is no god but Him. Choose Him as the One to take care of your affairs.*" (73:1-9)

Questions to Answer

1. Why did Muhammad earn two good nick-names and what were they?
2. How did Muhammad get a job working for a lady?
3. Who was Nafisa and what did she do?
4. List all of the children that Muhammad and Khadija had?
5. How did Muhammad find out he was going to be the last Prophet to the world?

Think About It

If you hear about something that is true, should you fight against it for no good reason? Explain.

Vocabulary Words

'Ali

What to Learn

Islam grew slowly at first.

A. Who Were the First Believers?

Angel Jibra'il came several more times to the Blessed Prophet in the coming months. He taught him how to make the Salat and wudu and then he taught him the most important Surah of the Qur'an, *Al Fatiha*. (1:1-7)

Zayd ibn Harith, who was the adopted son of Muhammad, also accepted the call of Islam and became a Muslim. He knew Muhammad well and was certain of the truth of what he declared.

One day, while Muhammad and his wife were both bowing in prayer, Muhammad's nephew, **'Ali**, who was a boy of about nine or ten, happened to walk in the room. He was surprised at what they were doing and stood and watched until they finished.

Then he asked his uncle, "*Who were you bowing to?*"

The Blessed Prophet answered, "*We were bowing to Allah Who has made me a Prophet and Who commanded me to call people to Him.*" Then the Prophet invited 'Ali to join him in the new way of life and to give up the idols.

He also recited some of the verses of the Qur'an to him and 'Ali was so overwhelmed with the beauty he heard that he was stunned. He asked to have time to ask his father's permission to accept the new teachings and rushed home.

'Ali spent the night in bed, tossing and turning, but he never spoke to his dad. Instead, he ran back to Khadijah and Muhammad in the morning and declared, "*Allah made me without asking my father, Abu Talib. So why should I ask my father now to serve Allah?*"

Next, Muhammad approached his good friend, Abu Bakr, who was a local businessman, with the teachings of Islam. Abu Bakr had known Muhammad for years and trusted him completely. He accepted Islam gladly

So the first Muslims were Khadijah, Zayd, 'Ali and Abu Bakr. For the next three years Muhammad preached to his close friends and relatives privately. His daughters accepted Islam as well as many of his friends and their friends.

The time was not right to go public, however, that is why Muhammad worked on gathering a small base of true believers. For now the Prophet would devote his time to teaching the new Muslims the basic teachings of the faith: mercy, justice, brotherhood, truth, peace and patience.

B. An Invitation to All.

After about three years, Muhammad had gained around thirty or so converts to Islam. They would meet in the home of a man named Arqam. There were both male and females, young and old, rich and poor among the believers. The idol-worshippers began to hear about Muhammad and his new ideas, but they at first thought it was some new fad that would eventually die out.

One day the Blessed Prophet received the revelation which said, *"Declare what you have been ordered and turn away from the idol-worshippers."* (15:94) This would mark the next level in the growth of Islam.

The Blessed Prophet first arranged a large dinner and invited all his relatives whom he had not yet approached about Islam. After the food was finished he stood up and declared the message of Islam and asked the people to accept it.

None of the elders were responding favorably and then they decided to leave. But 'Ali stood up and declared that he would follow Muhammad and help him in the cause. Imagine the courage of the young boy to declare publicly that he was a Muslim! The people just laughed, however, and went home. They began to insult the Prophet and his followers in the streets after that.

Not to be denied his right to call people to the truth, the Blessed Prophet tried a new strategy. He climbed to the top of a hill called As Safa and shouted for everyone to come close. The people in the streets nearby and in the marketplace saw him and came out of curiosity.

When they were gathered, the Blessed Prophet called out, *"People of Quraysh! If I were to tell you that I see an army ready to attack you on the other side of the hill, would you believe me?"*

The people started to feel a little edgy and replied that they would because Muhammad was always honest. Then the Prophet announced, *"So know- all of you- that I am a Warner and that I'm warning you of a severe punishment!"* Then he called on the people to declare that there was no god but Allah.

Abu Lahab, one of Muhammad's uncles, became red with anger and shouted, *"Did you gather us here for this?"* Then Abu Lahab made a horrible insult by saying, *"May you perish!"*

Muhammad was shocked but then Allah revealed the following message to him, *"The hands of Abu Lahab will perish! He will perish. Neither his wealth nor possessions will save him, for he will be surrounded by a fierce blaze. And his contemptuous wife, (whose slander) made (tempers) rise, shall join him, shackled in fibrous chains."* (111:1-5)

The reference to his wife was reflecting the fact that she was gossiping and telling people not to believe in Muhammad's message. She slandered him and incited people to anger against him. She also used to throw garbage on his doorstep.

C. The Attacks Begin.

After the Blessed Prophet and the believers started to preach Islam openly among the people, the leaders of the idol-worshippers became very hostile. Some of them sincerely believed in the power of the idols, others were afraid of angering the surrounding tribes who kept their idols in Mecca and still others thought that if the idols were abandoned that business would suffer in the city.

Abu Bakr had built a small Masjid in his yard and used to go there and pray and recite the Qur'an out loud. Many curious women and children would gather and listen to the magical words for hours. The Quraish Arabs then forbade their family members from going around Abu Bakr's house.

Soon the leaders of Mecca began to look on the Muslims as a threat that must be stopped. Families were told to bully their relatives who became Muslims and Muhammad, himself, was sometimes hit with rocks and things as he walked in the streets by the angry idol-worshippers. He was always insulted whenever he went to pray near the Ka'bah.

The idol-worshipping Arabs accused him of being a person who talks to evil spirits. Other people said he was possessed by a jinn while others said he was crazy. No one could explain why a man who never recited anything prior to this nor who knew any poetry was now giving messages which were unlike anything they ever heard before.

Prophet Muhammad was teaching that people were equal, regardless of color, that women had equal rights with men, that the powerful must respect the rights of the weak, that there will be an afterlife of either pleasure or punishment based on our deeds in the world and that idols were inventions of man's own hands. For these teachings the people ridiculed and harassed the Prophet.

Abu Talib once went to Muhammad and explained how the other Meccan leaders wanted to give him money or anything else if he would only stop preaching his message. Muhammad merely replied, *"My uncle, by Allah, if they put the sun in my right hand and the moon in my left, and asked me to give up my mission, I would not do it until either Allah made me victorious or I died (in the struggle)."*

Abu Talib was satisfied and told Muhammad to preach whatever he wanted to. Many other Muslims also were receiving poor treatment and sometimes worse. Those Muslims who had strong family connections usually only suffered teasing, insults and sometimes fist-fights.

But the Muslims who had few or no family connections were beaten, kidnapped and tortured or even killed. A slave of African heritage named Bilal ibn Rab'ah accepted Islam and when his master found out, he beat Bilal mercilessly and tied him down in the hot desert sand, under the bright sun. Then he had huge stones rolled over his chest and beat him until he would give up his new faith.

Sometimes, Bilal's master would dress him up on a suit of hot metal and make him lie in the desert sun until he passed out. Other times, crowds of young men would drag Bilal through the streets beating him. But Bilal never broke and endured the suffering.

When Abu Bakr found out what was going on, he rushed to the cruel man and offered to buy Bilal from him. He reluctantly agreed and Abu Bakr took Bilal to safety and freed him from slavery.

Another Muslim, a lady named Sumayah, was arrested by the Meccan leaders and tortured so badly by Abu Jahl that she died. Other Muslims also lost their lives at the hands of angry mobs.

One woman became so enraged when she found out her slave, Khabbab ibn al Aratt, had become a Muslim, that she used to beat him and put hot coals on his head! (Later on she became sick and the idol-worshipping doctor she went to told her she had to have her head burned with a hot poker to be cured!)

When a man named 'Umar found out his maid-servant had become a Muslim, he used to beat her so much that his arm got tired. But the maid-servant never left Islam and later on the man became a Muslim himself and freed her!

This period of persecution and torture of the believers went on for some time. Once, when Muhammad was praying in the courtyard of the Ka'bah, some idol-worshippers, led by the evil Abu Jahl, came and threw garbage on him.

Fatimah, Muhammad's beloved daughter, was nearby and when she saw it she came running to her father crying and cursing the idol-worshippers who stood nearby.

She removed the garbage from her father's back and sat and wept. The Prophet prayed to Allah to punish the idol-worshippers saying, "Allah, destroy the Quraysh." But he never fought back or threw garbage on them. By this he showed Fatimah the great patience he had. The time for self-defense had not arrived yet. (23:93-118)

Questions to Answer

1. How did 'Ali become a Muslim?
2. What happened at the big dinner the Prophet organized?
3. Why was Surah 111 revealed?
4. What did the angry idol-worshippers start to do to the Muslim converts?
5. Who was Sumayah?

Unit 6
Review Exercises

Vocabulary Review

On a separate piece of paper, write the meaning of each word below. Remember to write in complete sentences.

1. 'Ali
2. Judaism
3. Zakariyya
4. Tur
5. Zam Zam
6. Taurah

7. 'Esa
8. Banu Sa'd
9. Bani Isra'il
10. Madyan
11. Maryam
12. Zayd ibn Harith

Remembering What You Read

On a separate piece of paper, answer the questions below. Remember to answer as best as you can and write in complete sentences.

1. Why did the Pharaoh want to kill male babies?
2. What miracles did Prophet Musa show the Pharaoh?
3. Where did the name, "Jews" come from?
4. Describe some of the good qualities of Maryam.
5. Why did the Jews think that Prophet 'Esa was a threat to them?
6. Why did the city Arabs like to send their young children to the countryside?
7. Describe Muhammad's manners as a child.
8. How did Khadijah find out that Muhammad was a good worker?
9. Describe two ways in which the Prophet tried to call the idol-worshippers to Islam.

Thinking to Learn

Read the following statement and explain whether it is true or false. Write in complete sentences on a separate piece of paper and give examples to support your answer.

Muhammad had an easy life as a child.

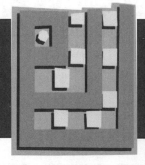

Unit 7

The Great Tests

25 The Meccans Take Action

Think About It

Why would a person be against the teaching of a belief different from their own?

Vocabulary Words

Bayya'

What to Learn

Muslims were victims of persecution and torture.

A. The Bribe.

'Utbah ibn Rabi'ah, who was one of the leaders of the Quraysh tribe, thought of a clever way to end the troubles that were happening in the city. For although the Muslims were being put to severe tests, still many people were joining Islam, especially among the young men and women of the city.

'Utbah went to the Prophet one day and gave him this offer, *"If you want money, we will gather our riches together so you will be the wealthiest man among us. If you want status, we will make you our leader, so that no one can decide anything without your consent. If you want power we will make you our king. Finally, if you are unable to cure yourself of the visions that you have been having, we will pay for all the medical services possible until your health is perfect again."*

But the Blessed Prophet Muhammad refused these tempting offers and instead recited Surah 41 of the Holy Qur'an to him. 'Utbah listened to the fascinating words and returned to the other Quraysh leaders in a state of wonder.

He told them that they should leave Muhammad alone because if he succeeds in his mission then all the Arabs would benefit. The idol-worshippers were not happy at all with 'Utbah's words and resolved to make life even more difficult for the Muslims.

B. The Attacks Grow.

The poets of Mecca were unleashed against the Muslims in a new war of words. They would tease Muhammad in the streets and ask why Allah wasn't giving him news of the market prices or why Allah didn't show Himself to the people. (11:12-14)

Allah revealed the following Ayat in answer to their cruel words, *"If We sent to you, (Muhammad,) a (message) written on paper that they could touch with their hands, the unbelievers would be sure to say, 'This is obviously only magic.' Then they say, 'Why isn't an angel sent down to him?'*

"If We sent an angel, then the matter would be settled at once and they would have no chance. If We were going to send an angel, We would send him (disguised) like a man and We would have made them confused about an issue they're already confused about. The Messengers before you, (Muhammad,) were mocked, but their insulters were trapped by what they mocked." (6:7-9)

It was Muhammad's habit to go out and greet arriving caravans and invite the people towards Islam. The Quraysh leaders arranged for people to go out as well and shout that Muhammad was a crazy man and that no one should listen to him. (25:7-9)

Allah revealed these Ayat to comfort him in his trials: *"The Unbelievers say, 'Don't listen to this Qur'an, but talk loudly when it's being read so you can gain the upper hand.'*

"But We will give the unbelievers the taste of a severe penalty and pay them back for the worst of their deeds." (41:26-27)

The Muslims received an unexpected gift in the form of one of Muhammad's uncles, Hamza, the lion-hunter. He used to spend long periods of time in the open desert and was known for his strength and bravery.

One day Abu Jahl, the bad-tempered idol-worshipper, was following Muhammad around in the streets insulting him and Islam. Hamza, who had just arrived in town from a hunt, heard about what was happening and went straight to the Ka'bah without greeting anyone.

When he saw Abu Jahl yelling at Muhammad, he hit him hard with his bow. Abu Jahl backed down and left the scene. Then Hamza declared his acceptance of Islam and took the oath of allegiance, or **Bayya'** to Muhammad. The Muslims felt happy while the idol-worshippers nearby were shocked.

The Blessed Prophet felt encouraged to teach further in public. He spoke out against idol-worship and called people to serve Allah, alone. On one occassion he told his followers that Allah has forbidden people to disobey their mothers, to keep what is not theirs, to take what is not theirs, to bury their daughters alive and to gossip or talk bad about others. (Bukhari)

People saw the wisdom in these teachings and as Islamic ideas spread the idol-worshippers felt more threatened. They would soon be forced to take action.

C. The First Escape!

The idol-worshippers intensified their persecution of the Muslims. More people were arrested and tortured. Abu Sufyan, the leader of the council of Mecca, thought of ways to stamp out Islam forever.

But the Prophet Muhammad knew he had to do something to protect those Muslims who had weak family connections. He hated to see his fellow believers suffering and was himself powerless to do anything about it. (6:33-36)

Then one day the Prophet received the instructions from Allah that he should send the weakest Muslims away from Mecca to a country across the Red Sea, in Africa, named Abyssinia. The king of that nation was a Christian named Najjashi who was known as a fair and wise ruler. If the weak Muslims remained in Mecca, they would be killed one by one. They had to escape.

Accordingly, the Muslims made secret plans to send out small groups to the coast where they could buy passage on a ship to Africa. The first group of Muslims, eleven men and four women, left the city by night and journeyed to Abyssinia.

There they lived in peace for a time. Then they received the false news that the idol-worshippers were no longer persecuting the Muslims, so they hurriedly returned to Mecca. Of course the persecution had not stopped and people were being beaten and harmed as much as before, so this time, the Prophet organized an even larger group of over eighty men and numerous women and children to escape to safety.

They set out secretly for Abyssinia and were gone even before the idol-worshippers knew what was happening! When they found out a few days later that their favorite- and easiest- targets were gone, they were filled with rage. They would bring them back by any means necessary!

D. The Debate in Abyssinia.

The Meccan leaders had some trade agreements with the king of Abyssinia and thought that they could use that to their advantage. They sent two of their best speakers, 'Amr ibn Al As and Abdullah ibn Abu Rabi'ah, to meet with the king, Najjashi.

After they arrived, about a week later, in Abyssinia, the pair gained an audience with the king.

They explained to him that there were people from Mecca in his country who left the religion of their people, but who were not Christians either. They asked the king's permission to seize them and return them to Arabia.

The king decided to hear the case of these people who left their fore-father's religion, as he was curious to know their side of the story. He thus ordered the leaders of the Muslims to his court for a hearing.

When they arrived, the king asked the head of the Muslim group, Ja'far ibn Abi Talib, *"What is the religion which you profess? What is this religion which has caused so much disunity among your people?"*

Ja'far stepped forward and declared, *"O King! We were in a state of ignorance and immorality. We worshipped stones and idols, ate dead animals, committed all sorts of injustices, broke family ties and treated our neighbors badly. The strong among us would exploit the weak as well.*

"Then Allah sent us a Prophet, one of our own people, whose family history, truthfulness, trustworthiness and honesty were well known to us. He called us to serve one God alone and to reject the stones and idols which we and our fathers used to worship.

"He commanded us to speak the truth, to honor our promises, to help our relatives, to be

The meeting hall of the king.

good to our neighbors, to stop killing and to not do fornication. He commanded us to stop lying and not to take the property of orphans or to falsely accuse a married woman of bad deeds. He ordered us not to associate anyone with Allah.

"He commanded us to establish prayer, to fast and to spend in charity. We believed in him and what he brought to us from Allah and we follow him in what he asks us to do and in what he tells us not to do.

"So our own people have attacked us, treated us badly and tried to take us back to the old bad ways and worship of idols. They made life unbearable for us in Mecca, so we have come to your country to seek safety and to live in justice and peace."

After hearing this beautiful speech, the king was inclined to the side of the Muslims. Then he asked to hear some of the verses of the Qur'an. Ja'far, like the wise Da'i, or caller to Islam, that he was, chose his Ayat wisely.

He recited the verses from Surah 19 which talked about Maryam and the birth of Prophet 'Esa. (19:16-33) After finishing, the king turned to the ambassadors from Mecca and told them he would never give the Muslims up to the Meccans.

The next day 'Amr ibn Al As returned for another meeting in which he tried a different approach. He told the king that Muslims deny that 'Esa (Jesus) was the son of God and that he was a Prophet only to them.

The king had Ja'far brought to him again and asked him about this and he replied that Islam teaches that 'Esa was Allah's Prophet, a spirit and command from Him and that he was born of a virgin named Maryam.

The king drew a line on the floor with his staff and declared that the difference between Christianity and Islam was no thicker than that line. The two Meccans returned to Arabia empty-handed.

Questions to Answer

1. What offer did 'Utbah make to the Prophet and how was it answered?
2. How did the Meccans try to keep the growth of Islam down?
3. Who was Hamza and what did he do?
4. How did the Muslims convince the Najjashi of Abyssinia that Islam was better than the Arab idol-worshipping religion?
5. Why did the Blessed Prophet send Muslims to Abyssinia in the first place?

Testing the Believers

26

Think About It

Why do you think the Meccans were so cruel and determined in their fight against the peaceful Muslims?

Vocabulary Words

Boycott   Ta'if   Yathrib

What to Learn

Islam found a new home where no one would fight against it.

A. The Boycott and Year of Sorrow.

Another boost to the morale of the Muslims was in the conversion of 'Umar ibn al Khattab. He was a strong and influential man in Mecca and was known for his standing among the people. When he came to Islam it had a good effect on the community.

Soon the Meccan leaders decided on a new strategy to punish the Muslims. They agreed to form a total **boycott**, or avoidance, against the clans of Banu Hashim and Banu Muttalib, from which many Muslims came. The idol-worshippers wrote on a piece of paper that no Arab tribe should have any dealings with these two clans nor should they sell them any food.

They hung this paper in the Ka'bah, which was the custom for official announcements and then sent armed men to force all the boycotted people out of town and into a small valley outside Mecca called the Shi'bi Abi Talib.

The Muslims spent three years in that desolate valley and suffered tremendous hardships. Revelations from Allah came to strengthen the hearts of the people and a food-sharing system was worked out so that everyone got a fair share.

But food supplies were always low and the few smuggled goods sent in by people who felt sorry for the Muslims were never enough. Visiting Arab tribes from the countryside, who came in during the pilgrimage months to Mecca, often complained to the Meccan leaders about their cruelty and advised that the horrible boycott should be lifted.

One day a group of the leaders were arguing about it and Abu Jahl declared that the boycott was a sacred law and could not be abandoned. But others around him wanted the pact removed. When they went to the Ka'bah to check on the paper, they found that the ink had been eaten by ants! Their "sacred law" was an empty sheet of paper!

The boycott was lifted and the clans of Banu Hashim and Banu Muttalib were allowed to return to their homes. Prophet Muhammad immediately resumed preaching Islam to the Quraysh and the Muslims worked to regain their strength.

But tragedy was soon to follow this positive turn of events. Muhammad's uncle, Abu Talib, who provided some measure of protection for him, passed away from old age. But even more tragic was the death of his beloved wife, Khadijah.

She had been his wife for nearly twenty-five years. She was the mother of his children and his support and source of strength. She was the first to accept Islam and the first to comfort him when Prophethood was bestowed upon him.

What helped Muhammad through these tough times was the fact that he had dealt with horrible loss before in his life. He lost his father, mother and grandfather in years past. But his grief was great and he called this year, *the Year of Sorrow.*

B. The Mission Continues.

The Blessed Prophet continued his mission, but now without any help or support from any powerful tribal leader. More of the Qur'an was being revealed all the time to give further shape to the teachings of Islam and people were still embracing Islam in a steady stream.

A note of joy later occurred when the Prophet was engaged to the daughter of Abu Bakr, A'ishah. The marriage would wait another three years until she was well into her teens, however, and in the meantime the companions asked the Prophet to marry a widowed Muslim woman named Sauda, which he did, as she had no family support. The Muslims remained united and supported and comforted each other..

After realizing that they couldn't break the spirit of the Muslims, the idol-worshippers began to show more boldness. It was bad enough that many of the Muslims had suffered beatings, insults and even death for their beliefs, but now the idol-worshippers were starting to make life unbearable for even those who had strong family allies.

The Prophet, who barely escaped being strangled to death one afternoon while praying near the Ka'bah, knew that a place of safety for the Muslims had to be found otherwise the Meccans were liable to resort to wholesale murder.

The Blessed Prophet, accompanied by his adopted son, Zayd, traveled to the hill-top city of **Ta'if,** which was to the southwest of Mecca. There they met with some of the leaders of the city and asked them to consider accepting Islam. The leaders refused and ordered Muhammad and Zayd to leave. Then the leaders of the Thaqif tribe unleashed their unruly children upon the pair by inciting them to throw stones at them.

The Prophet and Zayd ran out of town under a shower of rocks and stones. Just outside the city they found a small enclosed garden where they rested. The owner of the garden felt sorry for Muhammad and sent him a gift of some grapes while a shepherd boy brought them some water.

The Angel Jibra'il came to the Prophet and said he would destroy the entire city if he wanted him to. The Prophet declined the offer explaining that he was sent as a guide and a mercy to people. (21:107) Then the Prophet prayed to Allah and returned home from what he termed as *"the most difficult day of my life."*

C. A Light From the North.

The situation was getting worse for the Prophet. The idol-worshippers began attacking him personally and directing much of their anger at him. Once while he was walking, one of the Meccans threw dirt on his head and insulted him.

When the Prophet returned home, his daughter, Fatimah, saw him and began crying as she cleaned her father's hair and clothes. The Prophet consoled her saying, "*Don't cry, Fatimah. Your father has Allah for a protector.*"

Fatimah's two older sisters, Ruqayyah and Umm Kulthum, were now living at home again because their husbands were made to divorce them by the command of Abu Lahab, their father. Fatimah's third sister, Zaynab, had a slightly better husband who resisted the pressure to divorce his wife as an insult to the family of the Prophet.

For the next several months, the Blessed Prophet traveled from tribe to tribe outside of Mecca and offered the teachings of Islam to them. But although he made a few converts here and there, the tribes didn't commit to anything.

One evening, Muhammad found out about a small group of people who were visiting from **Yathrib**, a city to the north of Mecca. When he found out where there camp was he waited until nightfall and slipped out of the city in their direction.

When he reached their camp a few moments later, he approached the small group and began explaining the beliefs of Islam to them. The six people, who were all from the Khazraj tribe, embraced Islam joyfully. They felt it was right and were open-minded enough to listen.

When this group returned to Yathrib, they spread the news about Islam and made people curious about it. Yathrib was a mixed city with Jews, idol-worshipping Arabs and a few Christians, so the people were already exposed to many different religious ideas. Although most of the people were idol-worshippers, they were used to having new thoughts expressed.

D. The First Pledge of 'Aqaba.

The following year, twelve people from Yathrib came to Mecca for the pilgrimage season. But they weren't there to worship the idols. They were there to see Muhammad.

In a secret location called 'Aqaba, the twelve people embraced Islam and promised to obey the following six rules: that they would not make partners with Allah, not commit adultery, not steal, not kill their female children, not bring false charges and that they would obey the Messenger of Allah, Muhammad, in all that is good.

After the group made this promise, Muhammad told them, "*Whoever fulfills the pledge will be rewarded by entering Paradise after their death. Whoever neglects any part of it must be prepared to face Allah. He may forgive the person or He may not.*"

The Prophet sent one of his trusted companions, Mus'ab ibn Umair, to Yathrib with the group so he could teach them Islam and give the call to others in the city. As you will see, Mus'ab was very successful.

E. The Second Pledge of 'Aqaba.

The Prophet and the Muslims in Mecca weathered the insults and suffering inflicted upon them by the Meccans for yet another year. Then, in the thirteenth year of his Prophethood, a second, much larger group came from Yathrib to Mecca, representing both tribes of the city, the Auws and the Khazraj.

This time there were seventy-one men and two women to see the Blessed Prophet! Meeting at the same, secret location, 'Aqaba, this large group declared that they were Muslims and they even asked the Prophet to come with them back to Yathrib!

Just before the new Muslims took the oath of service to the Prophet, Abbas, the Prophet's uncle, told them, "*You people of the Auws and Khazraj! As you know, Muhammad has respect and status here due to his lineage. As you can see, his family and friends have protected him from the idol-worshippers who wish to destroy him. He is one of the most respected among his people. He refuses to join anyone but you.*

"*If you think you can carry out what you have promised in calling him to your city, and if you can defend him against his enemies, then the burden of proof rests in your hands. But if you are going to surrender him and abandon him after you have taken him with you, then you had better leave him here.*"

All the new Muslims promised to defend the Prophet with their lives. This second oath is known as the Second Pledge of 'Aqaba. The people then returned to Yathrib with the instructions to be ready to act if necessary.

Questions to Answer

1. What did the boycott mean for the Muslims?
2. Why did the Prophet declare one year his "Year of Sorrow?"
3. How did the people of Ta'if react to the teachings of Islam?
4. What happened at a place called 'Aqaba?
5. What did the people of Yathrib agree to do?

27   The Great Migration

Think About It

How do you think the idol-worshippers will react once they find out that the Muslims have a safe place to go?

Vocabulary Words

Hijrah   Medinat un Nabi

What to Learn

Islam became a nation in Medina.

A. The Muslims Migrate.

Although the meeting at 'Aqaba was held in secret, it didn't take long for the Meccan leaders to find out about it. They were angered that Islam was spreading despite all their best efforts to stamp it out. They decided to increase their persecution of the Muslims.

Although many of the less protected Muslims were still safe in Abyssinia, there were people accepting Islam all the time, so many new targets opened up for the idol-worshippers.

The Blessed Prophet held a secret meeting in which he ordered his followers to prepare to leave Mecca for Yathrib. The plan was for people to leave in small groups, by night, so the Meccans would suspect nothing.

Soon Muslims were sneaking out of Mecca every night and heading towards safety in Yathrib where they were welcomed with open arms by the Muslim community there. Islam was spreading rapidly and there were now hundreds of Muslims in that city.

After almost all the Muslims had escaped, only Muhammad, Abu Bakr, 'Ali and a few others remained. When the Meccans figured out what was happening they were filled with rage! They became fearful that Muhammad might be able to raise an army in Yathrib to attack them.

The Meccan leaders held a special meeting to discuss the situation. One of them proposed killing Muhammad and ending Islam once and for all. The others cheered and the plan was made that every family would contribute one of their warriors so they could all kill Muhammad together. That way the family of Banu Hashim couldn't take revenge for his death.

As the Meccans were hatching their evil plot, Muhammad received permission from Allah to emigrate. He asked Abu Bakr to have two camels ready for their escape. Later in the day, when Muhammad found out about the plot against his life, he hurried to Abu Bakr's house and told him the time had come to move. They would leave that night.

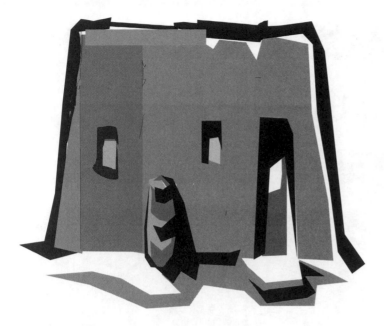

Muhammad returned to his house and asked 'Ali to return some money which was entrusted to him to its owners and then to go to Yathrib as well. When nightfall came, Muhammad, Abu Bakr and a Bedouin guide they hired, crept out of the city heading south, in the opposite direction of Yathrib.

'Ali returned the money to whoever it belonged to and then returned to the Prophet's house. He knew about the plot against his life so 'Ali made a brave decision. He made it look like someone was home in Muhammad's house and then lay on Muhammad's bed, covered by sheets and the green robe the Blessed Prophet owned.

The hours passed and all was quiet. It was almost midnight when the group of young men entered the house secretly. The blades of their spears and swords glinted in the moonlight. They all knew there would be no one to protect Muhammad now, and each one was eager to be the first to strike.

They filed into Muhammad's bedroom and circled around his bed. One of them wanted to see just how surprised Muhammad would be when he saw them, the moment before his death. He pulled away the covers and suddenly, all the men gasped in disbelief! There was 'Ali, lying in the Prophet's bed.

It would have been of no use to kill him and they didn't have the permission of their elders to do so anyway, so they stormed out of the house in disgust and sounded the alarm by shouting in the streets. Muhammad had escaped them! This was the **Hijrah**, or flight to Medina.

B. The Cave of Thawr.

When the Meccans were alerted to Muhammad's daring escape from death, they were enraged and gathered together in a confused mob, shouting and cursing. The men who were supposed to kill Muhammad the night before went out into the countryside in the hopes of catching him yet.

Muhammad and Abu Bakr were guided to a small cave south of the city called the Cave of Thawr. Not many people knew about it, but Abu Bakr's trusty guide, Abdullah ibn Urayqit, did. He left the pair there and took the camels away for hiding.

Only Abu Bakr's two daughters, A'ishah and Asma', and his son, Abdullah ibn Abi Bakr, and a servant named Amir knew about the men in the hide-out. During the day Abdullah would gather news of the Quraysh and in the evening he and his sister, Asma', would bring food to the cave.

Amir would graze a flock of sheep near the cave to cover up any tracks. Muhammad and Abu Bakr spent three long days in the cave, hiding from the Meccans who were scouring the countryside, hoping to claim the rich reward. The Prophet spent much of his time praying to Allah for deliverance

One afternoon a group of Quraysh warriors came upon the cave and asked a shepherd boy nearby if he had seen anything. The shepherd replied that he had not but that they might try looking in the cave.

When he heard the shepherd's answer from his hiding spot, Abu Bakr trembled and expected to be found. He retreated into a dark corner and remained motionless. Some of the Quraysh men climbed up the hillside to the cave entrance but then came right back down the hill.

Their fellow warriors asked them why they didn't enter the cave and the men replied that their was an unbroken spider's web and a pigeon's nest in the entrance. No one could be in there without breaking the web and causing the pigeons to flee.

Abu Bakr whispered to his friend, "*If anyone of them looked near his feet he would find us.*"

The Prophet replied, "*Abu Bakr, how can you fear for two men when Allah is the third with them?*"

The Meccans decided to head in another direction and left. Abu Bakr exclaimed, "*Alhumdulillah. Allahu Akbar.*" "*Praise be to Allah, Allah is the Greatest.*"

C. The Journey to Yathrib.

After the third day had passed with no success, the Meccans began to tire of the search. When Abdullah informed his father and the Prophet, they decided to continue their journey. Abu Bakr's servant brought three fresh camels to the cave and Asma' came along with some bags of supplies.

There were no ropes for them to tie the bags together so Asma', thinking quickly, ripped the extra cloth of her robe and twisted that into a temporary rope.

The guide led them further south and then looped around towards the west through unknown tracks heading northward again in the direction of Yathrib. He had to because now the Meccan leaders made a public announcement that whoever captured Muhammad would receive the reward of 100 camels. Every man with a sword jumped at the opportunity and went out in search of their prey.

A Meccan warrior by the name of Suraqa heard reports about three people being seen in the hills. He told everyone that the sighting was of someone he knew so they should forget about it.

But Suraqa told a lie, suspecting that the three were the fugitives whose capture would bring the reward. So he secretly set out a little while later in full battle gear heading in the direction of the reported sighting.

Sure enough, after several hours hard riding, he came within sight of the Prophet and his group. Suraqa urged his horse faster, but it stumbled and fell, throwing him on his head. When he regained his mount and charged forward again, the horse stumbled once more, throwing him on his head.

When he managed to get back into his saddle, he let loose a battle cry and charged headlong at the three. But his horse stumbled a third time, throwing him on his head. Suraqa began to feel that there was an otherworldly force preventing him from charging so he asked permission to approach Muhammad.

Suraqa introduced himself and promised that he would not tell anyone that he had found them. When Suraqa returned to Mecca he kept his word and said he didn't find Muhammad anywhere.

D. The Arrival in Quba.

The Muslims in Yathrib were eagerly awaiting the news of Muhammad's arrival. They heard the reports from Mecca about the unsuccessful plot to kill him, and of the chase and the reward for his capture. The Prophet was their teacher, friend and brother. If anything happened to him they would be heart-broken. A watch was kept and everyone waited in anticipation.

A few days later, under the harsh summer sun, Abu Bakr, the guide and the Prophet Muhammad arrived at a small town named Quba, just a few miles from Yathrib. The people of Quba were overjoyed at the arrival of the Prophet and came out cheering and waving.

A group of girls came singing a welcome song, *"We are the girls of Banu Najar, Oh what a wonderful neighbor is holy Muhammad."* The Prophet stayed in the town and rested for four days. They built the first public Masjid of Islam there.

During their stay, 'Ali came walking in from the desert. He returned the money to the owners, as the Prophet directed him, and came on foot, all the way from Mecca. The trip took two weeks. His feet were bruised and bleeding and the Prophet helped take care of him, himself.

E. The Joyful Entry Into Yathrib.

After his rest in Quba, the Prophet was ready to enter the city of Yathrib. The people there were also eager to welcome him. It was a divided city that had known much war. The two largest groups, the Auws and the Khazraj tribes, had fought many wars in the past and were tired of fighting each other.

The Jews of the city, who were divided into three clans and lived just outside of the city, often competed with the idol-worshippers for power and status in local politics and the few foreigners, Persians, Christians and others, looked on with worry at the disunity and instability of the city's people. Everyone saw in Muhammad a way out of that trouble. (2:151)

The day the Prophet arrived into the city was a day of celebration. Everyone came out and lined the streets to see the man they had heard so much about. The Muslims, both from Yathrib and the recent Meccan immigrants, thanked Allah and came to greet their trusted friend and guide.

As the Prophet's camel made its way through the crowds, the girls of Yathrib, not to be outdone by the girls of Quba, came out with a song of their own, *"The moon has risen over us at last. From behind the valley of Wadaa.. We must be thankful to the Lord every time we call upon Allah."*

From that day onward, the city was renamed, **Medinat un Nabi,** the City of the Prophet. It's now called Medina, for short.

When he entered the city, everyone wanted the Prophet to stay in his house as their honored guest. People started to argue and beg the Prophet to stay with them. The Blessed Prophet, whose wisdom in similar circumstances was displayed so long ago in the dispute about the Black Stone, announced that he would let his camel loose, and where ever it sat, that was where he would stay.

Everyone agreed with that wise solution and the camel stood up and started walking. After a few minutes, it sat down on a vacant lot owned by two orphans. The orphans came running and said they wanted to donate that land for the Prophet, but the Prophet, seeing that the pair were poor, refused and insisted on paying for the land with a fair price.

After the land was bought, the community joined hands to build the Masjid of the Prophet. While the construction was going on, the Prophet stayed in the house of Abu Ayyoub al Ansari, because the camel had hesitated by his door before moving on to the empty lot.

Houses and other buildings were made of mud bricks with wooden roofs in those days.

Questions to Answer

1. Why did the idol-worshippers want to kill the Blessed Prophet?
2. Why didn't the idol-worshippers look in the Cave of Thawr?
3. Who fed the Blessed Prophet and Abu Bakr while they hid in the cave?
4. How was the Blessed Prophet greeted in Quba?
5. How was the Blessed Prophet greeted in Yathrib?
6. How did the Prophet solve the problem of whose house to live in?

Angel Jibra'il Comes For a Visit

One day the Blessed Prophet Muhammad was sitting with a group of his companions when he said to them, "Ask me about anything."

The companions were very humble and they felt too shy to ask him any questions. Then a man appeared in the distance. He was walking along the road towards the seated people. As he got closer, everyone noticed that his clothes were white. Even though he must have just come in from the sandy countryside, there was no dirt on him at all. His hair was completely pitch black.

The mysterious man approached the gathering without saying a word. He walked right up to the Prophet and sat down in front of him, knee to knee. Everyone was amazed but they said nothing, wanting to see what would happen next.

"Messenger of Allah," the strange man said. "What is Iman?"

The Prophet answered, "It is declaring your faith in Allah, His Angels, His Books, the Meeting with Him (on Judgment Day), His Messengers, life after death and that you believe in Determination completely."

"You have said the truth," the man answered.

All the companions were surprised that this man seemed to be quizzing the Prophet as if he knew more than Allah's Messenger! They kept silent.

The man again said to the Prophet, "Messenger of Allah, what is Islam?"

The Prophet replied, "(Islam) means that you don't make any partners with Allah, that you establish Salat, pay the Zakat and fast during the month of Ramadan."

"You have said the truth. Now, Messenger of Allah, what is Ihsan (goodness)?"

"It is that you fear Allah as if you were seeing Him, because even though you don't see Him, indeed He sees you."

"You have said the truth. When will the last hour come (of the end of the world)?"

The Prophet looked at the strange man and said, "The one who is being asked doesn't know more than the one asking the question. I will give some of its signs, though. When you see a maid giving birth to her master, that is one of the signs of the end. When you see barefoot, naked and ignorant people in charge of the world, that is one of the signs of doom. And when you see shepherds of dark-colored camels excited about building tall buildings, that is one of the signs of the end. The (knowledge of the last day) is one of the five things that are unseen. No one knows them except Allah."

Then the Blessed Prophet recited this ayah from the Qur'an: "Indeed with Allah alone is the knowledge of the hour and He sends down rain and knows what is in the womb and no person knows what he will earn tomorrow and no person knows in what land he will die. Indeed Allah is the Knowing and Aware." (31:34)

Then, to the wonder of all those gathered there, the man stood up, turned around and walked back down the road from where he had come.

The Prophet said, "Bring him back to me."

Several of the companions got up quickly and went to look for him, but he seemed to have vanished. The man was gone and no one could find him! When everyone came back and said the man had just disappeared, as if into thin air, the Blessed Prophet told them, "That was Jibra'il and he came to teach you your way of life when you didn't ask (me)."

(Composite from Bukhari & Muslim)

Part A. Exercises.

Answer the following questions in complete answers. Use a separate piece of paper.

1. Why do you think Allah sent the Angel Jibra'il to the gathering?
2. What things did the Prophet list when he was asked about Iman?
3. What five things did the Prophet say when he was asked about Islam?
4. According to the Blessed Prophet, what is the definition of Ihsan?
5. What are two of the signs of the Last Day?
6. Which part of the conversation do you think was the most important?

Life in Medina

28

Think About It

How can a person bring many different groups together in unity if they are used to fighting and mistrusting each other?

Vocabulary Words

Muhajireen   Ansar

What to Learn

The Blessed Prophet was an excellent city leader.

A. What was the Prophet's Masjid Like?

The construction of the Masjid took about seven months. It was a simple structure made of mud bricks, wooden poles and a roof made of palm leaves. It was large enough to hold a good-sized crowd and the Prophet's house was built in a separate building next door through which a doorway opened up into the main Masjid area.

The Muslims of Medina were made up of two groups: those who escaped Mecca, who were called **Muhajireen**, or Immigrants, and the native Muslims of the city, which were called **Ansar**, or Helpers.

The Muhajireen were poor, given that they escaped with barely more than themselves. So one day, the Blessed Prophet gathered the Muslims together and announced that the two parties would be joined together in brotherhood. Every Ansar would adopt a Muhajir and share half his possessions with him or her.

The Ansar happily responded to the call and soon every poor Muslim from Mecca was given the means to earn a living. This built the bond of brotherhood strongly in the hearts of the people and helped to ease the suffering of the poor.

Because housing was still in short supply, there was an area of the Masjid reserved for the poorest Muslims. They could sleep there at night and rest for as long as they needed.

The Masjid was lighted at night by burning torches made of bundled straw. It was the special place where the community gathered to pray, talk, rest and meet.

B. The Prophet Takes Charge.

Everyone agreed that the Prophet was going to be the new leader in the city. It was clear to all that they couldn't get along on their own so right from the beginning the Blessed Prophet represented the highest authority in the city.

Because the Muslim community was growing and more and more people were accepting Islam, it became easier and easier for the Muslims to organize and feel at ease. Here Islam had found its home.

One of the first things the Prophet did upon entering the city was to make a treaty of peace and friendship between the Muslims and the Jewish tribes. The Jews had welcomed the arrival of the Prophet like everyone else and they had hopes he would join their religion.

The treaty spelled out the rights and responsibilities of both sides and was agreed to by both sides. The Prophet also made a treaty with the Christians of Najran, which was a land in north-central Arabia.

All of these treaties were made to show people that Islam is a faith of toleration. The truth of Allah is clear to anyone who has eyes to see. If a person is not yet ready to listen to their heart and accept Islam, you can't force them to be a Muslim.

Allah declares in the Qur'an, *"There is no forcing someone into this way of life. Truth stands clear from error. If anyone rejects evil ways and believes in Allah, then they have grabbed the strongest handhold that never breaks. Allah hears and knows all things. Allah is the Protector of those who have faith. From the depths of darkness He will lead them forth into light..."* (2:256-257)

Thus we see demonstrated one of the fundamental teachings of Islam: people have rights, whether they are Muslim or not, and as long as they are not fighting you, you must respect those rights.

C. The Adhan is Called for the First Time.

When the Masjid was being completed, everyone helped in its construction, even the Blessed Prophet who was over fifty years old. But soon the issue came up of how to call the people to Salat.

Some people suggested the use of a horn like the Jews used. Others thought a bell like the Christian churches in Palestine used would be good. In the end, the Prophet wasn't satisfied.

Then Allah sent a dream to one of the companions of the Prophet, Abdullah ibn Zayd. In it, he saw a man in green robes who recited some beautiful verses to him.

When he went to the Prophet and told him what he dreamt, the Prophet declared that the dream was a true one from Allah. (Islam teaches that some dreams come true and are given by Allah.)

So the Prophet asked him to teach the words to Bilal, for he had a beautiful and loud voice. Then, when the time came for the next Salat, Bilal stood up

on one of the walls of the Masjid and called out in a loud and clear voice: *"Allahu Akbar! Allahu Akbar! Allahu Akbar! Allahu Akbar! Ashahadu an la ilaha ill Allah. Ashahadu an la ilaha ill Allah. Ashahadu anna Muhammadar Rasul Allah. Ashahadu anna Muhammadar Rasul Allah. Hayya alas Salah. Hayya alas Salah. Hayya alal Falah. Hayya alal Falah. Allahu Akbar! Allahu Akbar! La ilaha ill Allah!"*

Everyone came running from all quarters of Medina to the Masjid to find out what was going on. 'Umar ibn al Khattab rushed to the Prophet and announced that he heard the exact same words in a dream the night before.

From then on, the Adhan, or call to prayer, has been the way Muslims call each other to Salat. Not an artificial tool such as a horn, bell or drum, but the melodious and pure human voice. For indeed, Islam was made by Allah for humans, not made by humans for each other's convenience.

D. The Community Grows.

The Muslims were beginning to enjoy a measure of stable community life in Medina. Islamic social and political teachings were growing and being implemented with wonderful results. By the second year of the Hijrah, the duty of Zakat was announced and this helped in further helping the needs of the poor.

Islam and Brotherhood

The Blessed Prophet once said:
"You will not enter Heaven until you believe, and you will not believe until you love each other. Let me guide you to something that will make you love each other: spreading the greetings of peace (Assalamu 'alaykum)."

(Muslim)

"When three people sit together, two should not talk secretely, leaving the third one left out since this will sadden him."

(Bukhari)

At the same time, the believers were being taught how people should behave in their personal lives. Neighbors should be kind to each other, the young should address the old in respect and a man and wife should be honest and faithful to each other.

Drinking alcohol such as wine was made forbidden and collecting interest money on loans was also outlawed. Other laws which were being revealed in the Qur'an covered such topics as respecting orphans, marriage laws and the rights of women.

To get an idea about the kind of brotherhood that was being developed, we need look no further than the example that the Prophet, himself, set.

There was a man who lived in Medina who had a very ugly face. He was so ugly that he was ashamed to be around too many people. One day he was in the market when he saw the Blessed Prophet walking down the street, coming in his direction.

The ugly man felt so ashamed that he started calling out, "Who wants to buy this worthless servant, (Me)!"

The man felt that low about himself.

When the Prophet came near him, the ugly man turned his face away and wouldn't look at the Prophet.

The Blessed Prophet asked him why he was looking away and trying to sell himself.

The man answered, "I'm so ugly and I'm no use to anyone."

The Blessed Prophet lifted up the man's head and smiled at him. "Allah has a use for you."

The grateful man cried tears of thanks and joy because he knew the greatest man he ever met accepted him, no matter what he looked like.

E. The Hostility of the Jews.

Not everything was peaceful in Medina. The three Jewish clans of Qaynuqa, Quraiza and Nadir began to regret having the Prophet Muhammad in the city. At first they thought well of him, but when they realized he was teaching a way of life that was different from theirs, they became angry.

Islam was teaching that the Jews of today were not following the true teachings of the Prophets of old and that the Prophet 'Esa, whom the Jews hated, was a real Prophet sent to them. In addition, some Jews were leaving their religion and becoming Muslims. Even a rabbi by the name of Abdullah ibn Salam accepted Islam along with his whole family.

Why did the Jews begin to hate the message of Islam when it was calling them to Allah and affirming the truth of the old Prophets? The answer lies in pride and arrogance. As much as the idol-worshippers of Mecca didn't want to give up their customs, no matter how ignorant, the Jews, also, didn't want to give up their ways, no matter how far away from real truth they were.

Soon the leaders of the Jews began to meet among themselves and plan ways to stop the growth of Islam. They decided to send people to the Muslim community who would falsely announce their acceptance of Islam. Then, when they gained access to Muslims circles, they were to confuse the Muslims and arouse doubt in people's minds.

The situation became so serious that one day a Jewish man tried to get the Auws and Khazraj Muslims fighting again over issues that were long forgotten. The Prophet rushed to the scene and repeatedly reminded the believers of their new bonds of brotherhood.

Allah revealed many Ayat in this period explaining to the Muslims how rebellious the Jews were against Him and that the Muslims should beware of their tricks.

Questions to Answer

1. How was the Masjid in Medina constructed?
2. How did the Blessed Prophet bring peace to the city?
3. How was the Adhan invented?
4. How did the Blessed Prophet demonstrate that in Islam, our looks don't mean anything, rather our Iman and Taqwa makes us valuable?
5. Why did the Jews of Medina begin to hate the Muslims?

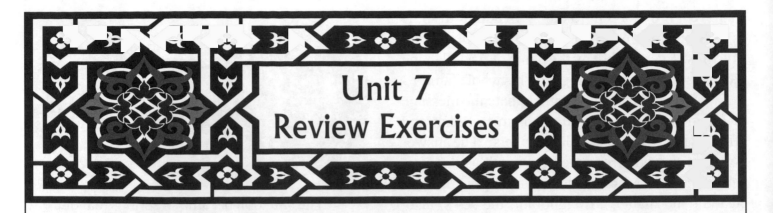

Unit 7
Review Exercises

Vocabulary Review

On a separate piece of paper, write the meaning of each word below. Remember to write in complete sentences.

1. Quba
2. Auws
3. Ihsan
4. Abdullah ibn Salam
5. Adhan
6. Ansar

7. Yathrib
8. Muhajireen
9. Khazraj
10. Thawr
11. Suraqa
12. Medinat un Nabi

Remembering What You Read

On a separate piece of paper, answer the questions below. Remember to answer as best as you can and write in complete sentences.

1. How did the Blessed Prophet respond to the offer of 'Utbah?
2. Describe four things that the Blessed Prophet was teaching that the idol-worshippers didn't like.
3. Who was Ja'far ibn Abi Talib and what did he do?
4. How did the Boycott of the Muslims get lifted?
5. What happened at Ta'if?
6. Why did Abu Lahab make his sons divorce the daughters of the Blessed Muhammad?
7. What happened at each of the Pledges of 'Aqaba?
8. Who was Suraqa and what happened to him?
9. How did the Blessed Prophet begin his rule in Medina? What sorts of things did he do?

Thinking to Learn

Read the following statement and explain whether it is true or false. Write in complete sentences on a separate piece of paper and give examples to support your answer.

Islam teaches that non-Muslims have no rights and must be forced to accept its teachings?

Unit 8

The Final Victory

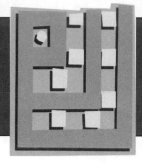

The Battle of Badr

29

Think About It

How can a small group overcome a much larger one?

Vocabulary Words

Ghazwa   Qiblatain   Sahaba

What to Learn

The Muslims won their first great victory at Badr beacause of their true Iman.

A. The Meccans Plot.

The idol-worshippers in Mecca never forgot the Muslims. They would periodically send out small raiding parties to attack the outskirts of Medina. Whenever the Meccans captured any Muslims they would often take them back to Mecca where they would be tortured.

The raiders would set fires to the crops and trees and cause trouble. In the minds of the Meccans nothing had changed and they were out to destroy the Prophet any way they could. After a few months the Prophet organized small groups of Muslims to go on patrol and defend against these attacks. Sometimes they found bands of enemy soldiers and a small battle would happen. These small battles were called **Ghazwas**. There were no major battles between the two sides but that would soon change.

Abu Sufyan, the leader of the merchants of Mecca, was leading a very large caravan of goods from Syria. When the Muslims found out about it from their long-range scouts, the Prophet saw that this might be a way to pay back the Meccans for all the suffering they inflicted on the Muslims.

At the same time, when the Muslims left Mecca during the Hijrah, the property they left behind was seized by the Meccans and stolen. So the Prophet began to organize a group to go and capture the caravan.

Meanwhile, Abu Sufyan, realizing that this was what the Muslims might try to do, sent a message ahead to Mecca asking for an army to be raised to go and fight any Muslims in the area. The Meccans marched out from the city with one thousand fighters, fully equipped and armored.

When the Prophet received the news of the Quraysh army coming, he called a meeting in which he asked the Muslims to support the fight against the idol-worshippers. The Muslims agreed completely and said they would follow Allah's Prophet and be strong in their faith.

Thus, the Prophet mobilized every fighter he could and left Medina with only 313 men. There was only one camel or horse for every three or four men so everyone, the Prophet included, took turns riding.

Thinking that Abu Sufyan would have to stop at an oasis called Badr, about eighty miles from Medina, the Muslims marched there and took up positions around the wells. But Abu Sufyan took the long way around the area and was headed safely to Mecca. (8:7-10)

The Muslim army sent scouts ahead as it marched because they didn't want to be attacked by surprise at any time. One group of scouts spotted a man who looked like a merchant. He was riding a camel at a slow pace and didn't notice the Muslim warriors speeding up on him from behind.

If he was a spy from Mecca then he would have to be stopped in his tracks! The Muslims captured him without a fight and brought him back to the main body of the Muslim army.

The Blessed Prophet came to see him and knew right away that the man was not a threat. But he might have valuable information about the Meccan army, so the Blessed Prophet asked him, "Where are you from?"

The man replied, "I'm from Mecca and am only a merchant."

Then the Blessed Prophet started to ask him a lot of questions about the preparations for war in Mecca and about the size and strength of the Meccan army. The merchant answered all the questions, and when he had finished, the Prophet said he go on his way.

But the man had a question of his own. He asked the Blessed Prophet, "And where are you from?"

If the Prophet said he was from Medina, then the man might figure out that they were Muslims. He might try to run back to Mecca and give away the Muslim position. At the same time, the Blessed Prophet couldn't tell a lie, because Islam taught that lying was totally forbidden. At the same time, the Blessed Prophet himself had always been an honest man, even before he became Allah's last Messenger.

So the wise Prophet gave an answer that was both true and clever. He replied, "We are from water."

His answer was based on an ayah from the Qur'an where Allah said He created all life from water. The man realized he wasn't going to get any more of an answer than this and continued on his way.

Meanwhile, the army of idol-worshippers that marched out of Mecca was in no mood to return to the city without a fight or battle. Even though Abu Sufyan sent a message to them that the caravan was now safe, Abu Jahl urged the army forward to beat the Muslims once and for all.

Accordingly, the army of wild idol-worshippers headed for Badr and sang songs about their brave ancestors and the glory of battle.

B. The Battle of Badr.

The night before the battle, The Prophet prayed to Allah for help against the overwhelming forces he was about to face. He ended his prayer with the words, "*Allah! The idol-worshippers have come with their allies to kill your Messenger. We need Your help, Allah, the help which You promised. If our small group is destroyed, then there will be no one left to serve You.*"

The next morning the Muslims gathered water supplies for themselves and then filled the wells with sand so the idol-worshippers wouldn't gain any benefit from them. (8:11-14)

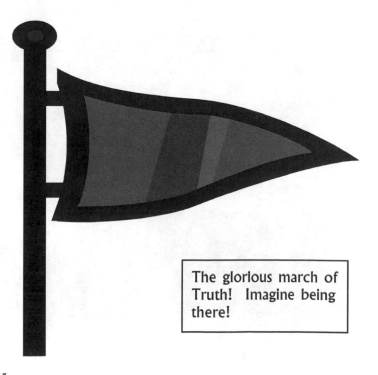

The glorious march of Truth! Imagine being there!

A little while later the Meccans came into sight, all one thousand of them. Many of them had horses and were eager for a fight. As was customary, individual duels were called for by the Quraysh. Hamza, 'Ali and 'Ubaydah ibn al Harith were sent to fight in hand-to-hand combat against three Meccans named Shaybah, Walid and 'Utbah. After a few minutes, and under the eyes of both armies, the three Muslims killed their three opponents.

The enraged idol-worshippers rushed forward in a mad charge and the two armies collided together. It was the seventeenth of Ramadan in the year 624 CE. The Muslims were fasting. (8:42-48)

C. The Fierce Fight.

The fighting erupted all along the battle line. At first the sheer weight of the idol-worshippers threatened to push the Muslims back, but the believers charged into battle without fear at all. They knew that a person who dies fighting in the cause of Allah would be rewarded with Paradise and so bodily injury mattered little. (8:15-19)

Bilal, who was fighting off a group of idol-worshippers, saw his old enemy, Ummaya ibn Khalaf, the same one who used to torture him and roll heavy stones on his chest. Bilal cried a fierce battle cry and charged straight towards him and killed him.

A **Sahaba**, or companion of the Blessed Prophet, by the name of Mu'adth ibn 'Amr engaged Abu Jahl in combat and struck him down and Hamza, 'Ali and the rest of the Muslims plunged right into the middle of the idol-worshippers, not even noticing that they were outnumbered!

The dust rose and the battle raged hotly as the heads of the Quraysh were struck from their bodies one-by-one. The Muslims chanted, "Allah is One! Allah is One!" and pressed forward. Allah sent angels to the battlefield to make the Muslims feel stronger and the idol-worshippers feel weak and scared. (8:9)

The Prophet Muhammad stood in the middle of the battle and was fighting as well. Once when a large group of idol-worshippers were charging towards him, Muhammad took up a handful of dirt and threw it in their faces and commanded the Sahaba around him to stand their ground. (8:24-26)

The Muslims stood firm and beat back the superior force. Finally, after several hours of fighting, the Meccans turned around and began running away. The idol-worshippers were beaten and filled with shame as the survivors walked back to Mecca. (8:30-37)

D. The Aftermath.

The Muslims remained at Badr for the rest of the day. They buried the dead Meccans right there

After marching all day in the hot sun, the Meccans found that the wells of Badr had been covered in sand. They had to fight while dying of thirst!

and collected the captured goods left on the battlefield, for later distribution.

The Muslims returned to Medina victorious and the people rejoiced. The prisoners that the Muslims captured were ransomed, which means that their families back in Mecca paid money to let them be released. Some, who could not afford to pay the ransom fee, were allowed to go free after teaching ten Muslims to read and write.

In the same year, the order came from Allah that Muslims should no longer pray towards Jerusalem, as they had been doing, but instead should pray towards the Ka'bah. The actual Ayat were revealed during Salat and as the verses came to him, the Prophet Muhammad turned from the direction of Jerusalem towards Mecca in the south. The Masjid where they were praying became known as the Masjid **Qiblatain**, or the Masjid of two Qiblahs.

This change signaled to the Muslims that their next great focus was to be towards cleansing Mecca, and the shrine of Ibrahim, of idol-worship. But it wasn't going to come easily, as you will see.

E. The Community Supports Itself.

The victory at the Battle of Badr made the position of the Muslims more secure than ever. Everyday people in Medina were announcing their acceptance of Islam, whether their background was Arab, Christian or Jewish.

In addition, the Prophet sent out groups of teachers to preach Islam to people wherever they went. More treaties were made with friendly tribes and the Muslims themselves were beginning to feel a confidence that they never felt before.

But this didn't mean that they were suddenly going to start living the easy life. They knew what the real purpose of their lives was and therefore didn't devote their time to just getting rich and living the good life.

Everyday there were new Muslims arriving who needed financial support, or food or shelter. Muslims stepped forward and donated generously, often all they had.

Abu Bakr, Uthman ibn Affan and many others led the way in donating for the cause. The Blessed Prophet had special Islamic studies classes for women and after class sometimes he would call upon them to support the Islamic cause and Bilal used to pass around a basket in which the women would donate gold, jewelry and silver. The women were actually at the forefront of encouraging the cause.

Once A'ishah had three dates and a poor woman came to her with her two hungry children. A'ishah gave the three dates to the mother and watched as the woman gave a date to each of her young ones.

The children devoured them quickly but still complained of being hungry. The mother divided her date in half and gave the pieces to her grateful kids.

The Prophet, himself, often didn't have any food in his house. He would give whatever he had away to those who were in need, forgetting even himself. His usual meal consisted of dates, barley and milk. He almost never had meat, bread or other things that were considered a luxury among the Muslims. He was a man who looked into Paradise, however. He knew that the best way to please Allah was in giving to others until it hurts.

Questions to Answer

1. Why do you think the Meccans wanted to fight the Muslims so bad?
2. Describe what happened in the Battle of Badr.
3. Who won the Battle and why?
4. What is the Masjid Qiblatain?
5. How did the Muslims support the cause of Islam financially?

Think About It

Why do you think the desire for revenge is so strong in some people?

Vocabulary Words

Hypocrite   Abbas

What to Learn

Loving this world too much makes a person forget their duty.

A. The Meccans Want Revenge.

The Meccans were filled with bitterness at their loss at Badr. Poets recited verses calling for revenge, Jewish leaders from Medina came to comfort the Meccans and Hind, the daughter of 'Utbah, called for a new attack. Abu Sufyan, her husband, vowed to take revenge. Eleven of his fourteen fellow leaders were killed at Badr while he was stuck in a caravan.

He wanted to show that he was a warrior as well. A few months later, Abu Sufyan secretly led two hundred armed men to Medina where they attacked a small orchard in the middle of the night and killed two people they found there.

When the alarm was raised, the Muslims gave chase but the Meccans were too far ahead to engage. To help their escape the Meccans were dropping their supplies as they galloped, thus the raid was called the campaign of Al Sawiq, or the Flour Campaign, after the bags of flour the enemy dropped.

But this raid had the opposite effect. Because the damage was so light, people started saying the Quraysh were weak and ran away in the night. Soon the Arab tribes which controlled the coastal roads to Syria were won over to the Muslim side and agreed to peace treaties. This loss of their trade routes northward angered the Quraysh even further.

The Meccans resolved to fight the Muslims again and raised money and supplies for months until they were ready. **Abbas**, the uncle of the Prophet, who still lived in Mecca, sent a secret note informing the Prophet of the Meccan's plans. Thus the Prophet began preparations of his own.

In the meantime, the Jewish tribe of Banu Qaynuqa rebelled against the peace treaty they signed with the Muslims and challenged the Muslims to a fight. The Muslims easily defeated the rebels and after the Banu Qaynuqa surrendered, the Blessed Prophet ordered them to pack their bags and leave Medina.

With a few days, all the Banu Qaynuqa tribe left Medina and moved out of Arabia altogether. They settled mostly in Palestine and elsewhere. One internal threat was gone, but the threat of the Meccans grew ever larger.

The Idol worshipping in Mecca soon formed an alliance of several tribes and marched out of the city with an army of three thousand men. Along with them came many Meccan women who wanted to keep their men from running away from the battlefield by making them feel ashamed.

The Prophet marched out of Medina with an army of one thousand warriors and a few Muslim women who would be the doctors and nurses. The two armies met on the far side of Mount Uhud, to the north of Medina.

B. The Battle Begins.

The Prophet began to arrange his men in defensive positions on the hill side when he noticed something strange. The men who were under the command of Ibn Ubayy didn't look like any Muslims he knew. When he asked, the Prophet found out that they were Jewish friends of his.

The Prophet explained that they could only stay and fight if they became Muslims. The Jews refused and so the Prophet ordered them to return home. Ibn Ubayy, who was a known **hypocrite**, or fake Muslim, decided to take all his men home. (6:25)

When he left, he took three hundred men with him. Imagine how the seven hundred Muslims who were left must have felt like, seeing the enemy, three thousand strong, assembling across the valley! (3:173)

The Prophet ordered fifty archers to go stand on another hill to guard a narrow pass through which the enemy might try a sneak attack. The archers were ordered not to move under any circumstances.

The position of the Muslims was good and the men were ready. The Prophet raised his own sword in the air and declared that anyone could have it if they fulfilled one condition. A man named Abu Dujanah came forward and asked what he had to do.

The Prophet replied, "*Strike the enemy with it until it breaks.*" Abu Dujanah happily agreed and tied a red scarf around his head, which was his way of saying he would fight to the death. After he took the sword, he started to dance for joy in between the two rows of the fighters, as was always his custom before entering battle. When the Prophet saw him performing his dance, he remarked that "*This* would *be hateful to Allah except under the circumstances.*"

The individual duels started between the two armies. The three Muslim champions, Hamza, Ali and Abu Dujanah, easily beat their Meccan opponents. The enraged idol-worshippers charged in a great mob as their women shouted that if they lost they would avoid them.

The Meccans crashed upon the Muslim lines like a tidal wave. The Muslims fell back but fought fiercely. The Muslims in the back rows were shooting arrows as fast as they could into the charging warriors but could barely keep up.

Small groups of Meccans charged together at different places to break the Muslim formations but were unsuccessful. Finally, Hamza shouted a fierce battle cry, "*Die! Die!*" and charged right into the middle of the idol-worshippers.

'Ali struck down the Meccan's flag-bearer and the Muslims shouted, "*Allahu Akbar!*" and advanced forward. Abu Dujanah saw one Meccan fighting a Muslim with his fingernails. As he drew closer to deal with the attacker, he discovered that it was a woman and that it was Hind, the wife of Abu Sufyan.

He moved away as he didn't want the Prophet's sword to ever shed the blood of a woman, knowing he wouldn't have approved.

Hamza, meanwhile, was leading a charge of Muslims and nearly broke through the ranks of the enemy. Then an Abyssinian slave by the name of Wahshi, came out of nowhere and struck Hamza down with a javelin throw. He was promised his freedom in Mecca by Hind if he did away with the man who killed her father.

When the Muslims saw that Hamza had fallen they fought even harder. A group of the Muslims broke through to the enemy rear and even the idol the Meccans brought had fallen off its camel and broke to pieces.

The Meccans began to retreat and run from the battlefield as the Muslims shouted their battle cries. The panicked idol-worshippers were dropping their swords and running without thought of their goods or camp.

Some of the Muslims began to halt and instead of pursuing the idol-worshippers, they were grabbing the captured goods of the battlefield. When the archers, who were stationed on the hill, saw this they wanted to go and get the loot also. (3:152)

Their commander told them not to go but all of them did except for about ten. The Meccan horsemen, under the command of Khalid ibn Walid, saw the opportunity and rushed through the pass, attacking the Muslims from behind. The few archers left on the hill were killed as well. (3:152)

The Muslims turned and panicked at the unexpected threat and the fleeing idol-worshippers turned back around and attacked again as well. The Muslims were caught between two forces! In the confusion, the Prophet, himself, was wounded by a strike to the mouth and had to be helped back to Mount Uhud. (3:153, 172)

The idol worshippers attacked the Prophet and those who stood by him with great strength. A Muslim woman, Umm Amarah, who had come along to nurse the wounded, saw the Prophet under attack and rushed to where the he stood and shot arrows at the advancing Meccans.

When her arrows were gone, she slashed and struck at the attackers with a sword until she herself sustained many wounds. In later years the Prophet would remark that no one had any better than what Umm Amarah had that day.

The Muslims retreated to the side of Mount Uhud and began climbing higher. Here they were able to make a stand and hold off the Meccans.

In the counter-attack of the Meccans, the Prophet's helmet had been smashed and part of the metal had caused a wound on his head. In addition, one oh his teeth was chipped. 'Ali used a shield to bring water to wash the Prophet's wound.

Fatimah, who came along with a group of women to be the doctors for the wounded soldiers, tried to stop the bleeding. When she saw it was too deep of a wound, she took some palm leaves and burned them quckly in a small fire. Then she took the ash and packed it into the cut and the bleeding stopped.

C. The Aftermath.

The Meccans proceeded to comb the battlefield for Muhammad. They wanted him dead and looked for him frantically. In the pause most of the Muslim soldiers were able to escape up the mountain and join the Muslim defenses there. One Meccan group came forward and called to the Muslims up on the side of the mountain, *"Where is Muhammad! Death to me if he lives!"*

The Prophet grabbed a javelin and threw it at the advancing group and killed the leader. The Meccans made repeated assaults up the hillside but could not break through the Muslim line. By noon that day, both sides were so exhausted that the fighting subsided. (3:154)

The Muslims returned to Medina while the Meccans retired to their camp and celebrated. The next morning, the Prophet assembled his battered army and marched out to meet the idol-worshippers again. (3:3:156)

Abu Sufyan found out about the Muslim army's new march and couldn't believe it. He sent a message to the Muslims that he would fight them again but then argued with his fellow leaders and allies about whether it was a good idea to fight them once more, for although many Muslims were killed, the Meccan army lost more men than that. (3:165-166)

The Prophet waited with his army at Uhud for three days and nights and lit huge bon-fires to let the world know he was there. Abu Sufyan decided against taking another chance with the Muslims and withdrew to Mecca. (3:160)

The lesson of Uhud for the Muslims was obedience. Obey your commander, obey the Prophet. If you disobey, you invite disaster. Although the Muslims didn't lose the battle outright, they did lose the chance for another stunning victory.

D. Reactions After Uhud.

Allah revealed many Ayat explaining to the Muslims why they did not win an outright victory at Uhud. They had been too concerned with worldly wealth, they disobeyed orders and they became shaken when some thought the Prophet was killed.

This reawakened in the Muslims their sense of duty and many people made supplications to Allah asking for forgiveness and strength. The hypocrites were publicly telling the Muslims that no one would have died if they had only declined to fight like they did, but Allah answered them harshly saying:

"What! When a single disaster strikes you, although you inflicted twice the punishment on (your enemies), you say, 'Why did this happen?' Tell them, 'It is from your own (fault) for Allah has power over all things...The hypocrites, who sat at home, say, 'If only they had listened to us they would not have been killed.'

"Tell them, 'Then keep death from coming for you if you speak the truth.' Don't think that those who were killed in Allah's cause are dead. No, they are alive, finding their supply in the presence of their Lord." (3:165,168-169)

In these and other Ayat, Allah put it clearly that no one can save themselves from death, even if they sit at home. No one will live forever so if you go out and strive in Allah's cause you will receive the best reward in the next life, where you're going anyway. (6:32)

The Muslims couldn't rest, however, for a new threat from home emerged. The Banu Nadir, another Jewish tribe that lived in the city, tried to kill the Blessed Prophet in an ambush.

They has asked the Blessed Prophet to come for a visit to their part of town and told him and his companions to sit against a wall while they made preparations for him to enter.

The Blessed Prophet felt that something wasn't right and then they noticed the people above and behind them on the roof with huge stones, just waiting for the signal to drop them on the men down below.

The Muslims quickly got up and left. After a series of street Battles, the Banu Nadir finally surrendered and were told to leave Medina forever. The same punishment as the double-crossing Banu Qaynuqa got! Some of the Banu Nadir people went to Palestine while the rest went to live in the far-away Jewish fortress-city of Khaybar.

The Blessed Prophet distributed the captured property to the poor Muslims and the situation of the poor improved so much so that everyone rejoiced. Life was getting better at home in Medina.

Questions to Answer

1. Why did the Meccans want revenge?
2. How did the Muslims learn about the size and power of the Meccan army and the plans of the idol-worshippers?
3. Describe what happened in the Battle of Uhud.
4. How did victory slip away from the Muslims?
5. What happened with the Banu Nadir?

The Battle of Khandaq

31

Think About It

Why is making a surprise move sometimes a good way to throw your opponent off?

Vocabulary Words

Khandaq

What to Learn

The Muslims faced the toughest challenge ever in the Battle of the Khandaq.

A. The Meccans Build Their Strength.

Abu Sufyan and the other leaders of Mecca were concerned that Muslim power was growing again. After the victory of the Muslims in some small battles with hostile Arab tribes, the Meccans resolved to attack the Muslims again.

A delegation arrived from the Jewish fortress of Khaibar consisting of the senior leaders of the Banu Nadir. Most of the Banu Nadir moved in with the Jews of Khaibar after they were forced to leave Medina and they were determined to take revenge against the Muslims.

The delegation met with the leaders of Mecca and urged them to attack the Muslims in Medina. The Meccans listened intently as they were still very much hostile towards Islam.

The plans were made after several more trips to and from Khaibar and Mecca. The Meccans would rally an army drawn from all the surrounding cities and towns, while the Banu Nadir and their allies would be waiting to attack the Muslims from behind.

After the date of the attack was set, the Jews sent messages to all the hostile Arab tribes in central and northern Arabia asking them to come and fight the Muslims as well. They even promised to the large tribe of Ghatafan a whole year's worth of produce from the orchards of Medina if they beat the Muslims. The Banu Nadir were determined to crush the Muslims for good.

When the time to march came, the idol-worshippers assembled an army of over 10,000 warriors, all fully equipped and armed for battle. This huge force, which Arabia had never seen before, marched towards Medina and the unsuspecting Muslims there.

B. The Defense Strategy.

When word of the huge mobilization of idol-worshippers reached Medina, everyone was struck with fear and panic. There had never been an army that huge in Arabia before. How could the Muslims hope to win against such a huge number of men, horses and war machinery?

The Prophet called a council and the Muslim leaders gathered for a strategy session. Going out of the city was out of the question. The Muslim warriors were barely over 3,000 in number and were poorly equipped.

One of the companions, a man by the name of Salman al Farsi, who was a skilled strategist, suggested a unique plan. He was from Persia and knew how wars were fought between large armies.

He suggested that they dig a huge trench, or **Khandaq**, around the exposed areas of Medina, while fortifying the city walls into thick barriers. With mountains encircling a good portion of the city, the main defenses could be directed towards one side.

The only weak spot was the eastern side of the city, where the last Jewish tribe, the Banu Quraiza lived. But they had a fortress that the idol-worshippers were unlikely to attack and they had a treaty with the Muslims and were still honoring it, as far as people could tell.

Everyone agreed with this plan and work began at once. The Muslims were divided into crews and everyone participated in the defense construction. Some were given the job of building and joining walls together while others were in the front of the city, digging the enormous trench.

The Prophet, himself, was out digging with the people and the Muslims sang songs while working to keep their spirits up. After many days of hard labor, the Muslims completed a trench, six or more feet deep and nearly eight feet, more or less, across.

When the project was all done, the weary Muslims were divided into defense units and stationed around the city and trench. There they awaited the arrival of a large enemy army.

C. The Huge Army Appears!

The huge idol-worshipping army first arrived at Uhud, hoping to meet the Muslims there, but seeing that they were not to be found, the leaders of the horde directed their troops to head for Medina.

Imagine how the Muslims felt seeing the huge army advancing in the distance. It was so large that it seemed to arrive from all directions, north, south, east and west. Men, horses and camels seemed to pour endlessly into the plain just outside the city!

The horde assembled and began beating war drums and chanting cries of battle. Muslim men and women looked on from their posts and knew the time for all out war had come. If they lost they would all be killed or sold into slavery.

The tribal leaders were about to order an all out assault on the city when they noticed the huge trench dug around the front of the city's walls. They became confused for this strategy was never known in the Arabian peninsula.

It was too wide for horses to get over and would stop any charge from succeeding. They cursed at the Muslims and after a few small assaults which were beaten back by Muslim archers, the idol-worshippers made their camps and prepared for a long siege.

D. The Siege of Medina.

It was winter and cold winds carried over the desert at night. The Muslims were safe and warm in Medina but the idol worshippers had only flimsy tents to keep out the chill.

During the day the idol worshippers tried to charge the trench in groups, only to be met with a rain of arrows. Any who made it through the trench were met with the determined Muslim guards and soon turned back.

Food supplies were low in Medina forcing many Muslim soldiers to tie rocks around their waists to press against their empty stomachs. But the defense of the city was holding and the horde of idol-worshippers began to lose their determination.

After a few days, the Meccan leaders realized that the siege might have to be prolonged for a long time. The Banu Nadir also began to fear. They worked very hard to assemble the tribes of Arabia under the Meccans and knew such an accomplishment might never be done again.

The Banu Nadir sent messages to the idol-worshippers begging them to keep up the attack and not to leave. Huyayy ibn Akhtab, the leader of the Banu Nadir, promised to get the Banu Quraiza, his Jewish cousins, on their side and to attack the Muslims from out of nowhere unexpectedly.

Then Huyayy went to the leader of the Banu Quraiza and tried to convince him to use his forces to attack the Muslims from behind. At first, the chief of the Banu Quraiza didn't want to join, because he had a treaty with the Muslims and wanted to honor it and he also knew what happened to the two other Jewish clans who tried to fight the Muslims.

But after Huyayy described the size of the Meccan army and the weakness of the Muslims, the leader of the Banu Quraiza, Ka'b ibn Asad, agreed to listen to the plans. Huyayy even promised to move all his Banu Nadir fighters into the strong fortress and help defend it should the Muslims discover their plot and try to counter-attack.

Finally Ka'b agreed and became convinced that they could wipe the Muslims out. The Banu Quraiza would attack the Muslims from behind on the same day that the idol-worshippers would make an all-out assault on the trench.

E. The Betrayal of the Banu Quraiza.

The news of the betrayal of the Banu Quraiza reached the Prophet and his companions quickly. They were shocked and dismayed. They had held off the idol-worshippers thus far and depended on the Banu Quraiza to hold the rear of the city safe.

A delegation consisting of the chiefs of the Auws and Khazraj tribes went to the Jewish settlement and fortress to plead with them to honor the treaty.

When they arrived the situation was far worse than they expected. The Jews were preparing for war and gathering weapons and supplies. The two chiefs tried to convince the Banu Quraiza not to break the treaty and that they might suffer a worse fate than the two other Jewish clans that were forced to leave Medina.

But the people of the Banu Quraiza began insulting the Prophet and declared the treaty was now over and worthless. The two Muslim chiefs hastily left the scene as the anger of the Jews began to boil.

The delegates returned to the Prophet and informed him of what had happened. The Muslims now feared that the idol-worshippers might circle around to the other side of the city where the Jewish fortresses were, and enter through the walls of the Banu Quraiza.

The Banu Quraiza, for their part, immediately cut off all food supplies to the Muslims and within days the Muslims began to feel the hunger. Women and children were fed in preference to the fighters so more stones were tied around waists to cut down on stomach grumbling.

The leaders of the horde, however, were elated. The news of the betrayal of the Banu Quraiza caused their spirits to soar and they thought that victory was in their grasp. The warriors began to dance and sing songs in expectation of the day of the attack.

The idol-worshippers planned a three-pronged attack, with Abu Sufyan leading the main body of men over the ditch. The Banu Quraiza were to attack from behind. (33:9-11)

The people of Medina became fearful as they watched the idol-worshippers preparing and moving their forces around. But the Prophet and the strongest companions remained firm, knowing that even if they died, they would win in the end by entering Paradise.

F. The Enemy is Divided!

Some of the Quraysh horsemen were so encouraged by their new fortunes that they attempted an assault of the ditch a few days before the main assault was to start. They found a spot where the ditch was narrow and attacked it fiercely until they actually gained a position on the other side.

'Ali ibn Abi Talib, and the other Muslim defenders there, rushed to the scene to engage the enemy in battle. 'Amr bin Wudd, who was a fearsome warrior, yelled a challenge to the Muslims for a hand-to-hand duel. 'Ali came forward and quickly killed him.

The other idol-worshippers, seeing their champion dead, ran back across the trench as fast as they could. But even though the front line was held for the moment, in the rear of the city, the Banu Quraiza's warriors were starting to descend from their fortress and occupy the houses close to the Muslim area of the city.

Many women and children were living in the walled houses there and there were few Muslim soldiers to spare to protect them. Safiyah bint Abdel Muttalib saw a Jewish scout skulking through the alley inspecting the Muslim defenses there. She asked an old man to go out and kill the spy. The old man refused out of his fear.

Safiyah then grabbed an iron rod and crept out in the street. Then she came upon the warrior from behind and killed him with one swift strike. Then she sounded the alarm and other women took up a careful watch on the back walls. Some Muslims stood on their roof tops and shouted, "*Allahu Akbar!*" all night to frighten the Jews and keep them from attacking.

The Prophet, seeing that the Muslims were being hemmed in on both sides, had no other choice but to attempt to divide his enemies. He sent a secret message to the leaders of the powerful Ghatafan tribe that if they withdrew, he would give them one third of the harvest of Medina for a year.

The Ghatafan were only there to appease their friends among the Banu Nadir and were growing weary of the siege which was over three weeks old now. This caused the tribal leaders to hesitate in their planning with the other tribes and the Meccans.

The Prophet also sent a man named Nu'aym to the Banu Quraiza. He was an old friend of the Jews and they didn't know he had become a Muslim yet. He pretended he was an unbeliever and convinced the Banu Quraiza that they shouldn't attack unless the Meccans promised them they would help them if the tide of battle turned against them. Thus the Banu Quraiza began to hesitate.

Then Nu'aym went secretly to the Quraysh camp and told them that the Banu Quraiza had broken the deal and went back to the Muslim side. After this he went to the Ghatafan camp and told the leaders there the same thing.

The next day Abu Sufyan, who believed the words of Nu'aym, sent a messenger to the Banu Quraiza telling them that the attack would begin tomorrow. The Jews replied that the next day was Saturday and that they wouldn't work or fight on their holy day.

Abu Sufyan was enraged at their disobedience and sent them the message that if they didn't attack tomorrow that the deal would be over and that the Quraysh would attack them as well.

The Jews refused again and said they would not make any attacks on any days unless the Quraysh promised to protect them from the Muslims. Abu Sufyan was completely convinced now that the Banu Quraiza went back on their secret deal with him.

When Abu Sufyan went to the leaders of the Ghatafan tribe, he found out they also wanted to postpone any attack while they considered Muhammad's offer of free produce for a year. Abu Sufyan was bitter with anger.

G. The Wrath of Nature.

That very night, as the confused and divided idol-worshippers slept uneasily in their tents, a wind

began blowing over the plain. Within the hour the wind was followed by a raging storm!

The hundreds of exposed tents started to fall down, sand whipped in the faces of men and horses and the idol-worshippers were thrown in confusion. Some of the leaders met hastily together, as the winds howled through the frightened horde, and they suggested a retreat. They saw in the storm evil signs and thought the Muslims might take the opportunity to attack.

Every man grabbed whatever supplies he could pile on his horse and began to move as the storm continued to swirl all about them. By the time the morning had broke, the field of battle was empty. The idol-worshippers, both Meccans and their tribal allies, went home.

The Muslims rejoiced at this miracle which saved them and shouts of "Allahu Akbar!" rang through the streets. The Blessed Prophet and the grateful Muslims gathered in the Masjid to give thanks to Allah.

H. Punishing the Banu Quraiza.

One thing still had to be done. The Banu Quraiza had betrayed the Muslims in their greatest hour of need. They broke the treaty which they signed and affirmed. They joined the enemies of the people of Medina and would have shown no mercy if they would have won. The time had come to deal with these traitors.

The Prophet ordered the Mu'adhan to proclaim as part of the Adhan, "*No good Muslim will pray the 'Asr prayer except in the quarter of the Banu Quraiza!*"

The Muslims immediately mobilized and began an assault on the Jewish fortresses. The Banu Quraiza held off the Muslim attacks, which were led by 'Ali, for twenty-five days and nights. Inch by inch the Muslims pressed forward. During one assault, 'Ali picked up a huge door and used it as a shield while he led a charge of Muslim fighters.

Eventually the enemy surrendered and the Muslims could breath easier once more.

Questions to Answer

1. How were the Meccans able to gather such a huge army?
2. How did the Muslims plan their defense?
3. How was the Blessed Prophet able to divide the enemy?
4. Why did the Banu Quraiza double-cross the Muslims?
5. How were the Muslims able to defeat the enemies outside and inside the city?

32

A Time for Peace

Think About It

After having to defend themselves so many times, explain why a rest period would be good for the Muslim community.

Vocabulary Words

Hajji   'Umrah   Ridwan

What to Learn

Islam continued to grow and won more new believers every day.

A. The First Islamic Pilgrimage.

After the siege of Medina was lifted, the prestige of the Muslims was raised in the eyes of the surrounding tribes of the region. Hundreds more were accepting Islam every week and the Prophet sent many companions to different towns and villages to teach Islam to the people.

But as Islam was making good progress among the hearts and minds of the people, another issue remained unresolved. The Ka'bah, the shrine built by Prophet Ibrahim so long before, was a house of idol-worship. The Meccans kept statues and sticks in there that they worshipped and prevented any Muslims from approaching it.

One of the duties of Islam was to honor the practices of Prophet Ibrahim, and since Islam was for promoting the teaching of the One God, everyone felt a longing to go and make the Ka'bah a holy and pure place again.

One night the Blessed Prophet had a dream in which he saw himself, joined by other Muslims,

making a pilgrimage to Mecca. The next morning he came out and announced to the community that he was organizing an **'Umrah**, or lesser pilgrimage, to Mecca.

After the preparations were made, the Prophet set out with 1400 of his followers who were armed with nothing more than their travelers swords. It was the year 628 CE. This was the first pilgrimage in Islam which would re-establish the ancient practices of Prophet Ibrahim.

The Muslim pilgrims, or **Hajjis**, journeyed towards Mecca, praising Allah and rejoicing in their new effort for Allah's cause. The Prophet had no intention of forcing his way into Mecca, because it was the season of pilgrimage in the peninsula and all tribes observed a general truce and avoided fighting. That's why the Muslims were so lightly armed.

B. Peace Between Mecca and Medina.

When the Meccans learned that Muslim pilgrims were coming to their city they were shocked. They realized that it wasn't an armed invasion and were confused about what to do. If they attacked the Muslims all the other people of Arabia would see that the custodians of the Ka'bah, the Quraysh, had violated the truce months.

The Quraysh decided not to allow the Muslims to enter the city and sent out a cavalry group under the command of Khalid ibn Walid and 'Ikrima ibn Abu Jahl to turn them back. Khalid was the same military commander who had attacked the Muslims from behind at Uhud when the archers left their posts and 'Ikrima still had bitterness about his father who was killed at Badr.

When the Prophet learned that an enemy cavalry unit was approaching, he asked his followers if anyone knew of another way to Mecca. One of them did and he guided the Muslim pilgrims through some narrow passes.

When they arrived at a field called Hudaibiyah, the Prophet's camel stopped. Everyone thought the camel was tired, but Muhammad said, "*No, the camel is not tired. It has stopped by the order of Allah. By the One Who created me, I will accept any offers the Meccans make for peace.*"

When the Meccan cavalry finally realized they lost their prey, they returned to Mecca. Soon a message was sent to the Muslim camp ordering that no one would be allowed to enter Mecca.

Uthman went out to talk to some of the Meccans about letting the Muslims in for a pilgrimage and was delayed. Some Muslims thought he was killed, that's why he wasn't returning and they were angry and wanted to fight but the Prophet forbade them to fight except in self-defense if attacked.

He moved under a tall tree and took a pledge from all the Muslims there that they would fight to last man if the Meccans had killed Uthman and violated the holy months of pilgrimage. This is called the Pledge of **Ridwan**. A short time later, Uthman

returned from his discussions and everyone breathed easier. (48:18)

The Muslims made camp and an official delegation arrived from Mecca to discuss the situation with the Prophet. After many meetings and proposals an agreement was finally reached. A treaty was signed between the Muslims and the idol-worshippers. This pact is called "The Treaty of Hudaibiyah," and was signed in the year 628 CE.

The main points of the treaty are as follows:

1. There will be ten years of peace between both sides.

2. No hostile moves will be made by either side.

3. Both sides can make deals and alliances with whomever they please.

4. Any Meccan man who leaves and goes to Medina without the permission of his family will be returned to Mecca.

5. Anyone who leaves Medina for Mecca will not be returned.

6. There will be no pilgrimage this year for the Muslims, but they can perform it the following year for three days.

The Blessed Prophet accepted these conditions, although many of the Muslims did not like the part about returning Muslims to Mecca who came to Medina from that moment onward. When 'Umar ibn al Khattab complained about the treaty, the Blessed Prophet replied, "*I am the servant of Allah and His messenger. I always obey His commands, and He will never fail me.*" (48:24-26)

The Muslims then began their return journey to Medina with the good news of a ten year peace treaty. As Allah revealed Surah al Fet-h, or Victory. In one of the Ayahs it says, *"Surely, We have granted you a clear victory."* (48:1)

As you will see, it was the best thing that could have happened for the Muslims.

C. Using the Time of Peace.

The Muslims, now freed from the fear of Meccan attacks, made good use of the peace. The Prophet made numerous treaties with other tribes around Arabia and thousands of people were accepting Islam at every turn. Even Khalid ibn Walid, the military genius of the Quraysh, became a Muslim!

To eliminate another potential threat to Muslim safety, the Blessed Prophet marched an army to the hostile Jewish fortresses of Khaibar, three days to the north. After several battles, the Jews surrendered and agreed to live in peace. The Prophet allowed them to stay on their lands and even returned some religious scrolls to them that were seized in the fighting.

The Jews agreed to pay one half the yearly crops of Khaibar to the Muslim government and not to make any secret deals with hostile enemies. To cement the new arrangement, the Blessed Prophet married a Jewish woman named Safiyah who remained a firm and committed Muslim for the rest of her life.

In addition, the Blessed Prophet began the next phase of his mission by reaching out to the people of the world with the message of Islam. (34:28) He sent letters to the leaders of all the known empires, countries and cities that he could, inviting them to consider Islam for their way of life.

D. The Meccan's Big Mistake.

Two years had passed after the signing of the treaty and peace still remained. During this time, the Banu Khuza'a became allies of the Muslims while the Banu Bakr became allies of the idol-worshippers in Mecca.

One night, towards the end of the year 630 CE, the Banu Bakr, supplied with fresh weapons given to them by the Quraysh, attacked the camp of the Banu Khuza'a at night and caused much death and destruction. Then the Banu Bakr warriors carried off all their loot to Mecca where they took shelter.

The chief of the Banu Khuza'a went to Medina and complained about the injustice done against his people with a loud voice. The Prophet came out of the Masjid and was told the story of what happened.

The Prophet was angry at the senseless attack and killing done by the allies of the Meccans and sent a message off to Mecca which stated the following three options:

1. The Banu Bakr must pay compensation for the victims they killed.

2. The Meccans should break their alliance with the Banu Bakr.

3. The Meccans could declare the Treaty of Hudaibiyah null and void.

The idol-worshippers, who perhaps saw the victory of the Banu Bakr as a sign of more good fortune in their interrupted war against the Muslims, shouted that the treaty was now over. When the news of the Meccans response reached Medina, the Prophet knew the time had come for final victory.

After a few days, the Meccans realized they made a big mistake. Abu Sufyan went to Medina himself and begged for the treaty to be valid, or working, again. The Prophet refused to see him. Then Abu Sufyan went to Abu Bakr, Umar, 'Ali, Fatimah and others and begged for their help. They all refused to talk to him. Abu Sufyan returned to Mecca bitter and frightened.

E. The Liberation of Mecca.

The Blessed Prophet raised an army of ten thousand Muslim men and women and set out for Mecca during the month of Ramadan in the year 630 CE. He took great care to keep his army's departure a secret.

After a few days of travel, the huge army entered into the hillsides just outside of Mecca. There the Prophet ordered them to make camp. He asked each small group of soldiers to start a campfire. When the Meccans came out and looked upon the endless sea of campfires they became scared.

The Meccans had no hope of fighting such an army. They had few fighters in the city and all the famous warriors of Arabia had already gone over to the Muslim side. Abu Sufyan had no choice but to go to the Muslim's camp and see the Prophet Muhammad.

Abu Sufyan declared his acceptance of Islam and agreed to surrender Mecca peacefully. The Prophet told Abu Sufyan he didn't want any blood to be shed upon entering Mecca and that anyone near the Ka'bah, in their homes or even in Abu Sufyan's house would be safe.

Abu Sufyan then returned to Mecca and informed the people that he was surrendering the city as there was no hope of opposing the huge Muslim forces. He told them about Muhammad's promise of safety and that everyone should go home.

The next morning, the Prophet divided his army into three, massive columns and instructed each to enter Mecca from a different direction. Imagine the sight of ten thousand Muslims, dressed in white, entering victoriously into the city that only eight years before Muhammad had to flee from in fear of his life!

There was only one incident of bloodshed. Some idol-worshippers, following the son of Abu Jahl, 'Ikrima, attacked a group of Muslim soldiers, but they were quickly subdued by Khalid ibn Walid without much fuss.

The first thing the Blessed Prophet wanted to do was to clear the Ka'bah of all the idols. When he approached the sacred shrine, with all the Muslims and Meccans looking on, he gave thanks to Allah for the victory.

The keeper of the key to the Ka'bah door, who was still an idol worshipper, was brought forward. When he was asked for the key, he refused to give it. One Muslim soldier angrily snatched it away and gave it to the Prophet. The Blessed Prophet, however, handed it back to the keeper.

The keeper of the key was so amazed that he declared himself a Muslim and gave the key to the Prophet with his own hand. Imagine the jubilation and celebration as the Muslims threw the idols out of Ibrahim's shrine and tore them to bits! *"Allahu Akbar! Allahu Akbar!"*

The Prophet recited the following Ayah as the work progressed, *"Declare: The Truth is now clear. Falsehood is broken as it should be."* (17:81)

When that task was done, the Blessed Prophet addressed the crowd of Meccans who had come to watch, saying, *"People of Mecca! What do you think I am going to do with you?"*

They answered, *"Noble Brother, and son of a noble brother, only goodness."*

Then they held their breath to hear what their punishment would be. After all, these were the people who murdered, tortured and persecuted people only for saying they believe in one God and in justice.

The Blessed Prophet replied in words that are to this day famous for their nobility and mercy. He announced, *"No blame is on you this day. Go to your homes, for you are all free."*

Then the Prophet asked Bilal to climb to the top of the Ka'bah and give the Adhan for the noon prayer. Imagine the honor! No one has ever been permitted to call the Adhan from the Ka'bah's roof since that day in the year 630 CE. The Muslims prayed to Allah filled with emotion that day. It was a day that would live on in the hearts and minds of Muslims as a day of victory until this very day.

F. The Community Prospers.

The Muslims soon returned to their main job of living as good believers and teaching others about Islam. Many poor people converted to Islam every day and money from the public treasury was distributed regularly.

At the end of the month of Ramadan, Abu Huraira, a trusted Sahaba, was put in charge of distributing the charity goods and money collected to the poor people.

One person came up to Abu Huraira's charity table and started taking handfuls and handfuls of stuff. Abu Huraira grabbed him and said, "By Allah I will take you to the Messenger of Allah (to be punished for your greediness!)"

The man cried out, "I'm very poor and have a lot of mouths to feed!"

So he let him go. The next morning, the Blessed Prophet came up to Abu Huraira and asked, "What did your prisoner do yesterday?"

Abu Huraira replied, "Messenger of Allah! He complained that he was poor and had many mouths to feed so I felt sorry for him and let him go."

The Blessed Prophet said, "He told you a lie and he will be coming again."

Abu Huraira then went back to his table and hid himself to see if the man would return. When he came back and started stealing loads of food and other things, Abu Huraira jumpoed out and grabbed him by the wrist and shouted, "This time I'm for sure going to take you to the Messenger of Allah."

But the man cried even more and said, "Let me go because I'm very poor and have so many mouths to feed. I promise I won't come back again."

Abu Huraira felt sorry for him and let him go. The next morning, the Blessed Prophet asked Abu Huraira, "What did your prisoner do?"

He replied, "Messenger of Allah, he complained so much about being poor and all his many mouths to feed, so I felt sorry for him and let him go."

The Blessed Prophet said, "He told a lie and he will be back again."

Abu Huraira went and waited for the man to show up a third time and, sure enough, the man went up to the table and started grabbing arm loads of food.

Abu Huraira popped out of his hiding place and grabbed the man firmly. "This time I'm going to take you to the Messenger of Allah! You promised me you wouldn't be back and you broke your promise!"

The man said, "Forgive me for this and I will teach you some words which will benefit you with Allah."

Abu Huraira asked him, "What are they?"

"Whenever you go to bed, recite ayah 2:255, known as Ayat ul Kursi. If you do, Allah will appoint a guard for you who will stay with you and no devil will be able to come near you until morning."

Abu Huraira released the man and when he saw the Blessed Prophet the next time and told him what had happened, the Blessed Prophet said, "He spoke the truth this time, although he is otherwise an absolute liar. Do you know who you were talking to those three nights, Abu Huraira?"

"No," answered Abu Huraira.

"It was Shaytan."

Abu Huraira was amazed and went away, lost in thought.

Once the Blessed Prophet was sitting with a group of people and he said, "There are people from among the servants of Allah who are not Prophets or Martyrs, but who will be envied by them on the Day of Resurrection on account of how high Allah holds them in rank."

Someone asked, "Tell us, Messenger of Allah, who are they?"

"The Blessed replied, "They are the people who love each other for the sake of Allah, even though they are not family members and never exchanged property. I swear by Allah that their faces will be shining and they will be sitting in light. They will have no fear on the Day when humans will fear and they will not be sad when others are sad."

Then he recited the following ayah: "Indeed, for the friends of Allah there is no fear or sadness."

(Abu Dawud)

Questions to Answer

1. Why do you think the Muslims were happy about their first 'Umrah?
2. Why was going to Mecca a dangerous thing to do?
3. Why did the Meccans ask for peace and what were the terms both sides agreed to?
4. How was the peace treaty broken?
5. Describe the capture of Mecca.
6. What strange thing happened to Abu Huraira?

33 The Final Tasks

Think About It

What new enemies do you think were going to challenge the Muslims?

Vocabulary Words

Usamah   Jannah

What to Learn

The Blessed Prophet left the Muslims with the tools to succeed.

A. Organizing in Mecca.

The Blessed Prophet remained in Mecca for fifteen days. During this time, a number of important activities took place. The Ka'bah was cleaned of idols and paintings and rededicated to the service of Allah, alone.

Important Ayat about the Hajj and Zakat were revealed as well as more Ayat about relations among people. More treaties were signed with peoples, tribes and leaders all over southern Arabia and the administration of Mecca was organized.

From Yemen in the south to Syria in the north, Islam was gaining in strength and Muslim teachers were sent to the various peoples of Arabia and achieving great success.

Nearly everyone in Mecca, who were the Prophet's bitterest enemies before, became Muslims, after seeing how fair and just Muhammad was, and the few people who were hold-outs eventually converted of their own accord later. The Prophet then returned to Medina and worked on organizing the Muslims into an even stronger position.

B. The Road Ahead.

The Blessed Prophet made one last Hajj to Mecca. There he gave his famous "Farewell Khutba," in which he spoke to the Muslims about being true to the Qur'an and his example and to always remain faithful to Allah.

He declared that no non-Muslims would ever be allowed in Mecca ever again and that those who heard his words should tell them to others. After completing the Hajj he returned to Medina to live out the rest of his days.

The Blessed Prophet succeeded in bringing Islam to his people even as he equipped them to bring it to other people and so on. The revelation of the Qur'an was complete and thousands were memorizing it, learning it, living it and teaching it.

An entire generation of people grew up as Muslims and were firm and committed believers. The growth of Islam was well into the international stage and there was no need to fear that it would ever be in danger of destruction again, such as when the idol-worshippers tried so many times to suppress it.

The Prophet was getting old and was now 63 years old. He began to turn his attention to the northern borders of Arabia again, where the armies of Persia and Byzantium lurked. The Prophet called for the mobilization of an army to go to Palestine to put an end to the dangers of the Byzantines once and for all.

Shortly thereafter the Blessed Prophet Muhammad became ill and had to limit his activities. The Muslims became worried at his condition. The Prophet's illness continued to increase and the Muslims became worried for his health. He was old and didn't have the health of a young man anymore, although he was always active and ate a very healthy diet.

C. The Prophet's Health Worsens.

One morning, Muhammad found A'ishah, one of his wives, complaining about a severe headache. She was holding her head with her hands and muttering, *"O my aching head!"*

The Prophet, who had begun to feel even more ill, replied, *"But rather, A'ishah, my own head!"*

The Prophet, however, still kept up with his duties as best he could, meeting with delegations from tribes that wanted to accept Islam, teaching men and women about their Deen, exhorting the believers to live lives based on goodness and leading the Salat in the main Masjid in Medina.

The Prophet began to suffer a severe fever a few days later and found it hard to meet with many people. When he heard that some of the elder Muslims were grumbling about the appointment of the youthful **Usamah,** to head the army, the Prophet asked his wife, Hafsa, to pour some cold water over his head to reduce the heat in his forehead.

Then he entered the Masjid and addressed the people telling them that he made the choice of Usamah bin Zayd and that the people had no right to second-guess his decision because they also used to complain against his father, Zayd, who showed his bravery by being martyred in a previous battle.

The Prophet concluded his speech by saying, *"Didn't he make the best choice, who, when given the option of taking this world, the other world, or in submitting to whatever is with Allah, chose the last choice?"*

The Muslims realized that the Prophet was referring to himself and were filled with sadness. Abu Bakr began weeping and the Muslims fell silent. Usamah was chosen by the Prophet and no one would question it anymore.

When the Prophet's condition worsened, he asked that Abu Bakr be in charge of leading the prayers for him in the main Masjid of Medina. This signaled to many Muslims that the Prophet was tapping Abu Bakr to lead after him. Even when he felt strong enough to come into the Masjid for Salat, he asked Abu Bakr to continue leading Salat while he, himself, prayed behind him in the rows.

D. The Whisper to Fatimah.

One day, while his daughter Fatimah was attending him, the Prophet whispered something in her ear which made her cry. Then he whispered

The Muslim army was again preparing to march. This time to face the Byzantine Romans!

something that made her smile. A'ishah asked her what he said, but Fatimah refused to tell what she regarded as a personal secret.

One morning, the Blessed Prophet called to A'ishah and said to her, "*I have seven silver coins still in my possession. Please give them away in charity.*"

A'ishah agreed but then forgot to give them away because she was so filled with worry over her husband.

The fever burned in Muhammad's forehead and his body shivered with chills. The Prophet overheard Fatimah lamenting, "*Oh, the terrible pain my father is suffering!*"

The Blessed Prophet opened his eyes and said to her, "*Your father will suffer no more pain after this day.*"

Then he called out to A'ishah and asked if she had given away the coins yet. A'ishah brought them to him and said that she had forgotten. The blessed Prophet took them in his hands and said, "*What would you think if I went to meet Allah with these?*"

A'ishah took the coins and hurried to find some poor people to give them to.

As the Blessed Prophet's condition got worse, anxious Muslims filed in and out of his house throughout the day, some came offering medicines while others prayed for his health. Everyone felt confused and sick inside for the safety of the beloved Prophet.

In his last hour, as his head was resting on A'ishah's lap, the Blessed Prophet called out his last words.

As A'ishah tells the story, "*The Prophet's head was getting heavier in my lap. I looked at his face and found that his eyes were still. I heard him murmur, 'Rather, Allah on High and Paradise.' I said to him, 'By Him Who sent you as a Prophet to teach the truth, you have been given the choice and you chose well.'*

"*The Prophet of Allah passed away while his head was on my side between my chest and my heart. It was my youth and inexperience that made me let him die in my lap. I then placed his head on the pillow and got up to bemoan my fate and to join the other women in our sadness and sorrow.*"

It was the 12th of Rabi' ul Awwal, (June 8) in the year 632 CE (10 AH).

Later, Fatimah told A'ishah what was whispered to her. She said, "*The first time he told me that he would not recover from his sickness so I cried. The second time he told me I would be the first from his family to join him and I smiled.*" This prediction would soon come true.

The Blessed Prophet was the most loving person we can seek to learn from. His example was the living truth. May we follow in his footsteps and in the path of his companions, male and female. Ameen.

E. The Muslims Grieve.

With the Blessed Prophet having left this world, the new Muslim community had to try to make sense out of what his mission meant and how they were to get along without him.

When the Prophet was alive and with them, there were no doubts or uncertainties. All a person had to do was ask his guidance and you would be sure to receive an answer that was both wise and practical. But now he was gone.

When 'Umar heard the news of the Prophet's demise, he came running and drew his sword in anger. He declared that he didn't believe the Prophet was gone and that he'd fight anyone who said otherwise. Obviously, he was overcome with great stress at the thought of losing his beloved friend and guide.

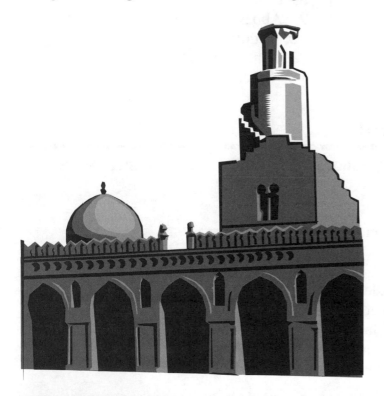

Abu Bakr came on the scene and when he saw 'Umar crying and holding up his sword, he went to his friend and announced in a loud voice, "*If anyone worships Muhammad, know that Muhammad has died. But if anyone worships Allah, then know that He is alive and cannot die.*"

Then Abu Bakr recited an Ayah from the Qur'an to drive the point home. "*Muhammad is no more than a Messenger. There were many Messengers who passed away before him. If he died or was killed, would you then turn around and run. If any ran away, it wouldn't do any harm to Allah. But Allah will reward quickly those who (serve Him) thankfully.*" (3:144)

'Umar accepted the wisdom of his friend's speech and slumped down into his friend's arms and wept at his heart-felt loss. A few hours later, when the time for the next Salat had come, Bilal began giving the Adhan.

When he came to the name "Muhammad" in the Adhan, he broke down in tears. People in the streets heard his pause and saw him weeping. Everyone else began weeping as well. After a few moments of gentle crying, Bilal resumed his duty and finished the Adhan. Then, in his sorrow, he vowed to never say the Adhan again.

The Prophet was buried in the place that he died. Soon afterwards, the elders of the Muslim community met and elected Abu Bakr to be the first Khalifa, or Steward, of the Muslim nation.

The Blessed Prophet fulfilled his mission. May Allah bless the Prophet Muhammad and give him the best in **Jannah** (Heaven) and make us among his company in the next life. Ameen!

Questions to Answer

1. What was the Blessed Prophet's Farewell Khutba?
2. Who was Usamah and why were some people against him?
3. What did the Blessed Prophet whisper to Fatimah?
4. Why do you think the Blessed Prophet wanted to give away the last of his money before he passed away?
5. How did Abu Bakr bring the Muslims back to their senses after the blessed Prophet passed away?

Unit 8
Review Exercises

Vocabulary Review

On a separate piece of paper, write the meaning of each word below. Remember to write in complete sentences.

1. Uhud
2. Khandaq
3. Banu Quraiza
4. Ghazwa
5. Abu Huraira
6. Abu Dujanah
7. Hajji
8. Hind
9. Abbas
10. Fatimah
11. Khalid ibn Walid
12. Sahaba

Remembering What You Read

On a separate piece of paper, answer the questions below. Remember to answer as best as you can and write in complete sentences.

1. Why did the Meccans attack the Muslims in Medina repeatedly?
2. Who was Abu Sufyan?
3. Describe some of the teachings of Islam.
4. Describe the events that led up to the Battle of Badr.
5. Describe what happened in the Battle of Badr.
6. Describe what happened in the Battle of Uhud.
7. Describe how the Jews tried to plot and plan against the Muslims.
8. What were the main events in the the Battle of Khandaq?
9. How were the Muslims able to take Mecca?
10. What signs did the Blessed Prophet give that he was soon going to pass away?
11. What did the Blessed Prophet stand for in his life?

Thinking to Learn

Read the following statement and explain whether it is true or false. Write in complete sentences on a separate piece of paper and give examples to support your answer.

Muslims were always attacking the idol-worshippers and trying to conquer them.

Unit 9

The Golden Age of Islam

34 Abu Bakr and 'Umar

Think About It

Why do you think some Arab tribes would rebel against the Muslims after the Prophet passed away?

Vocabulary Words

Yamama   Wars of the Ridda   Khawla

What to Learn

Abu Bakr worked hard to keep the Muslims united and he succeeded.

A. The Election of Abu Bakr.

You can hardly imagine the worry and turmoil that swept over the Muslim community after everyone heard about the death of the beloved Prophet! People were rushing from all over Arabia to Medina because they couldn't believe what they heard. What would become of the Ummah now? How would Islam survive without its great leader?

A day later a decision had to be made about the future of the Muslim community. The Blessed Prophet had left the Qur'an and the example of his way of life, his Sunnah, and now it was up to his faithful followers to carry the mission forwards.

A group of the Ansar organized a conference in the great hall of the Banu Sa'idah to decide what to do. Abu Bakr and 'Umar, as well as leaders from the Muhajireen and the Quraysh from Mecca quickly joined in the meeting. The issue was, of course, who should lead the community now that the Blessed Prophet was gone?

Some of the Ansar thought the new leader should be elected from among the them because they had provided protection for the Prophet and offered him a place to live. Some of the Muhajireen argued that only a Meccan should be chosen because Meccans were the first people to respond to the Prophet's call.

As everyone began to debate and argue, Abu Bakr stood up and said, "All the good things the Ansar said about themselves are true, but the Arabs only recognize the authority of the Quraysh. I suggest one of two men, accept one or the other as you like." He then took the hands of 'Umar and Abu 'Ubaidah and held them up for people to come and offer their bayya' to one of them.

People began to argue further and no solution seemed to be in sight. Finally, 'Umar suddenly declared, "Abu Bakr, how can anyone else fill the office as long as you're alive? You are the most important of the Muhajireen. You were with the Messenger of Allah in the Cave of Thawr, you led the Salat during his last days. Hold out your hand so that I may give my bayya' to you."

'Umar took Abu Bakr's hand and promised to be loyal to him as the first Khalifa of the Muslim Ummah. Everyone else immediately agreed and understood that the Prophet, himself, had given many clues as to his preference for Abu Bakr to succeed him. Suddenly everyone was surging forward and pledging their bayya' to him. Abu Bakr was elected as the first Khalifa, or Steward (Caretaker) of Islam.

B. Abu Bakr's Acceptance Speech.

The next day, as thousands more Muslims were pouring into Medina to give their bayya' to Abu Bakr, he stood before a huge crown and gave the following acceptance speech:

"O people, I have been elected your leader, even though I am no better than any of you. If I do right, help me. If I do wrong, correct me. Listen well, truth is a trust and lies are treason.

"The weak among you shall be strong with me until I secure their rights. The powerful among you shall be weak with me until, if Allah wills, I have taken what is due from them.

"Listen well, if people give up striving for the Cause of Allah, He will send disgrace upon them. If a people become wrong-doers, Allah will send disasters upon them.

"Obey me as long as I obey Allah and His Messenger. If I disobey Allah and His Messenger, then you are free to disobey me."

Abu Bakr's first duty was to lay to rest the Blessed Prophet, his beloved friend. After the Blessed Prophet was washed and wrapped in a burial shroud, he was buried right were he had lain when he passed away. This was on his own instructions. The funeral prayer for the Blessed Prophet must have seemed strange and empty as all the thousands of people were bidding farewell to the one person that had touched all their lives.

C. The Emergency Action!

Not everyone who had become a Muslim was sincere. Some Arab tribes, especially those far away from the area of Mecca and Medina, accepted Islam only because it seemed to be the trend. This fact became immediately clear when several of these tribes rebelled and declared that they would no longer pay their Zakah and do other Islamic duties.

Different Arab Bedouins began raiding Medina and creating all sorts of trouble for the sincere Muslims. To make matters worse, a couple of Bedouin leaders declared themselves as new Prophets of Allah! The most powerful of which was Musaylimah the Liar. These evil men did this even though the Qur'an called Muhammad the "Seal of all the Prophets."

Abu Bakr had few troops left in Medina as he just sent a large army to Syria to fight against the Byzantines and their allies. That army was under the command of a teenager named Usamah bin Zayd, whom the Prophet, himself, had appointed for the coming task. But Abu Bakr was still able to gather at least a small army to defend Medina against the increasing Bedouin attacks.

Then he ordered his small but tough army to go and subdue, or put down, the rebellions. Before any battle would begin, the Muslim generals would invite the rebels back to Islam and many tribes gave in without a fight, but a few unruly tribes were hungry for a battle and engaged the Muslims in war. But in battle after battle, the Muslims won victories over the rebellious Bedouins and made them sign treaties of peace. But the huge battle with Musaylimah the Liar, was soon to come.

At a place called **Yamama**, the Muslim army, which only had 13,000 soldiers, met Musaylimah's army of 40,000. After hard days of battle, the Muslims defeated the enemy and Musaylimah fell in battle. The danger of false Prophets was ended and all the Bedouin Arabs agreed to remain as faithful Muslims loyal to the Islamic government in Medina. These series of wars were known as the **Wars of the Riddah** and lasted only about a year. Abu Bakr had saved Arabia for Islam.

D. The Growth of the Islamic Nation.

One of the primary duties of Islam was to fight against evil rulers and to allow all people to hear the message of Islam. The Qur'an was totally against forcing anyone to become Muslim, it only called for getting rid of any evil rulers who would forbid people to hear the message.

The two great empires of the day were the Byzantines and the Persians. The Blessed Prophet had sent letters to the rulers of both lands inviting them to Islam and they both refused, even to the point of starting to fight against Muslims. The Persians had even supplied arms and money to the rebellious Bedouins to try and bring about the defeat of Islam. In the interests of self-defense, and in fighting against evil, the Muslims had to go on the offensive.

After the Wars of the Riddah were over, thousands more people flocked to Islam every month, seeing that Islam was going to survive after all. This swelled the numbers of Muslim soldiers, or Mujahideen, enormously. Islam started to make converts in Syria and Palestine as well, thanks to the preaching of Muslim merchants and travelers.

One Muslim leader, who lived near the border of Persian-controlled Iraq, came to Medina to ask for protection for his people from constant Persian threats and attacks. Abu Bakr sent an army of 8,000 men under the command of Khalid ibn Walid in 633 CE (12 AH) to engage the Persians in battle.

After a series of stunning victories, the outnumbered Muslims captured huge areas of the Persian empire. Within one year most of the lands of southern Iraq were firmly in the control of the Muslims. Muslim preachers and teachers entered every town and village and taught Islam to the people. Soon thousands were accepting Islam every day.

Muslims in Palestine and Syria were under threat of attack from the Byzantines so Abu Bakr ordered Khalid ibn Walid to move his army to Syria to meet the new threat. After a few important battles, the Muslims drove the Byzantines away and secured the entire northern frontier of Palestine. In one battle, a group of Muslim women were spotted by the Byzantines and were attacked. The women, led by sister **Khawlah**, picked up their tent poles and

used them as spears to fight the raiding enemy soldiers. The women held the enemy away and killed many of them, as the Byzantines only had short swords and were speared whenever they tried to get close. When Khalid's reinforcements arrived, they drove the Byzantines away. Islam was on the move.

E. The Changing of Leadership.

Two years and three months had passed with Abu Bakr as Khalifa. But he was very old and fell ill. While he was on his death bed, he called a council of the important companions of the Prophet and discussed with them who should lead after him. He suggested 'Umar ibn al Khattab should lead the Ummah and everyone agreed it was the best choice.

A few days later, after Abu Bakr passed away, 'Umar took the bayya' of the Muslims as the new Khalifa. He gave the following Speech:

"My fellow Muslims! Abu Bakr is with us no more. He has been successful in running the affairs of the Ummah for more than two years and completed some of the tasks begun by the Prophet.

"I wish the responsibility of leading the Ummah was put on someone else. I never wanted such a job. However, I promise you I will not run away from this position. I will carry out my duty to the best of my ability.

"I seek guidance from the Qur'an, the teachings of the Messenger of Allah, and the example set by Abu Bakr in running the affairs of the government. In this task I seek your participation and help. If I am right, follow me. If I do wrong, correct me so that we don't go astray."

F. A Major Defeat for Persia.

'Umar had no time to rest. Pressure from Persian soldiers on the Iraqi front was increasing and action was called for. A new army was sent from Medina to a place near the Euphrates River called Qadisiyyah. The people who lived in the area supported the Muslims and rebelled against the Persians because the Persian rulers had always been so harsh with them.

After a fierce battle, the badly outnumbered Muslims defeated the Persian army and took control of almost all of southern Iraq. As the message of Islam spread among the people there, thousands of Christians and Persians accepted Islam every day. Muslims would soon be forced to enter Persia itself for the final showdown.

Meanwhile, in the West, the Muslim forces facing the Byzantines in Syria were winning battle after battle. In almost every case, the Muslim army would only have to surround a city, cut off its supplies and ask the people to surrender, promising them that they would not be harmed.

Nearly every city in Syria fell to the Muslims this way and almost no actual fighting was occuring. The Byzantines were almost racing with each other to give up to the Muslims! By the way, the Muslim governments installed in each of the cities charged much lower taxes than the Byzantines ever did. This made the people doubly happy with Muslim rule.

After the Muslims took over the cities, life returned to normal for the people there. Because of the noble behavior of the Muslims, thousands of Christians were accepting Islam daily. After the Muslims took the huge city of Damascus, the Byzantine emperor, in far away Turkey, decided to

organize an army of 250,000 men to fight the Muslims.

At a place called Yarmuk, in the year 637 CE, an army of 40,000 Muslims defeated the Byzantines and forced them to retreat. In that same year, Jerusalem surrendered to the Muslims and 'Umar, himself, came to accept the surrender of the city. Palestine, Syria and Iraq were in Muslim hands for good.

'Umar helped to further organize the national Muslim government. The expanding Muslim world was organized into eight provinces each ruled by a governer appointed by the Khalifa. 'Umar reorganized the government system of tax collection and the treasury and ordered detailed accounts to be kept, in writing, of everything. This would be of help in raising the funds needed to face the growing threat of further attacks from the east.

Indeed, the Persians tried to launch further assaults against the Muslims in Iraq, but the Muslim armies were so successful in defeating these attacks that they followed the retreating Persians right into Persia, itself. Soon almost all of Persia would be in Muslim hands.

'Umar ruled as Khalifa for ten years. In that time, the borders of the Islamic nation were doubled and the numbers of believing Muslims were in the millions. Sadly, he was assassinated, or killed, by a Persian rebel named Feroz, who had come to Medina.

As he lay on his death bed from a knife wound, he appointed a committee of important Muslims to choose a new Khalifa within three days of his death. After a few days of debate, the choice fell on Uthman ibn Affan, who was a trusted companion of the Prophet. But as we shall see, the problems he will inherit may be too great for any leader to handle.

Questions to Answer

1. How was Abu Bakr elected as the Khalifa?
2. Who was Musaylimah?
3. Describe what the Wars of the Riddah were about.
4. What happened at Qadasiyyah?
5. Describe the growth of the Islamic nation diring 'Umar's time.
6. How did 'Umar get killed?

35 Uthman and 'Ali

Think About It

Why do you think Islam was spreading so fast to all the lands around it?

Vocabulary Words

Basrah   Khawarij

What to Learn

Muslims fell into disunity because they acted only on their emotions and refused to obey the Khalifa.

A. The Great Challenges.

Uthman became the leader at a time when Muslims were making strides on all fronts. To add to this progress, Uthman ordered the building of the first Muslim Navy. He also made sure that an official copy of the Qur'an was available in every main Muslim city.

Everything seemed to be going well for the Muslims, even new lands were added to the Islamic empire. But some new problems began to arise. Uthman was not as strict as 'Umar and was more shy about confronting people who did wrong. People loved the gentle character of Uthman, but when it became known that some of the Muslim governors in the provinces weren't behaving according to Islam, people began to complain that Uthman wasn't taking strong enough action against them.

Part of the problem was that the Muslim administrators in the new territories relied heavily on the system of local government that the Persians and Byzantines used. The Muslims were still not skilled at governing large cities and lands so they often left in place whatever city workers and tax collectors they found there.

At the same time, a few of the Muslim governors were taking advantage of the treasury and great wealth that the Muslim nation was gaining to enrich themselves and live in palaces. Uthman removed some of the corrupt governors but other governors, such as those in Syria and Egypt became so powerful that they sometimes simply ignored the Khalifa's written messages.

A third problem was that these most powerful governors were from the same family as Uthman and many people accused Uthman of playing favorites with them. Uthman was not, of course, but a few Muslims in Medina kept the charge up and soon opposition to Uthman spread.

On one occasion, a group of people came from the different provinces to complain about their governors. Khalifa Uthman listened to them and promised that he would take action and the people began their return journey home, satisfied that justice was going to be done.

On the way, an enemy of Islam named Abdullah ibn Sabah planted a fake letter on a man ordering all the people who complained about their governors to be killed when they returned home. He signed the letter as "Uthman."

When the people in the caravan found this fake letter, they believed that Uthman intended to murder them. Accordingly, they returned to Medina, surrounded Uthman's house and demanded he come out. When they showed him the letter they had found, Uthman said the letter was a fake and that he didn't have anything to do with it.

The small mob of angry people refused to believe him and they killed him. To make matters worse, they refused to run away and instead stayed in the city to press their case. The Muslims in Medina were shocked and in grief. Uthman was loved by all for his gentleness and kindness and now he had been cruelly murdered.

B. The Election of 'Ali.

'Ali was selected as the next Khalifa of the Muslims by a vote of the people in the great Masjid. Soon, people from all over Arabia came to give him their bayya'. But the immediate problem that faced him was the same one that faced Uthman: what to do about the bad governors in Iraq, Egypt and Syria. In addition to this, a large number of Muslims began demanding immediate punishment for the killers of Uthman.

'Ali was in a difficult situation. He decided to delay his investigation into the murder until the situation could be better understood and addressed. This was in keeping with 'Ali's intellectual mind. He was always against hasty decisions made through enflamed emotions.

But some people took this delay the wrong way and thought that 'Ali was refusing to bring the killers to justice. When A'ishah, the widow of the Prophet, heard about this, she joined with a group of people who decided to fight against the Khalifa to force him to punish the killers.

Meanwhile, 'Ali was taking action to address the problems before him. He sent written messages to all the bad governors asking them to step down from their posts. Some of the governors went voluntarily, but a few of them, most importantly, Mu'awiya of Syria, refused to even read the letter. Trouble would soon come from Syria but 'Ali had other matters to attend to first.

C. The Battle of the Camel.

A'ishah traveled with a group of like-minded people to the new Muslim city of **Basrah** to raise an army to confront 'Ali. They found some of the killers of Uthman in the city and executed them. Then they defeated 'Ali's supporters there. They soon gathered a huge army to march against the Khalifa.

When news of this reached 'Ali, he organized an army of his own and marched to Basrah to stop A'ishah and her supporters. He didn't want A'ishah, or anyone else, to take the law into their own hands. The evil Abdullah ibn Sabah was in 'Ali's army with many of his supporters, and when 'Ali asked him and his men to leave, knowing that they were suspicious characters, the evil troublemaker thought of a daring plan. As you will see, it will be the cause of a great disaster.

The two armies met outside of Basrah in the year 656 CE (36 AH). 'Ali and A'ishah met face to face and negotiated a peace agreement. After they returned to their camps, Abdullah ibn Sabah made his move.

Before anyone could stop it, a few of his men, who were hiding behind both armies, charged out swinging their swords as if the battle had begun. In the confusion, the men of both armies rushed to fight each other, thinking that they had been ordered to do so.

Thousands of Muslims were engaged in battle against each other. The Blessed Prophet once said that if two Muslims kill each other, they will both go to Hell-fire. Upon seeing the fighting, A'ishah became alarmed and tried to stop it. She mounted her camel and rode out into the battle trying to tell the people to stop, but her own army thought she had come to encourage them to fight more so the battle went on.

When 'Ali saw that A'ishah's presence was making the battle even hotter, he ordered some of his soldiers to cut down her camel so no one would see her any more. After 'Ali's men reached her and did it, they escorted her off the battlefield. 'Ali's army defeated the rebels and peace was restored. The affair was known as the Battle of the Camel, after A'ishah's ride into the battle.

D. The Battle of Siffin.

To save Medina from any more political trouble, 'Ali moved the capital of the Islamic empire to the new Muslim city of Kufah, near the border with Iraq. With the immediate trouble solved, 'Ali turned his attention to the rebellious governors.

He decided to replace every governor ever appointed by Uthman, thinking that they were weak and untrustworthy. But Mu'awiya of Syria again refused to step down and instead gathered an army to defend his position.

'Ali marched his own army from Kufah to a place in Syria called Siffin. There he found Mu'awiya's army ready to face him. 'Ali tried to start peace talks with Mu'awiya, but Mu'awiya refused saying that he would never negotiate until the issue of Uthman's killers was settled, once and for all.

A three day battle followed and 'Ali's army made steady progress against Mu'awiya's forces. When it looked like he was going to lose, Mu'awiya ordered his soldiers to hang pages from the Qur'an on the end of their spears so 'Ali would pause. The trick worked and Mu'awiya and 'Ali began negotiations.

A group of 'Ali's supporters were angry that 'Ali didn't go for the total victory and they rebelled against 'Ali. They are known as the **Khawarij**. They left the battlefield and returned to Kufah to prepare and army to attack 'Ali's forces.

'Ali and Mu'awiya pulled back their armies and returned to their own lands while the negotiations went on. 'Ali put down the revolt of the Khawarij fighters when he returned and then worked to strengthen his position in Kufah.

After several months of sending messages and proposals back and forth, both 'Ali and Mu'awiya agreed that they would let a new Khalifa be elected, and that neither one of them would run for the office.

But this was a trick on Mu'awiya's part. In a big public gathering, after 'Ali's representative declared 'Ali would step down as Khalifa, one of Mu'awiya's friends stood up and said that Mu'awiya would now be the new Khalifa!

This double-cross amazed everyone! The most angry people of all were the few rebel Khawarij fighters that had gone into hiding or who had pretended to make peace. They decided to kill both Mu'awiya and 'Ali and then to find a new Khalifa.

While they made their plots, Mu'awiya and 'Ali's armies made moves against each other from Egypt to Medina. Mu'awiya even briefly attacked and occupied Mecca and Medina!

Finally, one lone Khawarij man was able to sneak up on 'Ali and stab him. 'Ali ibn Abi Talib died in the year 661 CE (40 AH), just after Fajr prayers. The last of the true Khalifas who lived totally by the Qur'an and Sunnah was gone. The Khawarij agent sent to kill Mu'awiya failed to assasinate his target, however, though he did wound him.

Now new challenges presented themselves to the Muslim community, which was divided along political lines and badly in need of unity. Unity would soon come and a new line of Khalifas would arise, but it would not be completely according to the Sunnah and would cause even greater challenges to come in the future.

The period of rule of the first four Khalifas is known as the Khilafah ar-Rashidah, or Period of the Rightly Guided Khalifas. All four of those men were companions of the Blessed Prophet from the earliest days of Islam. All four of them were given the good news by the Prophet that they were guaranteed to go to Heaven, and all four lived simple and moral lives based completely on the Qur'an and Sunnah.

May Allah bless them and reward them for laying the foundation of a strong Ummah and may we learn from their noble example and re-establish the Islamic nation once again, using their example as our guide-post. Amin.

Questions to Answer

1. Why did people start to complain to Uthman?
2. What caused Uthman to be killed?
3. Why did 'Ali want a delay in investigating the crime against Uthman?
4. What causes led to the Battle of siffin?
5. Describe the troubles between 'Ali and Mu'awiya.

Skill Builder: Understanding Islamic History

Islamic history was only purely Islamic from the time of the Blessed Prophet Muhammad until the end of the rule of 'Ali ibn Abi Talib. After that, history continued to be made, but it was often only history with a Muslim flavor rather than history that served the Islamic cause. We say this because not all of the people and Khalifas that came and went were strict in following Islamic teachings. Many were good Muslims but most were only average or even weak in their Iman.

The next phase in Muslim history, after the time of the Rightly-Guided Khalifas, can be divided into two separate time periods. The first is known as the Ummayid Period, while the second is called the Abbasid Period. We will be examining some of the major highlights from these two periods to get an idea of the flow of Muslim history and what lessons it can teach us. In total this will cover about 600 years of Muslim history from the years 661 to 1258 CE (41-656 AH). The review questions at the end will help us to analyze and understand what has gone before us so we can better prepare ourselves for the future.

A. The Ummayid Period.

After the noble Khalifa, 'Ali ibn Abi Talib, passed away, Mu'awiya was able to declare himself the Khalifa of the entire Muslim world. The term Ummayid comes from the family name of the clan of Ummaya. All the Khalifas who will rule for the next 90 years will come from his family line. There was a lot of military progress on the frontiers of the Islamic nation with Muslim armies conquering Afghanistan, North Africa as well as reaching the borders of India. The new Muslim navy was making contacts as far away as East Africa and southern India and Islamic teachings were filtering into the lands of the non-Muslims like wild-fire.

But for all his achievements, Mu'awiya broke an important Islamic rule about choosing new leaders of the Ummah. Instead of letting the Muslims form a committee to elect a new Khalifa after his death, Mu'awiya decided that his own son, Yazid, would be the Khalifa after him. This outraged many Muslims but Mu'awiya had enough military power to crush any opposition.

When Mu'awiya passed away, Yazid then declared himself the Khalifa. Yazid was a known wine-drinker and lover of wealth. Many opposed him, including the grandson of the Blessed Prophet Muhammad, Hussain ibn 'Ali, who refused to accept Yazid as the new Khalifa. Yazid sent an army of 4,000 to crush this challenger to his power. At a place called Karbala, Imam Hussain was killed along with 72 of his followers.

Yazid even sent an army to attack Mecca where more Muslims had set up a rebellion against him. But Yazid died before the conquest of Mecca was finished. A period of confusion followed where several Khalifas came and went.

Finally, a series of strong Khalifas emerged who returned to the task of expanding the borders of Islam. Huge new areas in Central Asia, Europe, India and Africa were added to the Islamic state and converts were swelling the ranks of Islam at an ever faster pace.

One of the most famous of these Khalifas was named 'Umar ibn Abdul Aziz, who ruled from 717-719 CE (99-101 AH). He was known as an excellent Muslim and earned the nick-name, "the Second 'Umar." He never missed his Salat and ruled with justice and fairness. He even sent Muslim teachers as far away as Tibet and China.

During the rule of the Ummayids, Islamic learning flourished. Thousands of books were being written every year. Free public hospitals and schools were set up in every city and town and Muslim scientists and philosophers were busy making new discoveries. The rule of the Ummayids played a very great role in the strengthening of the Islamic community.

B. The Abbasids.

The Ummayid rulers were overthrown, however, after a series of wars and internal rebellions with a group known as the Abbasids. The Khalifas of this line were to rule for the next five hundred years and it was under their rule that the greatest progress was made in the arts, sciences, literature and medicine.

The most famous Abbasid Khalifa was named Harun ar Rashid, who ruled from the splendid and magnificent Muslim city of Baghdad. The city was so developed that it gained the nick-name, "the most civilized city in the world." It was organized into a circle pattern with even rows of city blocks and shopping districts that made it a major tourist attraction for travelers from all over the world.

The Abbasid empire gradually declined, however, in its later years, due to bad government practices and a weakness of Iman among many of the nobles and leaders. Some of the Khalifas were more interested in living in palaces, dancing and drinking alcohol than in holding up the banner of the Islamic Way of Life.

Abbasid rule was finally wiped out in 1258 CE, (along with the city of Baghdad,) when non-Muslim invaders called Mongols swept into the Muslim lands like a tidal wave. They conquered all of Muslim Persia and Iraq and unleashed a reign of terror against the Muslims there.

Eventually the Mongols converted to Islam, after they were settled in Muslim lands for around one hundred years and were able to appreciate and learn about the teachings of the faith. They even went on to become such strong Muslim rulers that they conquered all of Hindu India and a large part of southern Russia and Eastern Europe for Islam. But the power and might of the Abbasids was never going to be achieved by any Muslim empire ever again.

The Islamic World in the year 1000 CE

Review Questions.

1. Describe the achievements of the Ummayids.
2. Who was 'Umar ibn Abdul Aziz?
3. Describe the basic history of the abbasids.
4. Who was Harun ar Rashid?

36 A Famous Muslim to Know

Think About It

How are our Du'as answered?

Vocabulary Words

Imam Shaf'i

What to Learn

Muslims keep Allah in their minds in their daily lives.

A. Who was Nafisa bint Hasan?

There have been many famous Muslim women who were known for their Taqwa, Iman and wisdom. Islam teaches that men and women are equal before Allah and that both can rise to the highest levels of spirituality. As Allah said, *"Whoever does a good deed, whether they are male or female, and is a believer, will enter the Garden of Happiness. They will have an unlimited reward."* (40:40)

One of the most blessed women in Islamic history was Nafisa bint Muhammad Hasan, who lived around the year 700 CE. She was born in Mecca but eventually moved to Egypt. She was married to a famous Muslim scholar named Is-haq ibn As Sadiq.

Soon after her arrival, the people of Egypt began to admire her greatly. She was known for her simple lifestyle and devotion to Allah. She was so trustworthy that when the great Islamic scholar, Imam Shaf'i, visited Egypt, he heard her saying some Hadiths he didn't know and he learned them from her and taught them to others on the authority of her word alone.

B. The Missing Red Bag.

To understand how devoted to prayer and Iman she was, we can give, as an example, the story of a certain poor woman who had four daughters that she could barely feed. Whatever small amounts of money she made came from the yarn she and her daughters would spin and sell in the market.

One Friday, the mother wrapped a large bundle of yarn in a red cloth bag and set out for the market-place. Her plan was to spend half her earnings on a book for her daughters and the other half would be used to buy food for the week.

Along the way, however, a large bird swooped down and grabbed the red bag in its talons. Then it flew away. Seeing her yarn being taken away like that caused the woman to faint.

When she woke up, she worried that she wouldn't have anything to feed her family. She sat down and cried tears of sorrow. Some people passing by asked her what the problem was and when she told them, they suggested that she go and see Nafisa.

The woman went directly to Nafisa's house and told her the whole story of what happened with the bird. Nafisa felt sorry for the woman and prayed to Allah to let her property be returned. Then Nafisa told the lady to sit down.

After an hour had gone by, a group of sailors suddenly arrived at Nafisa's house. The captain said, "Assalamu 'alaykum, sister. A very strange thing has happened to us today. We were sailing into port when

a small hole opened up in our ship's bottom. Water began to gush into the ship and we knew we would drown if we couldn't stop it. We tried everything to stop the leak but nothing worked.

"Suddenly, a bird carrying a red bundle flew overhead and dropped what it was carrying on our heads. By the will of Allah, we used that bundle to stop the leak. We brought the bag of yarn and also 500 gold coins with us to offer to you as a way to thank Allah for his help."

Nafisa cried out, "My Lord! My Allah! You are kind and generous to your servants."

Then Nafisa called to the poor old woman who was still sitting in the other room to come to her. When the poor woman saw the wet bag of yarn she cried out in amazement. But before she could collect it and leave, Nafisa asked her, "How much money would you have sold that bag of yarn for in the market?"

"Maybe 20 or 30 silver coins." The poor woman answered.

Nafisa then gave the woman the 500 gold coins for the bag of yarn. The poor woman was so overjoyed that she ran home and distributed the money among her daughters. Afterwards they never had to work again and instead they all became students in Nafisa's Qur'an classes.

A few weeks later a man came running to Nafisa's home, begging to be protected from the governor of Egypt who wanted to punish him unjustly. She made a du'a for him and sent him on his way saying, "Allah, the Mighty, will cover the eyes of the unjust from seeing who you are."

The man was soon captured by the ruler's men and brought before the court for punishment. When the soldiers said they brought the prisoner, the ruler asked, "Where is he? I don't see him."

The soldiers replied, "He's right here in front of you."

Again the ruler complained that he couldn't see him.

Then the soldiers told the ruler that they heard he had visited Nafisa and she prayed for him so that the eyes of the unjust would not be able to see him.

The ruler was confused and thought for a minute. He lowered his head and cried, "So, my injustice has become so great that merely through people's prayers Allah covers my eyes! My Lord! I repent of my evil! Forgive me!"

Then the ruler lifted his head and saw the prisoner standing before him. The ruler prayed for him, kissed his head and gave him a new set of clothes to wear. Then he set him free in thanks. Afterwards, the ruler gathered all his wealth together and gave it to the poor. He sent one hundred thousand gold coins to Nafisa as way to thank her for helping him come back to true Iman.

Nafisa took the money and gave it all away to the poor. One of her students suggested that they save a little of the money so they could buy some food to break their fast that day. Nafisa instead gave the woman the bundle of yarn in the red bag and said, "Go sell this yarn in the market and use the money to buy our food."

Questions to Answer

1. Which famous scholar so trusted Nafisa that he accepted whatever she said with full trust?
2. How did the poor woman lose her yarn? Why was it bad for her?
3. How did Nafisa answer the poor woman when she came crying?
4. How was the poor woman helped in the end?
5. How did Nafisa help a bad ruler learn to be a good Muslim again?

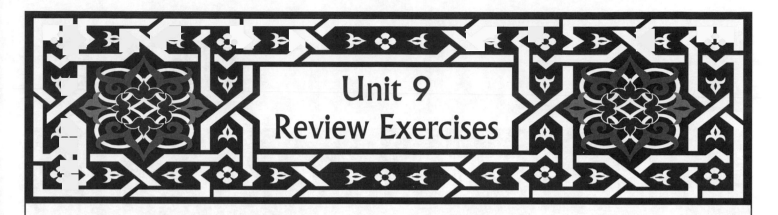

Unit 9
Review Exercises

Vocabulary Review

On a separate piece of paper, write the meaning of each word below. Remember to write in complete sentences.

1. Siffin
2. Byzantines
3. Yamama
4. Khawla
5. Qadasiyyah
6. Yarmuk
7. Abu Bakr
8. 'Ali ibn Abi Talib
9. Abbasids
10. 'Umar ibn al Khattab
11. Wars of the Ridda
12. Khawarij

Remembering What You Read

On a separate piece of paper, answer the questions below. Remember to answer as best as you can and write in complete sentences.

1. Who was Nafisa bint Hasan?
2. Describe the famous Abbasid capital of Baghdad.
3. How did Mu'awiya trick 'Ali into stepping down as Khalifa?
4. Describe two of the battles between the Muslims and the Byzantines.
5. What was the Battle of the Camel about?
6. Describe what happened during Khalifa Abu Bakr's rule.
7. Who made a false letter that got Uthman murdered?
8. What does the term Khilafah ar Rashidah mean, and who does it apply to and why?
9. What were the two main problems that Khalifa 'Ali had to face?

Thinking to Learn

Read the following statement and explain whether it is true or false. Write in complete sentences on a separate piece of paper and give examples to support your answer.

After the passing away of the Blessed Prophet, Muslims were never threatened by any nations or powers again.

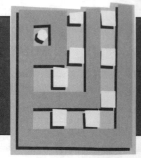

Unit 10

Islamic Arts

Think About It

What effect does art have on people?

Vocabulary Words

Calligraphy   Arabesque   Architecture
Minara

What to Learn

Islam has art forms all its own.

A. Beauty and Islam.

The Blessed Prophet once remarked, "Allah is beautiful and loves beauty." (Hadith) And indeed we find that in His creation there is a lot to admire. The mountains, the clouds, the animals, plants and oceans are all beautiful. The entire universe is an example of Allah's artistic ability.

Allah says, "*You won't find anything out of order in the creation of the Merciful. Look again, do you see any flaws? Again- look a second time. Your eyes will come back to you tired and weary.*" (67:3-4)

Many times people like to make their own art as well, using their own talents and creativity. Some people like to paint, others draw, some will write while others will use their bodies or voices to make art. The desire to express ourselves through art is in every one of us and is a reflection of the special qualities that Allah has endowed every human being with.

There are many forms of art. Islam, being the complete way of life, guides us in the expression of our creativity. This is important because what may

be good art to some people may, in fact, be bad for us and hateful in the sight of Allah. For example, in the museums of most non-Muslim countries, you will find endless statues and paintings of naked people or false gods. Non-Muslims call that shameful stuff art, but we just call it ignorance and the madness of Shaytan.

Allah says, "*Can a person who was dead that We gave life and a light to so he could walk among people (in truth) be the same as a person who is buried under darkness from which he cannot escape? And in the same way, the unbelievers think their (bad) deeds are good for them.*" (6:122)

The definition of good art, according to Islam, is any form of creativity that raises a person's thinking, brings joy to the heart, and makes us reflect on the glory and beauty of Allah's world and our way of life within it. Bad art, according to Islam, makes us depressed or confused, makes us feel ashamed and promotes bad values and unIslamic ways.

Muslims have been some of the greatest artists in the world, and Islamic art has been praised by both Muslims and non-Muslims for its beauty, simplicity, elegance and spiritual focus. From the earliest days of Islam, up until the present day, Muslims have been making world-class art. They do it to glorify Allah and to bring people's hearts and minds closer to Allah.

"The Middle East."

In general, Muslim artists have used every type of art form that is known to our world. From pottery, poetry and painting to architecture and drawing- Muslims have done it all- and done it very well. In this unit, we will explore some of the artistic achievements that Muslims have made and see examples of their works. You will be delighted and amazed and may even be influenced to get in touch with the artistic side of your own self.

B. What is Calligraphy?

One of the most respected Muslim art forms is called Calligraphy. **Calligraphy** means to write words in a fancy and artistic way. The main reason why this art form developed was to write the ayat of the Qur'an in a beautiful and noble style. People love the Qur'an so much that its very words themselves become the art.

Calligraphy in Islam began from the very first years of the Islamic state and continues to be practiced by Muslim men and women all over the world to this very day. In this lesson you will see examples of calligraphy done my modern Muslim artists as well as some from hundreds of years ago. Many Muslim countries hold calligraphy contests every few years where artists can compete for the top honors and recognition.

You will often find fancy calligraphy used as decoration on the walls of Masjids and other important places. Try to trace the designs you see on this page yourself, or make up new ones using Qur'anic words or ayat. Your teacher may be able to show you more about how to do it.

C. Muslim Architects.

Another form of art is called architecture (arki tek chur). **Architecture** means to design buildings, monuments and other places to be seen or used by people. Every community needs buildings and public spaces for people to move around in and Muslims have created some of the most beautiful buildings in the world! If you've ever had the chance to travel to a Muslim country you might have seen some of those beautiful buildings.

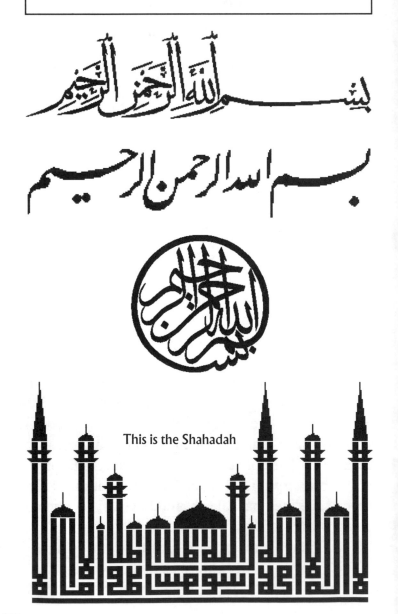

How Many Ways Can You Write Bismillahir Rahmanir Raheem?

This is the Shahadah

182

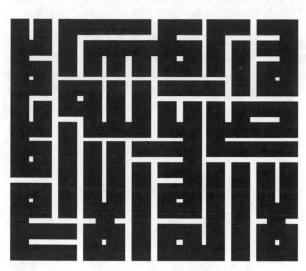

This is the Shahadah

"Indeed Allah is beautiful and He loves beauty."

"Allah"
Repeated over and over.

An ayah from
the Qur'an

A whole boat load of praises for Allah and the Blessed Prophet Muhammad!

Spotlight
Famous Muslim Women Calligraphers

The art of calligraphy began right from the beginning of the Islamic world. There have been many great calligraphers whose names are still remembered by Muslims to this day. Both men and women participated in this great art form and examples of Islamic calligraphy, both ancient and modern, decorate the walls of Masjids all over the world.

Every Muslim city has its famous calligraphers. During the Islamic era, when Islam was the supreme way of life in Muslim lands, calligraphers were respected and considered to be the finest artists. In the Muslim city of Cordoba, Spain, about 700 years ago, there were over 170 female calligraphers who made beautiful copies of the Qur'an in very artistic calligraphy.

They used to work in shifts, day and night, and the glow of all their candles and lamps used to provide light for three city blocks! One of these repected women was A'ishah bint Ahmad. She was an expert at a calligraphy style known as Kufic. She had an extensive library and also wrote poetry. She was always an invited guest at state dinners and exhibitions.

One of the most beautifully illustrated copies of the Qur'an ever written was done by a female calligrapher by the name of Zulaykhah Khatimi al Sa'di. She completed her project in Turkey in about the year 1276 AH (1859 CE). The book is now on display in Jeddah, in Arabia.

Ridaa bint al Fath, who lived in Baghdad, about 800 years ago, had such beautiful penmanship, that she earned the nickname, "the Glory of Womanhood." She was a Hafizah, or memorizer of the entire Qur'an, as well as a Muhaddithah, or authority on Hadith. She used to sell her calligraphy and use her earnings to buy the freedom of Muslim prisoners of war. She was so loved by the people that when she passed away, the Khalifa, himself, led her funeral prayers.

D. What is Arabesque?

Muslim artists have generally avoided drawing pictures of animals or people directly. This is because there is always a danger of people worshipping a picture as an idol. It may sound strange to have to worry about this but history is full of examples of people worshipping paintings and drawings of men and animals. All a Muslim needs to do is go into a Christian Church or Hindu Temple and see the people bowing and praying to pictures and drawings and then he or she will understand.

The Prophet said, "Whoever makes an image in this world will be asked to put life into it on the Day of Resurrection, but he won't be able to do it." (Bukhari)

Muslim scholars say that the only way any pictures of people or animals are allowed is if they don't look very real, are meant for children and are obviously not to be taken seriously. The computer-made graphics used throughout this children's book are like that. They don't look very real and no one would think to worship them.

The art form that Muslim painters and sketch artists created so that they could express themselves, without making animals or people, is called the art of Arabesque. **Arabesque** means fancy designs and drawings.

Many Arabesques are shape-pictures made up of repeating patterns, or "Infinity-Art." Many times such art is created with the help of algebra and advanced geometry, another Muslim invention. Other times, Arabesques will include patterns made up of flowers and flowing borders with nature scenes.

Almost every Masjid in the world has walls and hallways full of decorative Arabesques and many books published in the Muslim world over the last thousand years have had their pages decorated with fancy, colorful designs. This type of art is so special and requires such skill that it takes years to master.

Study the examples of Arabesques that you see displayed here and notice the detail and exact spacing. Try to draw a few of your own if you can!

E. Working Together.

Because the Masjid is the main building to be used by Muslims throughout the week, Muslim architects and calligraphers have often joined forces in designing Prayer Halls that will inspire and humble all those who enter inside. Because the main open space in any Masjid is flat and needs to be clear so people can line up for prayer, the walls, inside and out and roofs were usually the targets for special designing.

Many Masjids have curved domes on their roof. Almost all have tall **Minaras**, or Minarets, for the Mu'adhan to call people to prayer, and you can often find beautiful fountains and gardens in or around the Masjid. Some of the most famous Muslim builders and their achievements are to be found in the pictures in this lesson.

Simple, spiritual, beautiful and inspiring: these are the goals of Islamic art and Muslims have found their way to making those goals a reality. Perhaps the artist in you will come out and you'll create art that will move people to glorify Allah and feel uplifted in their hearts.

Masjid al Aqsa,
Jerusalem, Palestine

Badshahi Masjid,
Lahore, Pakistan

Taj Mahal, Agra, India

Salimiyya Masjid,
Edirne, Turkey

Questions to Answer

1. Why do people like to make art?
2. What is good art according to Islam?
3. What is calligraphy?
4. Name one famous Muslim woman calligrapher and mention some facts about her.
5. Describe what Arabesque is.

Skill Builder: Making Arabesques

An Arabesque design is made up of patterns that often repeat themselves. Sometimes Arabesques will form shapes that look like flowers. This is called Floral Design. Other times there will be endless, complex patterns that seem to go on forever.

To make an Arabesque you will need some tools to use. These tools are: A pencil, A ruler, A compass, a protractor, a thin-tipped marker and colored markers.

You will use the markers last, after the basic design has been made. Follow the directions and examples below and you will have created a basic Arabesque design. If you would like more information about Islamic art there are a lot of books you can read. Good luck and good art!

A. Making an eight pointed star and tile.

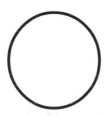

Use your compass to draw a circle

Use your ruler or protractor to make these lines.

Add 2 diagonal lines

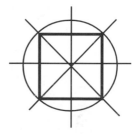

Draw a box shape

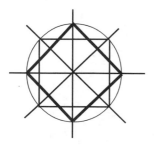

Draw another box shape, but slanted this time.

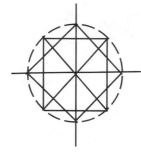

Erase the dotted lines of the circle

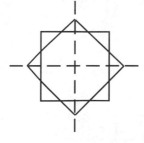

Erase the diagonal lines inside of the eight-pointed star

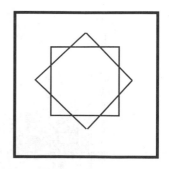

Draw a square around the star and erase the remaining inner guide lines.

187

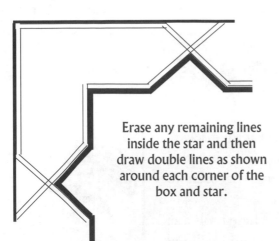

Erase any remaining lines inside the star and then draw double lines as shown around each corner of the box and star.

Then choose a floral pattern style and fill in the empty spaces with hand-drawn images. Many artists would put some Arabic calligraphy in the center to complete their work.

Then you have an Arabesque!

38 Islam and Writing

Think About It

Why are books so important?

Vocabulary Words

Tajweed Martyr Tafseer

What to Learn

Islam encourages all kinds of good writing.

A. Muslims and Reading.

Islam has always encouraged people to read and write. Do you remember the very first word that Allah revealed to the Prophet Muhammad? His first command was, "Read." And ever since that time, Muslims have been very interested readers as well as excellent writers.

The first and most important book to read is the Qur'an. The Qur'an was made by Allah, the best author of all. If you take a good look at what styles of writing that the Qur'an contains, you will find many different techniques used such as stories, ryhming, declarations, mystery, suspense, excitement, predictions, essays as well as many other literary methods.

All the best ways of conveying the message were used by Allah and as Allah pointed out, no human will ever be able to make something as beautiful as the Qur'an. Muslims are encouraged to read it, learn from it, think about it and memorize it. We are even taught how to say it out loud beautifully! That is called **Tajweed** reciting.

The Blessed Prophet Muhammad encouraged every Muslim man, woman and child to learn how to read and write. "Talabul 'ilmi faridatun 'ala kulli Muslimin wa Muslimat." "Learning knowledge is a required duty on every Muslim man and Muslim woman." (Ibn Majah)

Another time he said that when a person is reading that it is beautiful in the sight of Allah. On another occasion, he said that the ink of a scholar is more noble than the blood of a martyr. A **martyr** is someone who gives their life in a war for Allah's cause. That means that Islam believes that using your brains is more valuable than using your brawn!

As the fourth Khalifa, 'Ali ibn Abi Talib once remarked, "The beauty of writing is the tongue of the hand and the elegance of thought."

Muslims have taken their duty to read and write to such a high level that for most of the last 1,500 years, since Islam was born, Muslims were the only people in the world who had schools for everyone to learn how to read. Five hundred years ago, the average person in Europe or China couldn't even read one word, while in the Muslim world, there were libraries everywhere and schools in every town and city.

The only reason many Muslim countries are backward today is that about three hundred years ago, many Muslims became lazy about following Islam and they stopped encouraging people to learn. Our Ummah became weaker because of it and Allah let the non-Muslims of the world take charge as a punishment to us.

Now Muslims have woken up again and everywhere they are learning to read and write again. Insha'llah, as Allah wills, we will become stronger every year until we will get Allah's good favor again. May Allah help us all to learn as much as we can to make this happen!

B. Books and the Muslim World.

Muslims have been some of the greatest writers in the world. The first kinds of books that Muslims wrote in the early days of Islam were mostly about Hadiths, Shari'ah and the beliefs and practices of Islam. They had to do this because so many people were becoming Muslims that they needed thousands of books to teach everyone. This also helped to spread interest in reading.

As the years passed and Muslims became settled all over the Middle East, North Africa, Asia and Europe, new types of writing began to come out. For example, many Muslims began to write books which talked about the Qur'an and how to understand it. These kinds of books are called **Tafseer**, or Commentary.

Some of the great writers of Tafseer books were people like Muhammad Fakhr ud-Deen ar-Razi, Muhammad at-Tabari, Mahmoud Zamakhshari, Isma'il Ibn Kathir and al-Qurtubi. All of them studied the Qur'an with great care and wrote about the meanings of the ayat and how and why they were

revealed to the Holy Prophet. Muslims to this day consult these Tafseer writings for understanding and reference. Some of the books written by the classical, or previous scholars have been translated into English also.

Around a thousand years ago, Muslim writers branched out into new kinds of literature. In addition to the books about Islamic law, the Hadith and the Qur'an, Muslims began writing detailed books about science, history, geography and travel. By this time there were many colleges and universities in the Muslim world and the light of knowledge was spreading in all directions.

Muslims were also great writers of fiction stories and adventure novels during this time all the way up until the present day. There are some famous collections of stories that are translated into English. One of these is called, "The Thousand and One Nights." The stories of Ali Baba and the Forty Thieves, Aladdin and the Lamp and Sinbad the Sailor come from this book.

Most of the great stories of the Muslim world, however, are not yet available in English. Most of the stories in the past were written in Arabic, Urdu, Farsi or Turkish and have not been translated yet into English. But many have been and you can find more and more great books to read all the time written by great Muslim authors.

In addition, a new generation of Muslim authors in North America and Europe are busy writing good books for both Muslims and non-Muslims to read. Maybe you're a great Muslim author-to-be yourself. Only Allah knows.

C. Muslim Fables.

A fable is a story that is not always true, but is meant to teach a lesson. Some fables involve fantastic events such as talking animals or wily Jinns. When you remember that Islam teaches that animals have their own ways of communicating, then the fables don't always seem quite as far-fetched. Here are examples of some fables that come from the Muslim world. See if you can catch the lesson each one is teaching.

The Cat Who Went to Mecca

A Fable From Jordan

A long time ago the king of the cats went on a pilgrimage to Mecca. When he returned, the king of the mice felt like he should come and pay him the traditional visit of congratulations on his safe return as a Hajji, or pilgrim. He said to his fellow mice, "Tradition demands that we go to his house and welcome him back formally."

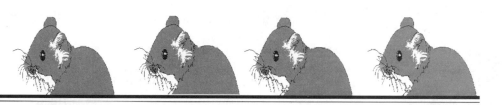

But the mice were not convinced. "The cat is our enemy; how can we go near him in safety?" The king explained, "Now that he has been to Mecca and become a Hajji, he is no longer free to do what was allowed before. These days he remains at prayer from morning till night, and he always makes dhikr on his prayer beads."

The mice were not persuaded. "You go and call on him and see if he changed," they said. "We shall wait for you here."

So the king of the mice set out for the home of the cat. When he reached it, he found a crack in the wall which he just managed to squeeze through. When he poked his head out the other side and looked around, he saw the king of the cats with a white kufi on his head. He was praising Allah, murmuring prayers, and every now and then bowing in sajda and glorifying his Maker.

The king of the mice decided that the cat had really changed his ways and strode confidantly towards him saying all the customary greetings. But as soon as the king of the cats caught sight of him, he dropped his dhikr beads and pounced towards him! And but for Allah the Preserver, he would have bitten the mouse's tail right off.

The king of the mice jumped back into the crack in the wall and ran all the way back to his subjects. "How is the king of the cats after his Hajj?" they asked. "Let's hope he changed for the better."

"Never mind the Hajj," said the king of the mice. "He may pray like a Hajji, but he still pounces like a cat."

The Woodcutter Without a Brain

A Moroccan Folktale

Two woodcutters were walking in a forest when they saw lion tracks on the road. "This is the mark of a lion," said one. "What should we do?"

"Let us go on our way and do what we have to do." said his friend. So they continued along the path and each collected a load of firewood. When it was time for them to return, the first man said, "By Allah, let us take another way home!"

"No, this path is shorter," said his friend. The first man said, "I saw lion tracks on the road, and I will not return that way, by Allah!" And he took a different rocky path that lead higher up into a mountain.

The second woodcutter returned the way they had come. When he reached the place where they had noticed traces of a lion, he found the lion himself sitting in the middle of the road. "Assalam 'alaykum, uncle lion," stammered the man.

"Wa 'alaykum assalam, O son of Adam," said the lion.

"*Wha..Wha...* What are you doing here?" asked the man.

"I am sick," replied the lion, "and I need the brain from the head of a man to cure me. Allah in His mercy has led you to me and is offering me your brain, alhumdulillah."

"Listen, O lion," said the frightened man, "for what I am about to tell you is the truth. I am a brainless fellow. If I had the least bit of brain I would not have returned this way after knowing their were lions around. The one with the brain is up there, beyond the rocks!"

The lion thought for a moment and then said, "May Allah grant you happiness," and he began climbing up the mountain to find the other man.

The Poor Imam
A Legend From Central China

A long time ago there was a poor but very learned Imam. He often gave away to the poor whatever he received, such as money and clothes. All the while he himself became poorer and poorer. All he could afford to live in was a small hut with a roof made of straw.

He would say to himself, "The Holy Prophet, may he be blessed, told us, 'Be in the world like a stranger. Save yourself from Hell even if only half a date (given in charity).'" So he knew that he didn't want to have a lot of stuff that would get in the way of living a simple life.

One day a rich man named Ma Wang heard about the poor Imam's great knowledge. He invited him to a dinner in his mansion out of admiration.

Because the poor Imam didn't have any nice clothes, he came to the dinner in a shabby cloak and pants. All the wealthy men looked down on him when he entered the room and so he was seated in the back of the room at a table reserved for common people.

Then, a few minutes later, another Imam came in to the dinner. He was dressed in very fine clothes and looked very rich. When all the wealthy people saw him they asked him to sit in the place of honor.

A few weeks later, for some reason, this rich man gave another dinner. He invited the poor Imam again, but this time the Imam told the messenger that he would rather not go this time. He said, "It would probably be better if you only invited the rich Imam who sat at the place of honor."

The messenger replied, "Please, you were invited by Ma Wang. Be sure to come, but this time you had better come in fine clothes."

As it so happened, the poor Imam received a donation of clothes from a well-to-do family who wanted to get rewards from Allah for giving in charity. The Imam was about to go and distribute them to the poor when a thought came to his mind.

Later that evening, when it was time to go to the dinner, the poor Imam put on a very fine over-coat and shoes that

he found in the pile of donated clothes. When he arrived at Ma Wang's house, all the rich guests were so impressed with his rich clothes that they asked him to sit at the seat of honor.

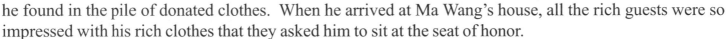

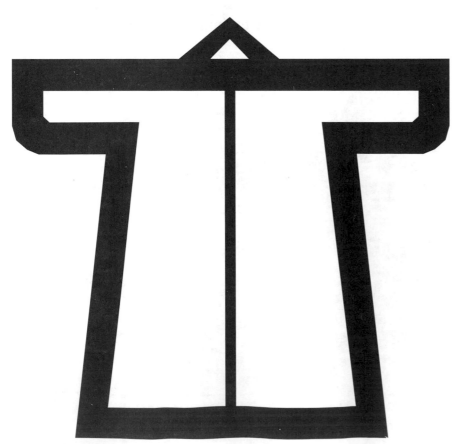

The servants brought bowls of hot soup and placed them in front of everyone. The poor Imam saw all the rich people sitting around the table and looked at their greedy and hungry faces. Everyone lifted their bowls to start drinking their soup and they invited the Imam to also start.

But the poor Imam simply stood up, took off his expensive over-coat and shoes and put them on the table.

"These are my coat and shoes, please help yourselves," he told the amazed people. Everyone began to ask why.

The poor Imam replied, "I must donate these to the poor. You don't respect knowledge. You only respect clothes. So I see you are really the poorest people of all and deserving of charity!"

Once there was Muslim ruler, a Sultan, on a voyage in one of his large ships. Among the people on the ship was a young man who had never been on a boat before. He looked out at the wide, blue sea and got so scared that he started to cry and yell. The rocking of the boat made him even more upset and he complained and yelled even louder.

Everyone around him tried to quiet him down but nothing worked. The Sultan and the sailors were very annoyed and thought that the trip was going to be a chore for them on account of this noisy young man.

Now on the same ship was a very wise Imam. He went to the Sultan and asked permission to bring this young man to his senses by any means. The Sultan was more than happy to give his permission and everyone watched as the Imam went into action.

He ordered the sailors to tie a few pieces of extra wood together. Then he

ordered that a long rope should be tied to the wood. Then he told the sailors to tie the other end of the rope to a mast and to throw the rest of it, and the wood bundle, overboard into the sea. When the wood bundle hit the water it began to be dragged behind the boat by the rope it was tied to.

Then the wise Imam ordered the soldiers to seize the yelling young man and to throw him overboard as well! The man screamed and yelled louder as he tried to resist the soldiers, but he was eventually heaved over the side of the boat to the amazement of all.

He hit the water with a crash and would have drowned but he saw the wood bundle coming by him and he splashed and threw his arms out until he just managed to grab it. He wrapped his arms around it and screamed and yelled as the waves kept crashing into his face.

Everyone on board the ship could relax now because, although the young man was still screaming, he was now some distance from the boat at the end of a rope. After a few hours, the wise Imam ordered the soldiers to pull the crude raft in towards the boat until it was near the back section of the ship, but not to pull it up into the ship.

The young man, who was still crying and wailing saw himself being pulled towards the boat and thought he was saved. But the rope was only pulled in far enough for him to touch the back side of the boat. When he was there, the Imam ordered that the rope holding the raft be cut.

Instantly the raft began to drift away from the boat and the young man panicked. He threw himself at the back of the boat and grabbed onto anything he could. He managed to cling to a few pieces of wood that were sticking out of the side of the ship and clung there for dear life. He sobbed and yelled but not so strongly this time.

After a little while, the Imam ordered a rope to be lowered to the young man. The man stopped his yelling and grabbed onto the rope. The soldiers pulled him up and he instantly ran into a corner and sat down quietly. He didn't say a word for the rest of the voyage and everyone could enjoy the trip in peace.

The Sultan was so happy with the wisdom of the Imam that he invited him to speak to all the sailors and guests on board. The Imam stood before them and said, "The young man didn't think much about the safety of the ship because he had never been exposed to the dangers outside of it. In the same way, we don't value the safety of Islam because we don't think of how dangerous it would be to lose the favor of Allah. The best Muslim of all is the one who understands why Islam is the best and safest way of life. People usually don't value the good until they fall into bad."

Questions to Answer

1. Why is reading and writing so important in Islam?
2. What are three types of books Muslims have been very good at writing?
3. What is the *Thousand and One Nights*?
4. Select one of the fables and explain the lesson that it teaches.
5. Write a fable of your own which seeks to teach a lesson.

196

Songs and Poems

39

Think About It

When can music become a bad influence on our lives?

Vocabulary Words

Qari   Daff   Qasidah

What to Learn

Singing and Poetry are allowed in Islam if they follow Islamic guidelines.

A. Poetry, Singing and Islam.

A'ishah went to the Blessed Prophet and told him about a woman who just got married to an Ansar man from the community. The Prophet asked her, "Did you send a young girl with the bride to beat a drum and sing?" A'ishah asked, "What should she say in her song?" The Prophet replied, "Let her say, 'To you we have come, to you we have come! So welcome us as we welcome you!"
(Tabarani)

People love to hear beautiful sounds. Nature has its own music made up of bird songs, flowing water and the wind rushing through the trees. People have also been given a way to make music with their voices. When the animals or natural world make their sounds, they are always praising Allah. People have a choice about whether to do the same.

The two most common art forms using the voice are poetry reading and singing songs. It seems a natural part of life to make words rhyme or to burst out in a few happy lines of song. So what does Islam say about this and what are the guidelines that we can follow so that our voices, also, will always praise Allah?

To begin with, both poetry and singing are allowed in Islam under certain conditions. But like every other part of life, Islam teaches us that there can be both good singing and poetry, as well as bad.

The Blessed Prophet Muhammad had many Companions who were skilled poets and they would recite poems and songs to stir the hearts of the Muslims for their Lord and way of life. At the same time, the idol-worshippers of Mecca had many poets as well, and they used their skills to attack Islam and say bad things about the Blessed Prophet. So we can see that poetry and singing can be good or bad.

The position of Islam on poetry and singing is clear. Poems and songs that call people to goodness, remembering Allah and to good and joyful feelings are allowed. But poems and songs that call us towards bad deeds, forgetting Allah or towards anger and hate are haram for us.

But before we go any further, we must understand some important things about our daily life as Muslims. The first thing to know is that Islam teaches that a Muslim shouldn't go around all day singing and listening to poems, as if there was nothing else to do in life.

For many people, Muslims and non-Muslims, music has become like a drug to forget Allah, forget themselves and to promote bad deeds. Most songs and music videos you hear on the radio or see on television call people to live a bad lifestyle and to do haram actions.

A Muslim must avoid seeing and hearing those things at all costs! Remember that this world is a testing ground and we surely wouldn't want to find ourselves remembering only the words of songs and poems and forgetting Allah's guide book for us!

B. The Qur'an is the Best For Listening Enjoyment.

For a Muslim, the first and best sound to hear is the verses of the Qur'an. That is the standard of our listening enjoyment and we should listen to the Qur'an being recited every day. The Blessed Prophet once said, "Whoever doesn't recite the Qur'an is not one of us." (Bukhari) We can either recite it out loud ourselves or hear it from others.

Once a man in Medina was reciting some ayat from the Qur'an when the Blessed Prophet walked by. The man saw the Prophet and stopped. Prophet Muhammad said to him, "Why did you stop? Please keep reciting."

The man felt shy and said, "You are the Prophet of Allah, I should listen to you reciting it."

The Prophet told the man to start reciting again because he, himself, liked to listen to it being recited also.

There are many different Qur'an recitors, or **Qaris**, that we can listen to. They each have their own style. Some reciters read slowly, others quickly, some have low voices, others speak in higher tones. A really good reciter can make people cry from joy, even if they can barely understand what the words mean! There are cassette tapes and CD's available almost everywhere and we can choose the reciter that our ears like to hear the most.

Some examples of famous Qur'an reciters in our own time are: Abdel Basit Abdus Samad, Khalil al Hussary, Qari al Minshawi, Abdel Rahman al Sudaisi, Sister Hajjah Roqaya bint Sulong-Amin and Shakir Qasmi. Do you have a favorite reciter?

So from all this we can see that singing should not be the main thing we look forward to when we want to hear beautiful sounds. The Qur'an is the best sound of all and that's where we should focus our listening attention first. Every year Muslims organize Qur'an reading contests all over the world to see who the best recitors are. Perhaps you can have one in your school as well!

C. Islamic Songs. (An-Nasheed)

As we learned before, innocent and good singing (ghinaa) is allowed under certain conditions. Even the Prophet sang songs. There are eight proper times for songs that have been accepted by Muslim scholars. They are listed as follows:

1) Singing before a battle so the Muslim soldiers can be filled with courage.
2) Singing songs of celebration on the 'Eid days.
3) Singing at weddings.
4) Singing when important people come.
5) Singing while working or traveling.
6) Singing to praise Allah. (Nasheed)
7) Singing when bored or lonely.
8) Singing to children to make them happy.

A common type of Islamic song is called the Nasheed. In this form of singing, the words of the song are about the praises and greatness of Allah. Another common form of song, especially for Muslims from parts of Asia, is called the Qawwali. The main theme in these songs is usually asking Allah to bless the Prophet Muhammad.

One of the most important rules about singing is this: while small children can sing songs as they like in front of anybody, older girls and women should <u>never</u> sing in front of older boys or men. This is so the men don't think bad or tempting thoughts.

In addition, Muslims should not dance and jump around like maniacs. If the song we are listening to makes us want to dance, then we shouldn't be listening to that kind of song. We are human beings and Allah wants us to have self-respect. We shouldn't dance and act like monkeys!

There are good reasons for these rules. If you look at many Christians in their churches, they sing loudly and dance around like they were going crazy! This bad behavior is no way to pray to Allah or to praise him! All the Christians do is sing and dance one day a week and the rest of the week they forget about their religion and its rules. And if you look at the wider society and see what people do, you find that music and singing are used to promote bad deeds and make people act badly!

In addition, singers come out with almost no clothes on and some act like they're angry or want to beat people! In addition, the words of most songs are about drinking alcohol, dancing, dating, taking drugs or feeling hopeless. They are abusing the beauty of the human voice. Only innocent singing for goodness is true music.

D. Islam and instruments.

What about Islam and musical instruments? Muslim women were allowed the use of a small hand-drum called a **daff** for their celebrations and community festivals.

As for other types of instruments such as flutes, guitars or pianos, Muslim scholars feel that these should be avoided, based on several Hadiths from the Prophet Muhammad who warned that using instruments would make us forget Allah. After all, the human voice is the best instrument of all and hearing the Qur'an read well is nicer than the biggest collection of instruments ever played.

It may be hard to understand why instruments, besides the hand-drum, are forbidden, but the answer is all around us. The people who listen to music the most are the least likely to pray, learn the Qur'an and do good deeds. The Shaytan uses music to put your soul to sleep and bury your Iman under sweet, but deadly melodies.

Take a look at people when they are lost in some music and remember that they are lost in another way also. A little song and a little poetry are fine in Islam but too much of it can deaden your soul. Beware of the tools of Shaytan and move closer to the real reason you're alive: to love Allah and follow His good way of life.

E. Examples of Islamic Songs.

Now we will take a look at some of the famous songs of Islam that Muslims have sang through the centuries up until our own day. Perhaps you can write some Islamic songs of your own or make a chorus group in your class.

The next time you feel the urge to sing, sing about Allah, the Prophet or something good and noble in this world. Allah hears your voice and will reward us for any good we do.

When the Muslims were digging the trench around Medina before the Battle of Khandaq, the Blessed Prophet Muhammad sang the following song:

"By Allah, if not for Him,
We'd never be guided,
Nor gave nor prayed.
So send down peace
And make firm our stand.
The others fought against us.
And when they wanted trouble,
We refused, We refused."

The Muhajireen and Ansar began singing in response:

"We are the ones who've pledged ourselves to Muhammad; that we will stay forever faithful in Islam."

Then the Prophet sang out in answer,

"O Allah, there's no good but from the Akhirah, so bless the Muhajireen and the Ansar."
(Bukhari)

When the Blessed Prophet entered Medina after fleeing Mecca, the people greeted him with this song:

The full moon has risen over us
From the valley of Wadaa'
Now we owe it to show thankfulness
Every time we call on Allah"

O you who were raised among us
Coming with a word to be obeyed.
You have brought to this city nobleness
Welcome! best caller to Allah's Way

(In Arabic the song goes like this:)

Tala'al badru 'alaynaa
Min thanee yatil Wadaa'
Wajabash shukru 'alaynaa
Maa da'aa lil lahidaa.

Ayyuhal mab'oothu feenaa
Ji-ta bil amril mutaa'
Ji-ta shar raftal Madinah.
Marhaban yaa khayra daa.

Modern Muslims have written a few more lines which go as follows:

A piercing light has arisen.	*Tala 'al nuru mubinu*
A light of the best Messengers,	*Nuru khayril mursaleen*
a light of security and peace.	*Nurul amin wa salaam*
a light of truth and certainty.	*Nurul haqqin wa yaqeen.*
A light of security and peace,	*Nurul amin wa salaam*
a light of truth and certainty	*Nurul haqqin wa yaqeen*
spreading over us,	*Sata'a ula 'alaynaa*
a mercy to all worlds.	*Rahmatan lil 'alameen*

F. Islamic Poetry.

The word for Islamic poetry in Arabic is **Qasidah**. Muslims have a rich tradition of Qasidahs that goes all the way back to the earliest days of Islam. The object of Islamic poetry is to uplift a person's mind, to bring a smile to the face, to tell a story and most importantly, to remember Allah and His beautiful world.

Everyone in the Muslim world loves good poetry and it's always been that way. In fact, in the Muslim city of Basrah, the Abbasid rulers held poetry reading competitions every week! Some of the best poetry in the world has been written by Muslims. The Khalifa Umar ibn al Khattab actually encouraged new Muslims from non-Arab lands to learn poetry as a way of helping them to learn the Arabic language. Maybe you can have a *"Qasidah Contest"* in your class!

There are many famous Muslim poets in Islamic history. They wrote mainly in Arabic, Urdu or Farsi. Among the most famous poets of all were Jalaluddin Rumi, Bashshar ibn Burd, and Dabal al Khuzai. Famous modern poets are Muhammad Iqbal, Ayesha bint Mahmood and Abd al Hayy Moore. The different forms of Muslim poetry range from subjects about Allah to events in every day life. We will see examples of many Muslim poets here.

Poems by Mevlana Jalaluddin Rumi

(From the book, "Al Mathnawi")

The Ladder

These words are the ladder to Heaven,
Whoever climbs them reaches the roof.
Not the roof of the sphere that is blue.
But the roof that goes beyond the visible stars.

The Safest Place

The safest place to hide a treasure of gold
Is in some deserted, forgotten place.
Why would anyone hide a treasure in plain sight?
And so it is said,
"Happiness is hidden beneath sadness."

Allah's Call

Listen, O drop, give yourself up without regret,
And in exchange gain the Ocean.
Listen, O drop, bring this honor on yourself,
And in the arms of the Sea be safe.
Who else is so lucky?
An Ocean calling to a drop.
In Allah' Name, in Allah's name, sell and buy at once!
Give a drop and take this Sea full of pearls.

A Rose Talking

What Allah said to the rose,
And caused it to laugh in full-blown beauty,
He said to my heart,
And made it a hundred times more beautiful.

The Angry Chickpea
(Rumi)

Look at the chickpea in the pot,
How it leaps up when it feels the fire.
While boiling, it continually rises to the
top
And cries, "Why are you setting the fire
under me?
Since you bought me, why are you
roasting me up and down?"
The housewife keeps hitting it with the
ladle.
"No!" she says, "boil nicely now,
And don't leap away from the one who
makes the fire.
It's not because of hate that I boil you,
But so that you might gain flavor,
And become nutritious and mingle with
the spices.
This affliction is not because you are
despised.
When you were green and fresh,
You were drinking water in the garden:
That water-drinking was for the sake of
this fire."

The Poet:
Mir Mu'izzi

Written upon the pages of the Earth
and sky,
The line: "Therefore take heed, you
who have eyes."

The Poet:
Reshma Baig

My Special Place

My special Place is in the park
Leaning against tree bark
Under a tree
Listening to the birds sing free
Breathing in the air
Staring everywhere
And seeing how special my place is to me

I think that I shall never see
a candyland with chocolate trees
with jelly hills and candy bees
birds that fly with marshmallow wings
houses made with M and M things
roads that are made with strawberry tarts
and everybody with sweet little hearts.

The Poet:
Abu Nuwas

Allah's Forgiveness

Stunned by the great amount
of my sins,
I saw hope, Lord,
and laid it side by side
With that great mercy
that is only Yours,
And measured both with a ruler
up and down.
My sin is great,
but now I know,
O Lord,
That Your forgiveness
is even greater!

Muhammad 'Attar Nayshaburi

(From the book, "The Flight of Birds to Union.")

They observed a Presence without qualification and description.
Beyond Perception, reason and Understanding.
If the spark of His Self-Plentitude were to be cast,
A hundred worlds would burn in one moment.
A hundred thousand esteemed suns,
A hundred thousand moons and stars, even more.
They observed them all in wonder,
Coming like atoms in a dance.

Sa'di Shirazi

(From the book, "The Bustan.")

Beware the Shaytan!

I will not say, O Brother, what the spiritual tune is,
Until I know who is listening to it.
If he begins his flight from the tower of the spirit.
The Angels will not keep up with his soaring.
But if he be a man of error, vanity and play,
The Shaytan will grow more powerful in his brain.
The Rose is torn apart by the morning breeze,
But not the log; for it can only be split by an ax.
The world feeds on music, drunkeness and pride.
But what does the blind man see in a mirror?

Sa'di Shirazi:

My Philosophy of Life

"I am joyful in the world because the world is joyful in Him."

Sa'di Shirazi:

On Praising the Prophet

Balaghal ula be kamaalihe.
Kashafad duja be jamaalihe.
Hasanat jami'u khisaalihe.
Sallu 'alayhe wa aalihe.

He taught first with his perfection.
Then revealed his beauty.
Goodness were all his qualities.
Peace be upon him and on his family.

The Poet: Abu Sa'id

Friendship

The high point of friendship is
When you expect nothing.
What value does a good deed
Have if you expect a reward?
The giver of the gift is more
Valuable than the gift.
The gift by itself is worthless
Even if it's a philosopher's stone!

The Poet: Omar Khayyam

Me and Thee

There was a door
to which I found no key.
There was a veil
past which I could not see.
Some little talk awhile on Me and Thee
There seemed-
and then no more of Thee and Me.

Abdel Rahman Jaami.

What is poetry?
The song of the bird of the mind.
What is poetry?
The likeness of the world of eternity.
The value of the bird
becomes clear through it,
And one discovers whether it comes from
the oven in a bath house or a rose garden.
It composes poetry from the Divine rose

A Poem by Abu al-Atahiya

Strength

Youth, free time and greed are seeds
Made for the corruption of men.
To escape evil, we must break with it.

When my share of time runs out
The mourners will give me little
comfort.

My memory will slip away,
Forgotten by friends.
My love will leave space for newer
friends.

Questions to Answer

1. Explain what Islam says about singing and poetry.
2. Why can some kinds of music and singing be dangerous to our Iman?
3. What makes the Qur'an the best thing to listen to for enjoyment?
4. Under what 8 conditions is singing allowed in Islam?
5. Which of the poems presented in this lesson is your favorite and why?
Write that poem on your paper and then give your answer after it.

Unit 10
Review Exercises

Vocabulary Review

On a separate piece of paper, write the meaning of each word below. Remember to write in complete sentences.

1. Masjid
2. Hafizah
3. Tajweed
4. Minara
5. Arabesque
6. Muhaddithah

7. Calligrapher
8. Daff
9. Qasidah
10. Ghina
11. Nasheed
12. Architecture

Remembering What You Read

On a separate piece of paper, answer the questions below. Remember to answer as best as you can and write in complete sentences.

1. How are Muslims encouraged to do art by the natural world?
2. Why do Muslim artists avoid painting or drawing people or animals that look too realistic?
3. What is one feature of Arabeque art?
4. How have Muslims decorated their Masjids?
5. What is the purpose of books of tafseer?
6. What did the Prophet say about learning and our duty as Muslims?
7. For most of the last thousand years, where have most of the world's schools and colleges been, in the Muslim world or Christian world? Explain your answer.
8. What was the lesson in the story of the Poor Imam?
9. What is a Qari?
10. Why are most instruments discouraged in Islam? Which instrument is allowed?
11. Write down one poem from this unit that you really like and memorize it for your test.

Thinking to Learn

Read the following statement and explain whether it is true or false. Write in complete sentences on a separate piece of paper.

Islam forbids all music, singing and poetry.

Reference Section

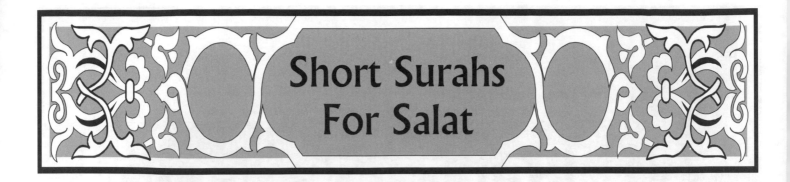
Surat An Naas (#114)

بِسْمِ اللهِ الرَّحْمٰنِ الرَّحِيْمِ

قُلْ اَعُوْذُ بِرَبِّ النَّاسِ ۙ

مَلِكِ النَّاسِ ۙ

اِلٰهِ النَّاسِ ۙ

مِنْ شَرِّ الْوَسْوَاسِ ۙ الْخَنَّاسِ ۙ

الَّذِیْ یُوَسْوِسُ فِیْ صُدُوْرِ النَّاسِ ۙ

مِنَ الْجِنَّةِ وَالنَّاسِ ۠

Bismillahir Rahmanir Raheem

Qul ow dhoobee Rabbin naas.
Malikin naas, Elahin naas.
Min sharill waswa sil khanas.
Al ladhee yoo was weesoo fee
soodoor in naas.
Min al jinnati wan naas.

<u>* English Meaning *</u>

"In the Name of Allah,
the Compassionate Source of All Mercy."

Declare: "I seek safety with the Lord of Humanity, the Ruler of Humanity, the God of Humanity, from the subtle temptations of evil whispered into the hearts of people through ways unseen and by other people."
(1-6)

Surat Al Falaq (#113)

بِسْمِ اللهِ الرَّحْمٰنِ الرَّحِيْمِ

قُلْ اَعُوْذُ بِرَبِّ الْفَلَقِ ۙ

مِنْ شَرِّ مَا خَلَقَ ۙ

وَمِنْ شَرِّ غَاسِقٍ اِذَا وَقَبَ ۙ

وَمِنْ شَرِّ النَّفّٰثٰتِ فِی الْعُقَدِ ۙ

وَمِنْ شَرِّ حَاسِدٍ اِذَا حَسَدَ ۠

Bismillahir Rahmanir Raheem

Qul ow dhoobee Rabbil Falaq
Min sharri maa Khalaq.
Wa min sharri ghawsiqin
edha waqab.
Wa min sharrin nafa thatee
fil 'ooqad.
Wa min sharri haasadin
edha hasad.

<u>* English Meaning *</u>

"In the Name of Allah,
the Compassionate Source of All Mercy."

Declare: "I seek safety with the Lord of the Dawn from the fear of (danger in) His creations, from the fear of approaching darkness, from the fear of magic and from the fear of the jeaolous one when he resents."
(1-5)

208

Surat Al Ikhlas (#112)

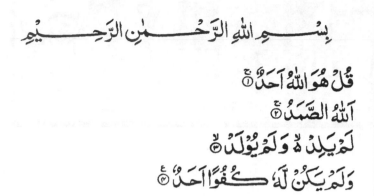

Bismillahir Rahmanir Raheem

Qul hoowa Allahu ahad.
Allahu Sawmad.
Lam Yalid wa lam yulad.
Wa lam yakoon lahu kufuwan ahad.

* English Meaning *

"In the Name of Allah,
the Compassionate Source of All Mercy."

Tell everyone: "He is Allah the One.
Allah is always forever. He doesn't have any
children and He was never born, and there is
nothing the same as Him."
(1-4)

Surat An Nasr (#110)

Bismillahir Rahmanir Raheem

Edha jaa'a nasrullahi wal fat-h.
Wa ra aiytan naasa yad khuloona fideen
illahi afwaja.
Fasab bih behamdi Rabbika wa staghfirhu.
Innahu kaana tawwaba.

* English Meaning *

"In the Name of Allah,
the Compassionate Source of All Mercy."

When the help of Allah arrives causing victory,
and you see people entering the lifestyle of Allah in
crowds, glorify your Lord and seek His forgiveness.
He is the One Who Accepts Repentance.
(1-3)

Surat Al 'Asr (#103)

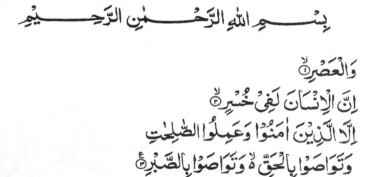

Bismillahir Rahmanir Raheem

Wal 'Asr.
Innal insaana lafee khusr.
Illel ladheena 'aamanoo wa 'amilus saawlihati wa
tawwasow bil haqqi wa tawwasow bis saber.

* English Meaning *

"In the Name of Allah,
the Compassionate Source of All Mercy."

The passing of time (or history) is proof that
people are truly lost. Except for those who have faith,
do what is right, and who teach each other about
truth and patience.
(1-3)

Where Do Muslims Live?

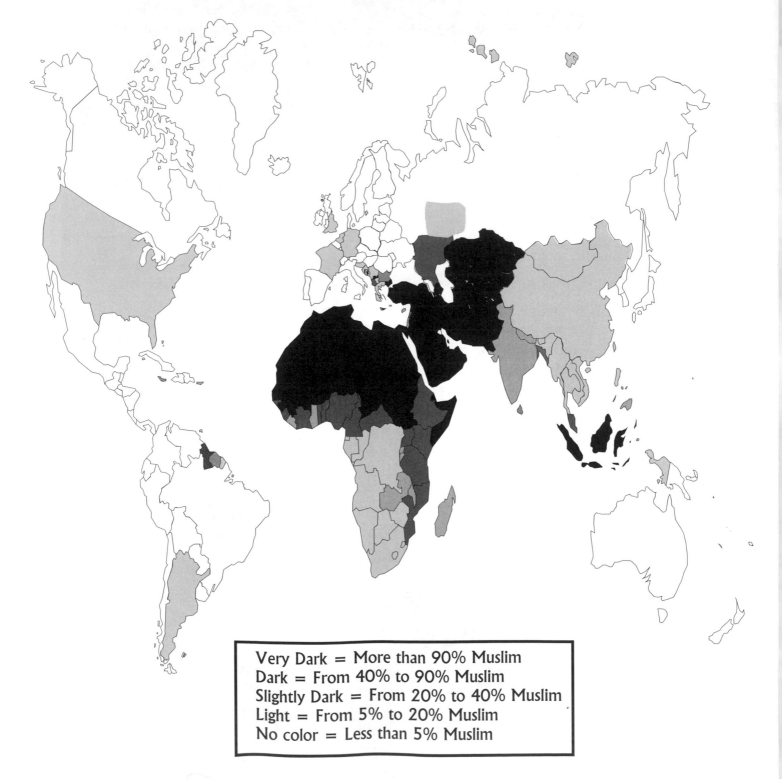

Very Dark = More than 90% Muslim
Dark = From 40% to 90% Muslim
Slightly Dark = From 20% to 40% Muslim
Light = From 5% to 20% Muslim
No color = Less than 5% Muslim

Selected Index